Date Du

You Stand There
making music video

You Stand There
making music video

by David Kleiler, Jr.
and Robert Moses

Three Rivers Press / New York

Published by Three Rivers Press
a division of Crown Publishers, Inc.
201 East 50th Street
New York, New York 10022
Member of the Crown Publishing Group

Random House, Inc. New York, Toronto, London, Sydney, Auckland
http://www.randomhouse.com/

THREE RIVERS PRESS and colophon are trademarks of Crown Publishers, Inc.

Self treatment courtesy of David Kleiler/X-Ray Productions/Zoo Entertainment. All rights reserved.
Foo Fighters treatment courtesy of Jesse Peretz/X-Ray Productions/Capitol Records. All rights reserved.

Printed in the United States of America
Design by Blue Brick Design, New York

Library of Congress Cataloging-in-Publication Data

Kleiler, David.
      You stand there : making music video : the ultimate how-to guide and
behind-the-scenes look at the art of music video / by David Kleiler and
Robert Moses. — 1st ed.
      p.   cm.
         1. Music videos—Production and direction. I. Moses, Robert.
II. Title.
PN1992.8.M87K64 1997
791.45'657—dc21
97-23968   CIP

ISBN 0-609-80036-1

10 9 8 7 6 5 4 3 2 1

First Edition

acknowledgments

David and Bob owe many thanks to many people, including: Alicia Potter for ace historical research and reporting; Lisa Sacks for her sharp eye and valuable opinions; Chris Wise, Jin Pak, Paul Krygowski and Sue Wozny at Blue Brick for flair and forbearance; Eileen Wilkinson and Catharine Tarver for editorial assistance; Eric Rachlis and Michael Shulman at Archive Photos; Lori Reese and Kelly McLaughlin at Retna Photos; Tim Spitzer at DuArt; Holley Bishop and Kim Witherspoon for sage counsel; Eleanor Ramsay for advice and proposal design; and Tim Haley and all at Working Media in Boston for their boundless patience and encouragement. Some were instrumental in setting the book in motion: Sherri Rifkin at Harmony launched us with enthusiasm; Dina Siciliano took over for Three Rivers with authority, and weathered sunny days and stormy E-mails. Tabitha Soren steered our proposal to a safe home. Chris Lombardi and all at Matador have been generous with time, thoughts and material; Mark Kates at Geffen has offered his counsel, words and encouragement.

For Noreen and the little one who shares a pub date with this book.
— Bob

Deepest thanks to my love, Roxana. Thanks to Mott for sharing so many You Stand There moments. Thanks to all of my friends who help me laugh at myself and keep things in perspective: Patrick Amory, Jon Easley, Jessie Givelber, Sarah Goodman, Char Hamer, Chris Lombardi, Josh Philips, Rafi Simon, Alison Tatlock, Clay Tarver, the Vapneks and Bill Wolfe. Special thanks to Bob Moses for his patience, hard work and for giving me the Clash's "Tommy Gun" single when I was 11. Thanks to the bands I've worked with, the folks who've helped me on shoots and all of the interviewees in this book.
— David

contents

You Stand There
making music video

I can't see anything. I hear only the tidal sloshing of a waterbed in the dark. This means I have to go to the front desk, the last thing I want to do. If the proprietors of a pay-by-the-hour love shack at the New Jersey mouth of the Lincoln Tunnel knew what we were doing, they would kick us out — or worse, ask for real money. My co-conspirator and cameraman, Mott Hupfel, successfully convinced them that we had to have the honeymoon suite for an afternoon tryst and assured them it would just be the two of us. A blown fuse ten minutes after check-in means it's my turn to do the talking.

Scott, the sexy guitarist for Girls Against Boys, sweats on the waterbed wearing a red satin pajama top and a Gibson SG as we hurriedly conceal any evidence of our production. We unplug the CD boom box, break down the lights, pack up the Hi8 video rig and hide everything in the closet.

Dodging the gaze of a surveillance camera, we sneak Scott back into the van parked outside, where the rest of his band patiently

prologue >

wait. He likes the honeymoon suite with its red carpet, heart-shaped waterbed and mirrored walls, but mutters under his breath about our shooting there without permission.

It's about three in the afternoon on what has to be the hottest day of the year. Sweat runs down the crack of my ass as I waddle over to the office with greasy smudges on my T-shirt. At the desk, I shout lame explanations through bullet-proof Plexiglas, "You know, we were playing loud music . . . laying on the waterbed . . . air conditioner cranked . . . " Understandably suspicious, the desk clerk shuffles cautiously to our room, where Mott lounges on the bed wearing a We-weren't-doing-anything-bad smile. My heart is pounding, and I'm making silent supplications: Please, just let us stay. I keep one eye on the door, worried that one of the band members will sashay into the room at an inopportune moment. Frowning, the motel guy opens the fuse box with his key, switches the circuit breaker and suggests we turn down the air conditioner. The moment he leaves, we scramble to replace lights, smuggle Scott back into place and start shooting.

The fuse blows three more times in the next 45 minutes, making our lives a bad silent slapstick. When the lights sputter and expire, we pack up our equipment and remove the rocker. Increasingly sweaty, grimy and sheepish, I return to the front desk each time to beg for a fuse adjustment. The clerk grows even more puzzled. What were we doing in there? Why was I so sweaty? Why did we need so much . . . electricity? At a certain point, the desk clerk doesn't really want the answers to those questions. Finally, Mott figures out how to open the fuse box without a key.

As the sweltering sun smears the late afternoon, we lead a tiptoe parade of rockers past the watchful camera. We shoot each band member individually so as not to crowd the room or make too much noise and, therefore, don't get any shots with the drummer. But by one in the morning, I'm fearless. The gods of electricity have kept the AC flowing for the past nine hours and I want to start shooting master shots — wide shots of all four band members, including the drummer and his kit. He sits down at his set after wedging it onto a small strip of red-carpeted floor next to the bounding waterbed where his bandmates bob up and down and starts to play. Our playback system is only a CD boombox and it's no match for crashing cymbals in the 12-foot-square room, but it puts up an awful, distorted struggle.

Interrupting our second take, motel guy calls to complain frantically about the noise. He struggles for the right expletive to describe the sound, the horror. Terrified of the scene he may confront in the room, the desk clerk begs us to leave from his perch behind the glass. High on chaos, I weakly explain that we've just invited some friends in from out of town. The rock band laughs. Feeling only a little guilty, I want to say, "You know what? We're making a low-budget rock video here and there's nothing you can do about it."

prologue

Flanked by renowned music video directors at a College Media Journal Festival panel, I told my Girls-Against-Boys-in-the-motel story. The audience in the New York City auditorium came to hear how music videos get made and how they could participate in the fun. Someone asked, "What crazy things have you done to shoot a video cheaply?" and I listened patiently as most of my colleagues described mild scenes of using a skateboard for a dolly or a bungee cord for a crane. As they talked on to an increasingly restive audience, I realized that my stories were funnier and more instructive because my production circumstances were more dire. If they had production value, I had anecdote value. Which production to describe? Shooting at a chemical plant on the day it was sold so we wouldn't get thrown out in the confusion of the property changing hands? Maybe the one where we used an overhead projector as a primary light source because we didn't have enough money for real lights. When the audience responded with laughter and appreciation, I realized that through **introduction >**

total desperation I had gained a unique perspective on videomaking — and filmmaking — that I could share.

Why share it now? Music videos have become so embedded in our popular culture that they are now an accepted route to directing not only television commercials but also feature films and network television. As we'll also see, music video making illuminates the filmmaking process and can be a method of learning that process. Each of the steps in music-video production that we'll describe (including many more stories like the previous one from me and other directors), and the decisions that are made at every step, are mirrored on film and television sound stages all over the world. As long-time director/producer/video commissioner Nancy Bennett told me, "Music videos are amazing teachers because you can approach them with little exposure to common production practice and just by the nature of the process pick up the common practice. It's training by hellfire but there's a lot that can be learned about putting across a story as a filmmaker."

SCOTT OF GIRLS AGAINST BOYS

Over the last 15 years, music videos have developed their own aesthetics, genres and visual language. The medium has settled into an established — some would say commercially calcified — form. "Personally, I think that music video is the ultimate expression of pop culture today," claims Randy Sosin, a video commissioner at A&M Records. "It's short, it grabs your attention, it's completely disposable, it's everything that encompasses pop culture and it's something that's extremely immediate the world over. Everyone understands a music video. From Latin America to China to Kuala Lumpur, you put on a music video for Madonna, Brian Adams or Sheryl Crow and it's something that's understandable."

We no longer hear that a film or commercial has an "MTV look." That "look" is now so ubiquitous in our youthful pop culture that the quick cuts and jerky camera movements that the phrase once implied have now become commonplace. We will provide a way of finding meaning in what many assume to be simply a "look," and a way of reading a medium that may at first appear to be a random collection of musical set pieces. We're at

introduction

a turning point in both music and music video at which both the commercial and creative communities are searching for new forms and new means of expression (witness MTV's launch of all-video M2 and its VJ-less techno program, *Amp*). Making a music video can be a personally rewarding experience of the creative process, and maybe we'll help inspire a younger musician or fan to take up the camera and join that exploration.

Making any music video is creatively and aesthetically challenging. Breaking through the stylistic or genre conventions to a new concept is, perhaps, more of a feat than ever, and interpreting a song visually, an art. When a video does make the leap to the attention of a wider world, it owes much to the resourcefulness and ingenuity of the director who conceived it, not to enormous budgets or major-label support. It is still possible for a first-time director to see his/her work beamed to millions. The budget for the Girls Against Boys video was $2,000, and I had money to spare. Though it was shot on Hi8 video and not film, and wasn't up to broadcast television's technical standards, the video was shown on MTV's *120 Minutes* and it saw airplay in Europe. From the chaos and anxiety of the honeymoon suite/indie-rock sweat lodge came an internationally televised video. Music-video networks have created one of the few means for the severely underbudgeted to access the mass media.

Every day there are thousands of video directors at work on projects aimed at those music-video networks, but we generally only hear about those few who end up on Hollywood sets. True, David Fincher, Michael Bay, David Hogan, F. Gary Gray, Tamra Davis, Hal Hartley and Jonathan Demme all have music videos in their past. But being a successful video director doesn't always translate into a successful film career, nor do all music-video directors aspire to Hollywood careers. In *You Stand There* we'll hear from directors such as Jesse Peretz and Spike Jonze, who are making the transition to feature films and big-budget commercials, and also from directors who have made hundreds of videos for minuscule budgets — and they have strikingly similar feelings about their work.

When you direct a music video, you do learn about the production dynamic. You learn about the players in the crew and that unteachable skill of working with different types of folks to get something done. You follow a project from its conception to its execution to its completion. You deal with money and how to spend it creatively. You figure out how to integrate your aesthetic goals while making everyone else happy. You acquire the invaluable talent of making other people feel like *they* came up with one of *your* ideas. You figure out how to "save" your project through editing or finding creative solutions on the set even if the shoot has gone wildly out of control. These dynamics are part of a larger, universal filmmaking process.

Notwithstanding the dire production circumstances, I followed that process when shooting the Girls Against Boys video. By agreeing to the job, I first had to conceive an idea for the action in the video, then I had to figure out how to get it done for little money, then shoot it with a crew of one other person, cut it with an editor who worked for free, and deliver the finished piece to the record company. As we follow the music-video production process, we'll meet the people who perform in, direct, shoot, edit, budget and distribute music videos. Chapters One, Two and Three present what happens before the first rocker steps in front of the camera: the treatment, the conceptual underpinning of the video, and some thoughts on music-video aesthetics and history to help you conceive your own video or understand the work of others; the budget — yes, a creative endeavor, and even more so when money's tight; and preproduction, arguably a more critical process than the shoot itself, especially if you're also the producer.

If Chapters Three and Four follow the planning and logistics that we think of as "producing," Chapter Five presents the tasks most of us think of as "directing": running the set, keeping up morale and getting unembarrassing performances out of rockers who can't act. Everyone can imagine the inspired director standing on set yelling "cut" and "action" with the cast and crew eagerly executing their every whim. As you'll hear from many directors in this chapter, the reality can be rather different. Chapter Six enters the editing suite to explore the underestimated process at the heart of music videos. Included is an in-depth discussion of telecine, that magic tool that snatches MTV airplay from the jaws of disaster, as well as different editing systems and editing styles. Finally, in Chapter Seven, you'll hear about what to do with your video creation: how videos get on MTV, the record label/rep/director dynamic, and what steps to take if you want to make more music videos — and even get paid to do it.

Ultimately, this book stresses the creative process rather than discussing technical details. Besides, first-time music video makers generally get stumped by issues beyond basic filmmaking information. I remember that my first concerns were "How do you really lip-synch the footage?" and "How do you get the film to look so cool and grainy when it's transferred to videotape?" Making a low-budget music video can be like writing a song or a short story. Both of us authors believe the experience of playing in bands helped us understand the creative process: Just like the group dynamics, the sudden flashes of inspiration and the compromises you make while playing in a band, music video making forces you to work with people, explain your ideas clearly, and figure out which processes, people and tools work best and which don't work at all. All creative endeavors follow the arc of conception, execution and completion, and in music videos, this all unfolds rather quickly.

introduction

In his inimitably charming, romantic way, Minutemen bass player Mike Watt often shouted "Now go out and start your own band!" as he walked off the stage. His band proclaimed that punk rock changed their lives in a romantic ballad called "History Lesson" and carried the torch for the "do-it-yourself" punk-rock ethos. This ethos created a vision of punk rock as a communal experience in which people infused with creative energy could make music away from commercial demands, without the latest equipment, and sometimes without knowing anything at all about making music. The point was to get out there and play. We say, "Now go out and make your own video!" Maybe the videomaking process doesn't offer the same rush of punk-rock adrenaline as starting a band, but there *is* something subversive about making a video for $2,000 and watching your own personal vision enter the media slipstream. We believe that everyone reading this book is visually literate enough to go out and direct; what matters most is having a point of view. The do-it-yourself philosophy means having enough faith in your point of view to teach yourself how to work in the medium. Besides, technical information is too easily made anachronistic: In a few years,

television will be made in a digital format that we're just starting to hear the whispers of now. The joy of making a low-budget video is the baptism by fire, the learning while doing.

Director Adam Bernstein defines a director as "the least skilled person on a set, the one person who doesn't have a craft," and Jesse Peretz talks about "The Wizard of Oz curtain factor," the feeling of being qualified to

DAVE (RIGHT) AND MARK E. SMITH (THE FALL) CONFER

direct only by virtue of having opinions. We discovered that many directors, especially when they're starting out, have identity crises about directing. We say the only way to become a director is to start, and start only with the intention of doing something fun and fulfilling. "I like to do things," says director Julie Hermelin. "I like to be out there and engaged with the world, and I discovered that using a camera was a fun way to be engaged with the world while doing something artistic."

As we scout locations for a new project, Mott and I engage in philosophical conversations about what makes a good location. We talk about spaces that have visual depth and search for never-before-seen vacant lots and alleyways. Over time, I have gained a new fascination with my surroundings. Potential locations are everywhere, and I just want to shoot. I imagine music videos wherever I look. When Mott and I pass cool-looking places in his girlfriend's car, we shout "You stand there." It's a command to the hypothetical band members in a hypothetical video and shorthand for our newfound ability to look at the world as a backdrop: "We could shoot there," or "Let's shoot over there." We imagine forcing frail rockers to perch on precarious places. We make ourselves ruefully laugh by saying "You stand there" whenever we see particularly absurd, treacherous locations such as sewage treatment facilities or buildings on fire.

From this tongue-in-cheek battle cry comes our title and the slogan for our DIY philosophy. We hope that by showing you how music videos are made and who makes them, you'll be inspired to make your own. Go ahead. Embarrass yourself and your rocker friends. Con your underemployed, director-of-photography-wannabe buddy into wasting an eighteen-hour day shooting your video. Make *her* figure out how to use the barely functional, borrowed 16mm spring-wound camera. Placate the rest of your sad-slack, unpaid friends on the crew with cold pizza. Hit the "pause" button on the CD boom box. Escort the rock band toward the abandoned building and ignore the enormous "Absolutely No Trespassing" sign that looms above. This is your shining moment. It's time to present the rockers to the camera. You boldly extend one arm toward the building and, with all the directorial authority you can muster, pronounce the magic words, "You stand there!"

introduction

Doug paces the perimeter of his tiny apartment in New York's East Village, surrounded by unexposed super-8 cartridges, overdue Kim's Video rentals, and posters for punk-rock shows and films by obscure Eastern European directors. He glances first at a poster and then a video box, then another and yet another in search of inspiration. He looks for a faded color, an odd shadow cast on the wall by the wind blowing the pull cord on the window shades, the face he makes as he pulls his hand across his unshaven stubble. Doug confronts more than a grooming disaster when he looks in the mirror. He faces a looming deadline. He has a phone meeting tomorrow at 9 A.M. and has to fax his treatment for Avenging Asteroid to the video commissioner at Bad Infinity Records, the Asteroid's manager and the lead singer. Doug punches in the advance cassette of the song one more time in pursuit of revelation and broods that his life and livelihood are reduced to winning an essay contest from hell. **dreaming >**

Not every director turns writing a treatment into a nail-biting film noir, but because it marks the first step in the music-video production process, and because it can determine which director gets a green light from a record-label video commissioner or band, music video makers often sweat putting their inspiration on the page. The challenge of the treatment is that it represents the first transformation of the most abstract art form, music, into evocative imagery.

Treatments are as individual as the directors who write them. Some read like classic dramatic writing. Others read like crazy prose poetry. Whatever the writing style, the treatment evolves into the blueprint for the video and is as important to a music video as a shooting script is to a film. It dictates the budget for the job and is the sacred text constantly referred to when drawing up the shot list. Like a contract, the treatment is the document that everyone involved in the production can point to and say, "Wait a minute, it says here that this is supposed to happen." If a record company feels that a video substantially departs from the treatment's description, it can even take its director to court.

> **TREATMENT**
> A short synopsis of a story written to present the idea for a movie, television program or music video; the game plan, the proposal, the pitch. Music-video treatments are generally one to three pages long and describe the action, the setting, the look and any specific film techniques that will be employed.

Though usually just one factor out of many, directors often get jobs based on who writes the "best" treatment. Guided by their record label's video commissioner, a band in need of a video chooses from a pool of potential directors, screening dozens of director's reels — a videocassette of a director's best or most recent videos — to determine a short list of directors with whom they would like to work. Then, the video commissioner sends the chosen directors a copy of the song to be presented in the video. The interested directors write a treatment and submit it to the commissioner and the band. If the band and the commissioner respond to a particular treatment ("Hey, I always wanted to do a parody of the Mentos commercials!") that director gets the job, and the band, video commissioner and director start to work planning the shoot.

When you're doing your first no-budget video, writing a treatment may seem like a pointless exercise. "My rocker friends aren't going to take me to court because I said something about jumping rabbits and I couldn't deliver the bunnies," you think. "Plenty of great movies have been made without scripts. Jean-Luc Godard shot *Breathless* from notes written on the back of an envelope." You are not Godard. A treatment should be written no matter how freestyle or low-budget the production. Writing a treatment forces you to translate music into imagery and order random thoughts into concise notions that you can communicate to others. If Godard's legendary envelope notes amounted to nothing more than a string of fragmented phrases that described his film — "black-and-white . . . jump cuts . . . handheld camera . . . groovy jazz soundtrack" — then the bespectacled auteur wrote what we would now recognize as a crude music-video treatment. As long as the words let a reader imagine the video for himself, it's a successful treatment.

How does one begin to visualize? That's a question central to all creative enterprises: writing novels, painting, composing and making music videos. Regardless of budget, it's important to pace the floor trying to articulate the images that fly through your imagination — even if the effort yields something that reads like bad beat poetry — because it's the first step in the creative process, visualization. Rendering a visual equivalent of music and musical tones has a long and distinguished history that extends back to the 18th century and a Jesuit priest's *clavecin oculaire* that attempted to demonstrate a correspondence between specific tones and colors. The most renowned attempt in our century was Scriabin's *Prometheus*, which featured a specially prepared *clavier à lumieres*. We have more complex tools now and, as a result of music videos and their various antecedents, assume at least a commercial correspondence between music and image.

To get ideas flowing, Nick Tanis, a much-admired film production instructor at New York University, suggests that students daydream their short films, an appealing idea because it's inherently nonintellectual and image oriented. If you're stuck on how to shoot a scene or what should happen next in your project, Tanis encourages daydreaming to let your imagination wander. Sometimes these daydreams help formulate memorable, lyrical images that are powerfully effective onscreen.

This daydream process works perfectly for music video. Once you've exhausted all the associative techniques ("This lyric makes me think of this," or "This chord makes me think of that"), you need to pause for a daydream. The more I listen to a song, the more cluttered my brain gets with obsessive thoughts and images. That's when I relax. I take a walk or a drive and daydream the video, channeling the images from the recesses of memory. These memories can be randomly accessed, like using the step function on a laser disk player: images flutter by in fast forward, then, with the touch of a pause button, you freeze a random image. Treatment writing becomes a transcription of these daydreams.

VIDEO COMMISSIONER
The person at a record label who oversees music-video production, maintains relationships with reps and production companies, and assigns music-video jobs to appropriate production companies and directors.

Jesse Peretz maintains the youthful energy that he once burned off as the bass player for the Lemonheads, with whom he started his video career. Jesse directed the Foo Fighters' MTV Award-winning Mentos-commercial-homage video and finished shooting his first feature film, *First Love, Last Rites* in November 1996. He doesn't find free-association to be as helpful because he enjoys constructing narrative videos. "I'll try to get into what the song is about and then try to forget it," he explains. "I just try to find one thing that's going on in the song and forget the bigger picture. Trying to create a narrative that illustrates the song literally is a death wish. I always hear people talk about how they just free-associate and write down every image that pops into their heads. I have to say I've never done that at all. I just try to find one main thing like a location or a character. That will be the first hook. From there, I try to create some sort of narrative because making music video is mini-movie-making. I try to establish a main character through whom we experience the whole event and with whom we're supposed to identify."

JESSE PERETZ TAKES A BREAK

As enjoyable as lying around daydreaming might sound, most music-video directors hate writing treatments. Like naughty students cramming for final exams, they often wait until the last moment before feverishly imagining their masterpieces. Julie Hermelin, director of videos for, among others, PM Dawn, Sarah McLachlan, and Seven Mary Three, shines in Los Angeles's Silver Lake rock scene and is engaged to the guy who runs the indie-rock hangout, Spaceland. She is friendly, pro-arts, pro-community, and she and her music-video-producer friend Joy May put together a pro-choice benefit record a couple of years ago. She always waits until the day after the treatment is due to start writing, mostly because she's cautious about how to approach a creation that, at its heart, is not hers.

"There's a lot of doubt," she says. "Will they like it? Will they not like it? I don't know who these people are, and I'm not writing for me. That's something I've always felt very strongly about: As a director, you have to take into account that it's their song, it's personal to them. They probably have ideas about it that you don't know. So, as a director, I always have conversations with the band. For a couple of years, treatment writing was an incredibly hellish process where it would take me three or four days, battling it out and coming up with a zillion different ideas. Now I'm a couple years down the road, and I know my process. It takes me a good day cooped up in my house after the treatment's due. I can't get it in on time because if I have that time beforehand, there are too many what-ifs involved and I second-guess myself too much. It's not a matter of not having any ideas; it's having too many ideas and not being able to decide which idea is right. The pressure helps me focus."

"Well, sometimes [coming up with an idea for a video] is quick and sometimes it takes weeks," Spike Jonze says. Jonze first caught the video world's attention with his collaboration with Kim Deal on the Breeder's "Cannonball," though he first dabbled in the mass media as an editor of *Dirt, Sassy* magazine's brother magazine for boys. Many of the directors in this book refer to his "Sabotage" video for the Beastie Boys as the most influential video of all time. His winsome personality and inventive exploration of one, usually brilliant, idea per video have made him a favorite with bands and audiences. Jonze won an MTV Award for the Weezer video, "Buddy Holly." "Sometimes you have the nugget of an idea, then you take a while to figure it all out. There's no real science to it at all. The good thing about videos is that there's

JULIE HERMELIN GETS SERIOUS

not one set thing it has to be. You can take one simple idea, and if it's a strong idea, make it work for a whole video, as opposed to throwing in a million random things. You see a lot of videos that have this one great idea in it, and then the rest of it's junk. If the director was secure enough with that one idea and took that idea all the way, they could have figured out how build that one thing into a bigger idea." He describes his Wax video, "Southern California," which depicts a slow-motion dash by a man on fire, as an example of one visu-

KEVIN KERSLAKE *ENJOYS* **TREATMENTS**

al idea being taken all the way instead of just being a single element in the video. "You see a shot of a guy running down the street on fire. It's a strong enough idea that it can work for the entire piece," he says. "You just figure out more and more pieces to put into it. Okay, he's running down the street. Where is he going? What's everyone else doing? And who is around? You don't just take one idea and throw in a million other ideas. You take one idea and build it. That [image of the burning man] could have just been a shot in the video instead of the whole video."

Kevin Kerslake, director of renowned videos for Stone Temple Pilots, Nirvana and Filter, actually likes writing treatments and considers it one of his strengths. Kerslake considers every word carefully, and it's not surprising that much of our conversation revolved around experimental film of the '60s. His work has that feel. His videos impress (and influence others) because some of them seem solely concerned with the lighting, the color, and the texture of the film. He's also capable of producing videos that are totally narrative, "concept" videos — his Felliniesque carnival video for the Red Hot Chili Peppers' "Breaking the Girl," for example. More recently, the "Hey Man Nice Shot" video for Filter is vintage Kerslake. The rich blues and reds almost look as if the film itself is tinted or colorized, but were produced purely by Kerslake's film processing wizardry. It also features the flickery effects of Lightning Strikes — a powerful lighting unit that is a glorified version of a strobe light (Peter Care's flickery video "What's the Frequency Kenneth?" for REM and Kerslake's early Smashing Pumpkins videos are other examples. Lightning Strikes has become à la mode, almost the latter-day version of the smoke machines that polluted '80s videos.)

Kerslake's appreciation of art, photography and masters of abstract film such as Stan Brakhage shows in his treatments as well. "I wrote a one-word treatment for Soundgarden's 'Black Hole Sun.' I wanted to do something really crude and apocalyptic, so the treatment was: 'Scratch.' I also sent over an old film I did called *Dogflower*. I had dragged the film out to the parking lot and stomped all over it, twisted screws into it, all that stuff." Kerslake's career has placed him in the enviable position of developing treatments only for songs to which he "responds viscerally." After playing the song again and again to pick up mood, visual impressions, or the beginnings of a narrative, "I usually meditate in silence on where it should go. After it develops a bit, I'll go back, listen to the song, and see how things fit, or then I'll revert to silence. Sometimes I'll even put on ethereal music like old jazz or ambient stuff just to have a different atmosphere." The resulting treatments are little works of art in themselves. "I've turned in one-word treatments, paragraphs, three- to five-page treatments. They're all pretty fun to read and sort of challenging, and probably rooted more in beat poetry or something that uses language. It's a comparable language to the film, really."

Although some directors are able to reduce the pain by making treatment writing a systematic pseudo-science, video commissioners aren't always consistent in the way they deal with treatments. If a director is especially hot, video commissioners don't make him/her jump through the treatment-writing hoop. Also, bands, managers, video commissioners and record label A&R people often have a good, though usually very general, idea of what they want before they read anyone's treatment. "Sometimes the band has specific ideas," concurs Jonze. "Sometimes they just have vague ideas of things that they don't like. But either way, use the band [for ideas] because the video is them. Usually I work with bands that I respect. I want to know what they have to say, and it's fun to work with what they have to say. Like the Weezer thing ['Come Undone — The Sweater Song'], they're on the record cover just standing, like, 'This is who we are,' so that was kind of the idea: take that photo and turn it into a video. The process was talking to them, getting to know them and seeing what they were about. Sometimes people say, 'That video doesn't have anything to do with the song.' Or, 'If I didn't use that idea with that band, I would've done it with another,' or, 'How long had I had that idea sitting around?' Usually my ideas are pretty specific to the song, even though they don't look like they have anything to with it. I stockpile ideas but I never come back to them. You want to do a video that is as much them as it is you. As opposed to it being just them or just you."

Phil Morrison has directed videos for Sonic Youth, Yo La Tengo, Juliana Hatfield and other luminaries of the alternarock scene. He's made the career jump from directing

> **A&R**
> Shorthand for "artists and repertoire," the employees of record labels who sign bands to contracts and then watch over their careers, coordinating recording, touring, and publishing with the bands' representatives and generally acting as in-house advocates with the label's business affairs, marketing, sales, advertising, publicity and video departments.

GETTING STARTED:
ADAM BERNSTEIN

"I wanted to be a director and I thought music videos were the most exciting forum. I thought they were the coolest thing you could do. I was infatuated with them. I still love to do them, but I like to do a mixed bag of things, narrative and working with actors. I got started in music video because I had a job when I was 24 as a producer at the Nickelodeon network. My boss at the time was a guy named Jeff Darby who let me direct those little comedy segments shot on 16mm and video. I caught the directing bug. As things slowed down on that floor, I would go every day to the library at MTV Networks, which was two floors above, and take videos out of the library. I began to identify my favorite videos and they were almost exclusively directed by Tim Pope and Zigore Verbinsky. I kept an archive of my favorite videos. I had a little bit of money I'd saved up, so I quit my job and just started hunting for bands. This is 1985. A pal I went to college with went to high school with two guys in They Might Be Giants, and he suggested that I go check them out. So I went to a club called the Darinka on the Lower East Side and approached them backstage because I just thought they were perfect. I was looking for a band that would reflect my sensibilities because I had done a lot of comedy. I approached John Flansburg backstage and said, 'Look, I got fifteen hundred bucks. Do you need to do a video?' Initially they were very

>>>

rock stars to directing cultural icons, including the Energizer bunny and the Nike Ice Man Cooketh campaigns. A true descendant of the North Carolina music scene, Phil's trademark outfit includes horn-rimmed glasses, band T-shirt and Carolina oil-resistant work shoes. He speaks with the kinetic energy of his videos and his hands fly through the air as we discuss his work. "For me, the process of writing a video concept has been a total crapshoot," he says. "I've always just done it based on free-association. When it really works, it just miraculously leads into a solid narrative. When it doesn't, it's kind of a mess. I think that the ones that have worked are when I've had good conversations with the band ahead of time. I always ask them what they hate a lot more than what they like. Sometimes that can drive you crazy, because, like when I did Rocket from The Crypt. It was kind of confusing at first because when I asked the band what they really hated, they said, 'No slow motion, we hate it, we think it's bullshit, it's not what we're about, we're Rocket from the Crypt.' So then I said, 'Well, what videos have you liked, that have really captured a performance or non-performance really well?' They said, 'We really love that Lenny Kravitz video [Mark Romanek, 'Are You Gonna Go My Way?')]. They might not have remembered that it was 80 percent slow motion, you know? But I was still not allowed to use slow motion, and, in the end, it came out cool. Their next video, for 'Ditch Digger,' — that I thought was really good, better than mine — Spike did with total slow motion. So he won them over somehow."

Certain ground rules are set before anyone writes a treatment: the band refuses to act; the guitarist hates small children; the band's manager and friend loves that French movie *Breathless*, for example. "It starts in some really boring meeting where you're not paying attention," says Susan Solomon, a former commissioner with A&M Records, "and, all of a sudden the word 'video' is mentioned, and you're like, 'Whoa, I better wake up!' If it's a band you've never heard of, say it's their first single, you want to meet the band and see the art work that's been done. At A&M, we were in the creative department, which makes a lot of sense. The A&R guy inevitably wants to come in and tell you all about the band. The radio department says, 'Hey, we're going for alternative,' or it's a pop record, or an urban act. You categorize the market we're going into. Money's based on how many records they think they're going to sell, what the chances are of getting this on the air. So, you've got a budget, you've got a song, you've got all these comments, and you've got a band that may or not be involved. If they are, you talk to them. What are they like? What are they into? Videos they've liked may be out of their league. You say, 'Well, I might not be able to afford that, but let me give you some reels that I think you'll like.'

In long, awkward conference calls with directors, bands reveal their deepest, darkest video fantasies: "I've always felt that supermarkets symbolized alienation in late-period capitalism," or "I've always wanted to shoot in a bright, shiny Safeway. My mother left me in one when I was three . . . " The lucky director who happened to write, "The supermarket in this video represents alienation in late capitalism," or "We discover a lost child in the dairy aisle, no more than three . . . " usually gets the job.

Mark Kates, director of A&R for Geffen Records, worked on promotion and marketing with Nirvana as they built their career. He has been guiding bands that formed the cornerstone of what became labeled "alternative" since helping manage Boston's legendary Mission of Burma in the early 1980s. Affable and passionate about music, he has since signed Beck, Elastica, and Jawbreaker to Geffen, did the A&R work for the *Beavis and Butt-head Do America* and

distrustful, but eventually they came around to the idea that they were getting a video for free. At that point they didn't even have a record out. They had a cassette that was available at Final Vinyl on Second Avenue. I did the video for 'Put Your Hand Inside the Puppet Head.' We shot it in two eight-hour days, for the all-in price of $1,750. The video was finished during this wild period, that was like the Prague Spring of MTV, when MTV opened up their playlist to just about anything that was cool. The band did not have a record out, did not have a record in the stores. It got rotation on MTV."

<<<

Suburbia soundtracks, and handled A&R for Sonic Youth, Hole, Siouxsie and the Banshees/The Creatures, XTC, the Posies, Teenage Fanclub, the Sundays, White Zombie and others. Kates remembers Kurt Cobain as someone who brought the same attention to music video as he did to his cathartic music. "Kurt's an example of an artist who had spent a lot of time watching MTV and had very clear ideas about how he wanted to be represented in his videos, down to the look of the film, to the color saturation," Kates recalls. "He thought about that very specifically. He nailed it with 'Heart-Shaped Box,' and created — and it might not be the most memorable Nirvana song — one of the most memorable videos because it's so dramatic. That was the last video we made. We had a lot of conversations afterwards about other videos and other songs: 'Well, that might make a better single, because it would make a better video.' I remember at one point Kurt saying, 'You know, I just don't think I can top 'Heart-Shaped Box.' I really achieved something exactly the way I wanted to, and I don't even want to try.' " By the way, the saturated color of "Heart-Shaped Box" Kates remembers as being Cobain's idea.

Adam Bernstein has all the qualities that one imagines in a successful director: He's direct and articulate about his ideas and his work. A director of videos beginning in the halcyon days of the mid- to late-'80s, including work for B-52s, Public Enemy, the Beastie Boys, Run D.M.C. and Frank Black, Adam has often gotten inspiration from bands. "My creative approach doesn't change whether the budget is $5,000 or $500,000. In terms of cooking up ideas, sometimes a band plays me a song and I'll have an instant flash, an instant intuition. Sometimes the band comes to me with a little kernel of an idea that is absolutely brilliant. The Dead Milkmen always have a fucking great idea. Rodney Anonymous, who's a pop-culture freak says, 'Adam, for this video I'd like to do a Dario Argento movie.' I'd never heard of Dario Argento, then I'd rent three of his movies and think, 'How fucking genius is this?' And then they would just cut me loose. Basically, they planted the seed. I'd do tons of research and carry the ball. I would figure out how to adapt this cinematic idea to the song: what scenes do I employ, what images do I employ to get it across?"

Nancy Bennett, director and producer of videos for Tori Amos, Mr. Big, and Victoria Williams, just quit a lifelong smoking habit and it makes her energy seem even harder to contain. In her late 30s, Nancy is an earth mother who has nurtured many video-makers at the beginning of their careers. Her perspective on the business was formed by working for years as a video commissioner at Atlantic Records. While writing treatments she sometimes can find a voice echoing from a dimly remembered location. "Well, I think you're the summation of people you've met and the places and things you've seen," she says.

"For me, locations are the places that I've been. You know, a good example is the Beth Hart video I did. When I wrote the treatment, I was thinking about a location I saw in 1990 when we were doing a Tori Amos video with Melody McDaniel. It was a very strange Byzantine mosque/Middle Eastern–style amalgamation of architectures. It was just appropriate to me. I wrote the treatment with that in mind and it fueled my prose perfectly. When you have a place in mind or you have a visual clearly etched in your head, I think the words roll onto the page."

As a practicality, the treatment exists so the record company has some idea of what they're buying. Though, at first, you may not be writing for label executives, somebody, even if it's just your guitar-playing friend, has to approve your ideas. Some directors, however, have learned to be deliberately vague about production details or effects they want to create. "When writing treatments, I try to be evocative of what you're going to see, and at the same time try to remain non-committal," agrees Kerslake. "I try to build a ride, and most people who read this stuff will get it on that level. But when the businessmen step in and say, 'What the hell does this mean?', they're looking for a blueprint, clean lines and thorough descriptions: 'What am I going to get for my money?' I sometimes write addenda to clarify what was vague, or to assure people that they're going to get the [production] goodies."

On the creative side, you need ideas in the first place and generally you won't get any unless you come to grips with the proverbial blank page. Some directors profess not to write treatments for low-budget jobs or until they've been assigned the job. However, if making your video is going to be an experience of the creative process rather than simply shooting a bunch of film to see what comes out, write before you shoot.

Before visualizing a video, it helps to think about what type of video makes the most sense for the song. Perusing MTV may convince the casual observer that music videos are visually arresting arrangements of random images not dissimilar to Nike ads, or, at best, vague sort-of stories invented to organize those images. We've developed a way of thinking about or "reading" a music video that recognizes the evolution of two types of videos.

>>>

OUR BACK PAGES

Follow the bouncing ball as we digress into the history of music television to find the missing links of rock video:

Contrary to what a generation of television brats might say, the concept of merging music and imagery did not arrive with the invention of the cable box. Nearly 400 years before spiky-haired Billy Idol sneered, "I want my MTV!", a poet named Octavio Rinuccini expanded his verse into a pastoral play and set it to music. He titled it *Dafne*, and the first opera was born in 1598. Meet music video's great-great-great-great-great grandfather. Perhaps more than any other combination of media, music and imagery has the power to lock into our memories and send us spiraling back in time.

Case in point: Ask any baby boomer about which *Ed Sullivan Show* episode he remembers best, and chances are it's the American debut of the mop-topped Liverpudlians harmonizing "I Wanna Hold Your Hand." Likewise, mention "Girls Just Want to Have Fun" to someone who was braving junior high in the mid-'80s, and the image of Cyndi Lauper tossing her multicolored locks crashes to mind as quickly as that hiccuping sound she makes. But the road leading us from Rinuccini to Lauper has been, just like the medium itself, far from linear. It zigzags from the theater to the movies to television to advertising. Still, despite the mishmash of influences, it's clear that no matter what the format, no matter what the decade, whenever

SHINDIG!

music and imagery are combined, someone sells a heap of records.

Thanks to Mr. Rinuccini, music video has some surprisingly highbrow origins. Like many art forms of the Renaissance, opera was created by reformers looking to rekindle the simplicity and humanism of the ancient Greeks. Into this new cultural offering they packed everything: acting, singing, instrumental music and storytelling. But it was not until 1637, when the first opera house opened in Venice, that the art form reached critical mass. By the end of the century, the Venetians had gorged themselves on nearly 400 productions. Opera and the mass-appeal musical productions of minstrel shows and vaudeville developed in suspicious parallel until several centuries later, when celebrated composer George Gershwin fused the gap between opera and Broadway with a grand opera based on Southern black life and music, *Porgy and Bess*.

Taking its cue from the Great White Way, Hollywood has been combining music with images for years. In the mid-'40s, elaborate movie musicals featuring the leggy likes of Brazilian bombshell Carmen Miranda and pinup doll Betty Grable distracted a nation beleaguered by war. Later on, with the advent of Technicolor, the genre dabbled in dreamy surrealism, with Vincente Minnelli's *Yolanda and the Thief* (1945) and *The Pirate* (1948) emerging as fanciful forerunners of the "MTV style." In addition to auditioning kick-line after kick-line of chorines, the studios were wising up to the fact that popular musicians could carry a bare-bones plot. A prime example is the 1944 musical *Atlantic City*, which relies on a marquee's worth of big-band and jazz musicians, from Louis Armstrong, Dorothy Dandridge, Buck and Bubbles, and Paul Whiteman and Orchestra, to inject verve into an otherwise unoriginal story about a boardwalk promoter. Likewise, the musician biopic came into vogue in the '40s with such hits as 1947's *The Fabulous Dorseys*, in which the big-band brothers play themselves in between, of course, playing their hit songs.

But long before original MTV veejay Martha Quinn was even a glimmer in Mr. and Mrs. Quinn's eyes, there were actual music videos on film. In the late 1940s, lindy-hoppers grooved to the Panoram Soundie, a jukebox with short film versions of artists' songs. While the so-called "soundies" enjoyed a brief period of popularity, by the 1950s they died out as Americans cozied up to the latest gizmo combining sound and image — the television. But the idea of pairing music and film didn't die. A decade later, a French company invented the next generation of soundie, the Scopitone. Although this video jukebox caught Europe's attention, few American acts created Scopitone films, and the machine never became popular across the Atlantic.

Back in Hollywood, a seemingly innocuous 1955 film signaled a tectonic pop-cultural shift. Director Richard Brooks' hard-hitting chronicle of one teacher's experiences in the New York City school system, *Blackboard Jungle*, became the first bona fide rock film. While the movie's credit sequence rolled to Bill Haley and the Comets's "Rock Around the Clock," the teenage audience rocked. They leapt to their feet, began dancing and ripped out the cinema seats in a rebellious frenzy. For the first time, music and film collided to explosive effect, sending a message to the entertainment industry that a steamroller youth movement was on its way.

After that combustible reaction, cinema and rock music forged a fast, lucrative friendship. Derivative flicks immediately followed, their see-through plots flimsy excuses to gather music's top draws. Frank Tashlin's *The Girl Can't Help It* hit the big screen a year after *Blackboard Jungle* in a blaze of Technicolor. It featured onscreen performances by Gene Vincent and the Blue Caps, Eddie Cochran, Julie London, Fats Domino and Little Richard. Meanwhile, Bill Haley returned to perform the eponymous song (twice) in *Rock Around the Clock* (much to theater owners' relief, the seat-ripping rioting was not repeated), and he made an appearance in the shameless "roxploitation" film, *Don't Knock the Rock*. That same year, director Edward L. Cahn put forth his equal-ly uninspired effort, *Shake, Rattle and Rock!* While these copycat films were unanimously razzed by critics, teens flocked to the theater to catch their jukebox idols in big-screen dimensions.

It wasn't long before Elvis himself was crooning on the celluloid stage. Critic David Marsh dubbed the King's passel of rock pics, "the last great series of Hollywood star vehicles." Indeed, there often wasn't much meat to these films, just fawning girls and a hip-twitching pop song every 10 or 15 minutes. But *Jailhouse Rock* (1957) yielded one of the iconic rock-movie moments with Elvis's slide down the pole and shimmying dance with a chair in the title-song sequence (choreographed by the King himself!). Hollywood cranked them out, one after another, from *Love Me Tender*, his first film in 1956, to 1969's embarassing *Change of Habit*.

Across the Atlantic, Britain was experiencing a youthquake of its own that also capitalized on the power of music and film. In 1957, the country's first pop idol, Tommy Steele, starred in a biopic titled, not surprisingly, *The Tommy Steele Story*, released just eight months after his first hit record. Bridging the gap between musical and biopic, it emerged as the country's first pop film and was followed by *The Duke Wore Jeans*. Lacking big production budgets, these rise-to-fame films avoided the chorus-singing crowds of Elvis's films and instead plunked the performing musicians in natural locales, on stage or in the studio.

Perhaps the liner notes to the sound-track to the 1969 film *Zabriskie Point*, which unites the Grateful Dead, Pink Floyd and the Youngbloods, best capture the relationship between music and image in the '60s: "It is more than just a case of a film today demanding the music of today. Contemporary music doesn't merely tell a story or set the mood; it is the story. It is the mood."

And what applied to film also applied to its cousin, television. In England, where the weekly chart countdown program *Top of the Pops* was already popular, shows like the perkily named *Ready! Steady! Go!* and *Oh, Boy* debuted. The latter was imported from England for a brief summer run in 1959 but was quickly dismissed by *New York Herald* critic Sid Bakal as "an appalling piece of trash." After Beatlemania washed over Britain in 1963 and America one year later, network executives on both shores of the Atlantic recognized the runaway poten-tial of rock-and-roll and television. Enter several fast-paced shows custom made for music-crazy teens.

In America, derivative shows such as *Hullabaloo, American Bandstand* and *Shindig!* hit the tube. For the first time, TV recognized its teenage audience as major consumers. *Hullabaloo* debuted in 1964 as one of television's first attempts to give rock-and-roll a big-budget, quality showcase in prime time. Each week, top acts per-

ELVIS, THE ROCK-MOVIE KING

formed current hits backed by elaborate production and frantic, miniskirted Hullabaloo Dancers. Acts appearing includ-ed the Supremes, the Ronettes, and Sonny and Cher. Rock impresario Brian Epstein, the manager of the Beatles, hosted a weekly segment taped in London that presented top British acts, including Marianne Faithfull, Gerry and the Pacemakers, Herman's Hermits and the Moody Blues. Epstein never brought his along his most famous protégés, however; they appeared after he left the show in 1966.

Based on the success of *Hullabaloo*, NBC recruited Jack Good, the British producer behind *Oh, Boy* and several similar shows. The result was the fast-paced, youthful *Shindig!*, hosted by West Coast DJ Jimmy O'Neil. The lineup for the fall '65 premiere included the Rolling Stones, the Kinks, the Byrds and the Everly Brothers. The Who made their American debut on the show later that year. *Shindig!* was a cut above the rest as it was broadcast live, for the most part, and the acts actually performed rather than lip-synching. Several regular acts were featured, such as Bobby Sherman, the Righteous Brothers, the Wellingtons, the Blossoms, Glen Campbell and Dana Loren.

But what about the top bands? For the most part, the Rolling Stones and the Beatles were too busy or too far away from the television studios to make personal appearances. As a result, record companies began shooting simple films and sending them to shows if the bands couldn't make it live. Most of the promos were crude by today's standards — a band would go to a sound stage and lip-synch their song as a camera crew caught the whole thing on film — but occasionally some bands took it a creative step further.

The Beatles were among the first. They scrapped the simple band-in-studio concept and created promotional video clips for "We Can Work It Out," "Penny Lane" and "Strawberry Fields." The Who and the Stones also dallied with this new format — the Who played a band of burglars for "Happy Jack" and the Rolling Stones spoofed Oscar Wilde's trial with Mick Jagger as Wilde and Keith Richards as the Marquis of Queensbury in their film of "We Love You."

As America grew fizzy with Anglophilia, the Fab Four set their sights on the big screen. Dubbed the *Citizen Kane* of jukebox musicals by Andrew Sarris of the *Village Voice*, their 1964 film debut, *A Hard Day's Night*, originally began as an excuse to squeeze a soundtrack out of the group. The film, directed by expatriate Richard Lester, follows the lads through a semi-fictionalized day in the life, all the while keeping up a breakneck pace as intoxicating as the electrifying soundtrack. In an homage to the avant-garde French New Wave and the British Free Cinema movements, Lester used super close-ups, hand-held camera shots and dizzying jump cuts to capture the frenzy of Beatlemania. Meanwhile, the music appears in a refreshingly organic style, rather than the forced musical breaks slapped into so many rock-and-roll films, not to mention the film musicals of the previous three decades.

The inevitable sequel, *Help!* (1965), bathed the Fab Four in color, with Lester, considered by many to be one of the founding fathers of music video, once again in the director's chair. While *Help!* boasted a bigger budget, it did not receive the same critical plaudits as its predecessor from the previous year. The Beatles bring their capers from London to the Salisbury Plains, from the Austrian Alps to the Bahamas as they chase a magical ring. Narrative takes second place to the music, which includes such gems as "Ticket to Ride," "You've Got to Hide Your Love Away" and "You're Gonna Lose that Girl."

The Beatles inspired a crop of imitators. The Dave Clark Five, Fab Four competitors in the teen magazines, starred in their own version of *A Hard Day's Night* called *Having a Wild Weekend* and its follow-up, *Catch Us If You Can*. Meanwhile, in 1966, television created a quartet of fun-loving moptops ready for zany adventure, *The Monkees*. The group's feature-film debut, *Head* (co-written by none other than Jack Nicholson), was the result of three days of smoking pot and rambling into a tape recorder. And it shows. Director Bob Rafelson (who later collaborated with Nicholson on the critically acclaimed *Five Easy Pieces* and most recently, *Blood and Wine*) created a bizarre, quintessentially '60s cult favorite around the band's sugar-pop tunes and kooky antics.

As the '60s closed, the convergence of film and music reached a darker, more experimental phase. The rock films created in the late part of the decade unnerve with hallucinatory visuals and hypnotic soundtracks. French New Wave director Jean-Luc Godard spliced in rehearsal footage of the Rolling Stones in his *One Plus One* (also

RICHARD LESTER DIRECTING

known as *Sympathy for the Devil*), while directors Donald Cammell and Nicolas Roeg intercut a Mick Jagger number in their 1970 release, *Performance*, which featured Jagger in his first dramatic role. In 1968, the Stones invited a bunch of friends, including John Lennon and Yoko Ono, Eric Clapton and Pete Townshend, to participate in their loosely organized *The Rolling Stones Rock and Roll Circus*, meant for British television. It finally debuted in the U.S. at the 1996 New York Film Festival. Of course, what's any experimental movement without an entry from Factory manager Andy Warhol? Sure enough, the artist/filmmaker keeps the camera trained for an unblinking 70 minutes on the band in *The Velvet Underground and Nico*.

Record companies soon discovered that films meant more exposure for their bands and in turn, higher record sales. While the clips were still few and far between, record labels started sending them to European and Australian television music shows when it was difficult for an act to tour on other continents. In the mid-'70s, both the creativity and the number of clips inched forward. A pivotal point came in 1975 when the band Queen hired an upstart director named Bruce Gowers to make a film for their unconventional single, "Bohemian Rhapsody." The song climbed to number 30 on the British charts and *Top of the Pops* began airing the clip. Suddenly, the song rocketed to Britain's number 5 and stayed there for more than a dozen weeks.

Suddenly "Bohemian Rhapsody" gave record companies the proof they needed to launch full-scale production. An expanding circle of European acts, in turn, made promotional clips for their songs, *Top of the Pops* increased its airplay of video clips, and a burgeoning music-video industry began in London. By 1978, the *Kenny Everett Video Show* debuted on British TV. Its host was a loopy British comedian, its director David Mallet, former assistant director of ABC's *Shindig!* The show featured in-studio performances as well as music videos.

America was a little slow to catch up. In 1977, Billboard, publisher of the music-industry trade publication, launched a division called Starstream that supplied clubs and other venues with promotional clips. Some record companies, including Warner Bros., an MTV parent company, started their own video departments that year and began to recognize video's potential. But the biggest push to launch the music-video industry came from the artists themselves, who saw not only sales but also the creative potential of the medium. Michael Nesmith of the Monkees, Todd Rundgren, Debbie Harry of Blondie, David Bowie and Devo explored video early on. Rundgren even began building a state-of-the-art video facility in his home, while the chameleon-like Bowie showcased his musical alter-ego in a narrative format in 1972's *The Rise & Fall of Ziggy Stardust and the Spiders from Mars*. On the underground scene, the merging of mediums gave way to an in-your-face wave of experimental film-making and punk rock. Derek Jarman had long been capturing the underground on super-8 when he filmed the Sex Pistols at Andrew Logan's St. Valentine's Day party in 1976. Similarly, Don Letts captured the middle-finger-waving rebellion of punk rock on super-8 with his *Punk Rock Movie*. Several independent record labels set up their own film companies. Ralph Records set the precedent with such films as the Residents' *Third Reich and Roll* (1978) and *Hello Skinny* (1980). In Britain, Mute Records inaugurated a film division to handle promotional needs and address the growing video market for concert films. Mute's *Halbe Mensch* (1985) by Sogo Ishii, is an imaginative coalition of experimental film and music that grew out of this influential movement.

By the fall of 1979, a program called *Video Concert Hall* began airing on several southern cable stations, while DJ Casey Kasem launched a half-hour syndicated video show called *America's Top Ten*. But by the early 1980s, late-night variety shows like *Saturday Night Live, Midnight Special* or the syndicated *Don Kirschner's Rock Concert* were the only programs airing rock. Television executives were gunning for mass appeal, and in their eyes, music-hungry youth was just too narrow a demographic.

Shortly thereafter, lanky ex-Monkee, actor and producer Michael Nesmith approached John Lack, a visionary executive at a company formed by American Express and Warner Bros. called Warner AMEX Satellite Entertainment Company. Nesmith showed Lack a surreal video for one of his songs, "Rio," plus a pilot for a program called *Popclips*, a show that exclusively featured video clips. He revealed to Lack his vision for a video radio station. Lack was blown away. He asked Nesmith to create another episode of *Popclips*, perhaps to be run on the new cable station for kids called Nickelodeon.

But Lack got to thinking. What about a whole network dedicated to rock and roll? He was convinced it would work. After receiving rave reviews for the video clips from test audiences, he commissioned Nesmith to create more *Popclips* shows. Nesmith delivered the goods in early 1980. But there was a problem. Many of the clips were too risqué for the kids' channel, and Lack thought the use of comedians like Howie Mandel detracted from the music. What about video DJs? Nesmith disagreed but made the changes, and *Popclips* debuted in the Columbus, Ohio, test market in March and garnered positive reviews.

In the spring of 1980, Lack decided that the time was right for an all-music channel. He envisioned the channel running clips as well as concerts and music news. Nesmith shook his head: He thought Lack's venture sounded too commercial. He approached the clips as an art form that consumers would buy and play at home on disk players and VCRs. Disgusted, Nesmith walked out on the project.

No problem. The plan moved forward. The executives decided that the channel would have to be as cutting edge as the music it played. There would be no separate programs with the exception of a Saturday night concert and a Sunday night movie. It would simply feature song after song, just like a radio station. This was indeed a radical notion because from the day it started, television had consisted almost exclusively of regularly scheduled 30-, 60- and 90-minute shows. But time was of the essence. A program that featured music videos called *Night Flight* had recently debuted on HBO. After numerous auditions, the executives discovered five "veejays" with the right combination of hipness, spontaneity and music knowledge — Nina Blackwood, Martha Quinn, Alan Hunter, Mark Goodman and J. J. Jackson.

On August 1, 1981, at 12:01 a.m., MTV debuted. The first video? A no-brainer: "Video Killed the Radio Star" by the British band Buggles. The influence was tangible. Within months, kids started looking for records by bands not typically played on mainstream American radio — Squeeze, Billy Squier, Talking Heads and the Tubes — but whose videos aired on MTV.

>>>

PIONEERS

These old-school music-video directors pioneered the medium. Flick on MTV today and you'll still see remnants of their narrative techniques.

MICHAEL NESMITH

Michael Nesmith may be best known as the Monkee in the wool cap, but his contributions to the music world stretch far beyond his stint as one of "America's Beatles." In 1979, the singer/songwriter/entrepreneur approached Warner AMEX Satellite Entertainment Company (WASEC) with a proposal to launch a music-video network. Great idea! He had already created one of the splashiest early videos (he called them "popclips") for his song "Rio." But Nesmith bowed out of the deal when he couldn't convince corporate bigwigs the videos should fulfill an artistic rather than a promotional purpose. A shrugging WASEC would go on to create MTV without him. Nonetheless, Nesmith is considered by most to be the father of music video.

BRUCE GOWERS

In 1975 the band Queen wanted a promotional clip for the grandiose single "Bohemian Rhapsody." Enter rising young director Bruce Gowers. The group asked if he could create a video that would bring their *Queen II* album cover to rocking life. In just two days they had it. The song was a colossal chart-topper, while the visually provocative video aired for nine consecutive weeks on Britain's *Top of the Pops*. Sales for the album skyrocketed, and suddenly the music industry was buzzing about the promotional power of music video. With this success, Gowers established himself as a director unafraid to push the medium's creative boundaries. He quickly rose to the top of the fledgling industry, creating videos for Genesis and Rod Stewart.

STEVE BARRON

With the plaintive wail, "I want my MTV," and blockheaded animated workmen, director Steve Barron's video for Dire Straits's "Money For Nothing" is one of the best-remembered videos in the medium's history. For most television viewers, the clip represents their first glimpse at the wonders of computer animation. Thanks to Barron's innovation, it was certainly not their last. He continued in this direction with the award-winning "Take On Me" video for the pop band A-Ha. Then came "Billie Jean." The first single to be released from Michael Jackson's monster-selling *Thriller* album, this clip elevated the medium to a theatrical new level in 1983 with its sophisticated narrative and moon-walking choreography. Barron later collaborated with the Human League, Rod Stewart and Adam and the Ants before directing such feature films as *Electric Dreams*, *Teenage Mutant Ninja Turtles* and *The Coneheads*.

BOB GIRALDI

In 1983 Bob Giraldi founded GASP!, one of the first music-video companies in the country. It was a good year. Soon after, the entrepreneur wrote and directed one of the industry's definitive music videos, Michael Jackson's chef d'oeuvre, "Beat It." From there, other popular videos followed: the Michael Jackson/Paul McCartney duet "Say, Say, Say," Pat Benatar's "Love Is a Battlefield" and Lionel Richie's "Hello," "Running with the Night," "Penny Lover" and "Ballerina Girl." His other collaborations include videos for Diana Ross, Stevie Wonder, Barry Manilow, Julio Iglesias, and Daryl Hall and John Oates. One of the entertainment industry's most successful commercial directors, Giraldi has directed television specials, films and hundreds of TV advertisements, including Miller Lite's "Tastes Great, Less Filling," and the literally incendiary Michael Jackson Pepsi campaign.

RUSSELL MULCAHY

From the moment young Australian filmmaker Russell Mulcahy burst onto the video scene, he was hailed as the industry's first auteur. And with good reason. His video for Buggles's

"Video Killed the Radio Star" was the first clip ever aired on a new all-music channel called MTV in 1981. Soon after, Mulcahy raised the narrative style of music video to near-epic levels with Duran Duran's "Hungry Like the Wolf." The clip portrayed the frilly band risking their lives and chasing babes as James Bond-inspired rogues on a sweeping, intercontinental adventure. The video not only sent squealing female fans clamoring around their TVs but also distinguished the band as one of the first groups to top the charts via a smash video. With his dramatic slow-motion shots and stylized, evocative imagery, Mulcahy emerged as the creative force behind a number of other hit acts, including Rod Stewart, Kim Carnes, Ultravox, and Bonnie Tyler.

GODLEY AND CREME

Lol Creme and Kevin Godley first made waves in the music industry as members of the British smart-pop quartet 10CC. After pursuing a successful career as a duo, they expanded their art-school adventurousness into video direction. Most famously, Godley and Creme directed Duran Duran's sensuously daring "Girls on Film," complete with oiled, writhing models, Herbie Hancock's funky "Rockit" and the Police's moody "Wrapped Around Your Finger." The pair broke into the top ten with their own single, "Cry," in 1985, accompanied by an award-winning, groundbreaking video that introduced computer-morped images of people's faces.

JULIAN TEMPLE

British director Temple rose to fame on the frilly coattails of the moussed, eyelinered heart-throbs of the '80s new romantic movement. One of the first music-video directors to weave a highly visual mini-narrative out of a three-minute pop song, Temple stepped behind the camera for such Reagan-era icons as Boy George and Duran Duran, and later for Tom Petty, the Rolling Stones, Neil Young, Janet Jackson and ABC. It's not surprising, given his talent for storytelling, that Temple landed a career as a feature-film director, helming several projects with an eye and an ear toward England's influential music scene. His first film, *The Great Rock 'n' Roll Swindle* (1980), is a fictionalized account of the Sex Pistols' story, while 1986's *Absolute Beginners* reinvents British pop history. Temple's most recent efforts include *Earth Girls Are Easy* (1989); *At the Max* (1991), a film of the Rolling Stones in concert; *Bullet* (1996), and *Burning Up* (1997).

DAVID FINCHER

Fincher is music video's most recent initiate into the pantheon of classic directors. Influenced by the lighting and composition of photography, the auteur's work includes "Love Is Strong" by the Rolling Stones, "Who Is It?" by Michael Jackson and "Bad Girl" by Madonna. Not bad. The rest of his credits roll like a countdown of the top videos of the '80s and early '90s: George Michael's "Freedom 90," Madonna's "Vogue" and "Express Yourself," Aerosmith's "Janie's Got a Gun," Paula Abdul's "Straight Up, " Jody Watley's "Real Love" and Don Henley's "End of Innocence." Not long after he conquered MTV, corporate America snatched him up to create award-winning television spots for Nike, AT&T, Chanel, Levi's, Coca-Cola and Budweiser. One of the most prominent video directors to parlay his distinctive style into feature films, Fincher made his big-screen debut with the sci-fi thriller *Alien 3* in 1992, followed by the chilling neo-noir *Seven* in 1996.

<<<

MTV patterned itself after Top 40 radio, using radio's non-linear, short-take formula to appeal to teenagers and young adults. The impact of MTV fever could immediately be seen on the *Billboard* charts. Bands like Britain's synthesizer-heavy A Flock of Seagulls, pretty boys Duran Duran, Australia's Men at Work and rockabilly throwbacks the Stray Cats parlayed their notice-me images into record sales via MTV. Without the medium, their hopes of cracking the American charts may have been significantly more modest. To further prove the point, the Stray Cats charted their touring itinerary based only on those cities that carried MTV. What you looked like suddenly had as much to do with success as what you sounded like, and in some case more. In 1983 Michael Jackson's "Billie Jean," directed by Steve Barron, "Beat It," directed by Bob Giraldi, and "Thriller," directed by John Landis, singlehandedly upped the artistic and budgetary ante of music videos with Jackson's choreography, elaborate productions and mini-movie narratives. All-time sales records tumbled.

While music video once turned to Hollywood for inspiration, the opposite was now true. Quick cuts timed to music, the trademark of the MTV look, influenced the making of soundtrack-driven movies such as *Flashdance*, *Purple Rain*, *Stayin' Alive* and *Footloose*, and even a television show, *Miami Vice*. Filmmaker Brian DePalma directed Bruce Springsteen's "Dancing in the Dark" video, while video auteurs Russell Mulcahy (Duran Duran's "Hungry Like the Wolf") and Steve Barron were recruited to feature-film work. This cross-pollination seems natural since the first generation of music video built on the well-established conventions of movie narratives and television concert and teen dance programs. Show the band. Close-up on the singer during the chorus. Cut between the song and the story. The next decade found more innovation as the medium found its own voice.

MTV pushed forward with new projects. It launched sister music channel VH-1 in 1985 and began rebroadcasting episodes of *The Monkees*, revitalizing the long-disbanded group's residual payments. But by 1987, MTV suffered its seven-year itch. A generation had grown accustomed to having access to music videos 24 hours a day and was numbed to the barrage of rapid-fire images. Viewership was down and competition was growing. MTV resorted to a strategy that went against the very core of its mission: It would run half-hour programs. The first, *Club MTV*, a dance show broadcast live from New York City's Palladium every afternoon, fit easily into the established format; the second, *The Week in Rock*, expanded the channel's music-news offering. The success of these two programs inspired MTV to add a wacky game-show, *Remote Control*, and a rap and hip-hop showcase, *Yo! MTV Raps*. Suddenly it was was open season on any programming that catered to the younger generation for MTV.

The '90s saw the trend continue toward blocks of music- and non-music-related programming. The acoustic showcase *Unplugged* debuted in 1990 with Squeeze, after rocker Jon Bon Jovi received plaudits for his acoustic performance of "Dead or Alive" at the channel's Video Music Awards. Soundtracks from *Unplugged* fueled a gold rush as aging rockers plundered their back catalogs to release the equivalent of another greatest hits collection, albeit a live, acoustic version. The *Unplugged* phenomenon created some odd spectacles: the ascension of Tony Bennett as a hipster icon? Rap unplugged? In 1992 *The Real World* picked its first seven strangers to occupy a house and have their everyday lives taped. That same year, Bill Clinton appeared on MTV's *Choose or Lose* forum, and animated pubescent morons *Beavis and Butthead* uttered their first annoying laughs and boosted the careers of White Zombie, among others. MTV has returned its focus to music programming with the advent of M2, the network's mostly satellite-distributed, all-music sister that offers more idiosyncratic programming, and new genre programming such as *Amp*, its techno/ambient exploration created by programmer Todd Mueller. MTV plans to morph again, recreating its schedule 15 years after beaming its first video, by adding 10 to 20 more hours of music videos per week and creating a nightly three-hour programming block for its non-music series.

MTV president Judy McGrath was quoted in *Variety* as saying, "It was never our intention to move away from music. We were pushed to do it in the mid-'80s to control our own destiny a bit. We just couldn't rely on a steady flow of product from the record companies. It's difficult to build a schedule when you don't know what records and videos are coming . . . With the music industry lacking a clear direction right now, we have an opportunity to try out a few new directions of our own." The network won't ignore the franchise it built with (higher-rated, after all) non-music programming, recently debuting the *Beavis and Butt-head* sister *Daria*; quiz show *Idiot Savants*; *The Rodman World Tour* with Dennis Rodman; the radio-on-TV show, *Loveline*; talk show from the public-access world, *Oddville*; *The Jenny McCarthy Show*; comedy showcase *Apartment 2F*; and its first sitcom, *Austin Stories*.

The videos themselves have taken a turn to the experimental and abstract, extending the exploration of the photographic videos of Matt Mahurin, Anton Corbijn and Sam Bayer that made icons of U2, Nirvana and R.E.M., among many others.

Amp displays videos from bands such as Aphex Twin, Tortoise, and electronica pioneers such as Kraftwerk and Tangerine Dream, sometimes with no band in attendance, sometimes with vaguely Germanic, machinelike camera movements and blurs of color.

For hints to MTV's and the music industry's future direction, catch M2 on satellite. McGrath described it to *Variety* as having a "far more freeform spirit" than MTV, and that it "embodies the kind of sensibility we want to borrow for MTV and belongs on MTV." M2 may also provide an insight into the future of broadcasting in general as it begins beaming over the Internet using chip-maker Intel Inc.'s "intercast" technology that allows a personal computer to receive a television signal. M2 will use intercast 24 hours a day and MTV itself will offer the service for two hours a day.

<<<

CINEMATIC AND PHOTOGRAPHIC VIDEOS

With a historical perspective, we can see that music videos come from a long tradition of marrying image to sound. In music video's less-than-epic-length part of that history, the form has already developed two distinct tendencies: the cinematic and the photographic. These general streams are the broad, wide tributaries into the ocean of music videos, and almost all videos feature elements of both. Most video directors, though, recognize the distinction even if they use their own terminology. "Early in the process," says director Adam Bernstein, "I tried to define the categories of music video: there's the performance video, there's the narrative video, there's the ethereal video, which relies on imagery and impressions. Then there's any mixture of those three."

The primary distinction between the tendencies in music videos is the degree of visual grammar — the commonly understood vocabulary of shot composition and editing — employed. Cinematic videos use traditional film grammar, and their treatments read like short stories, with narrative progression and storytelling devices. "Billy drives through the desert in an ice cream truck. To his surprise, he finds his bandmates hitchhiking along the road. When they arrive at a gas station, they smear their bodies with finger-paint and dance around in various stages of undress." Or, "After traveling by bike, car and airplane, Coolio pedals a Big Wheel to the house party to meet his girl, but she's gone because the party's over," and so forth. Early video directors such as David Fincher, Julian Temple, and Marty Callner pioneered videos that intercut a fully developed story with the performance, and the classic cinematic videos look like big-budget movies from the '80s. Callner's "Janie's Got a Gun" for Aerosmith defines the cinematic-video style. In the video, a young, rich girl, Janie, shoots her sexually abusive father. Dramatic scenes illustrate the father/daughter conflict, we see the murder and then follow as a detective tracks her down. Squad cars screech, police troops march, bright flashlight beams cut through misty rain-slicked streets. This minimovie features incredibly high-end production values, essential for any *Lethal Weapon*-era, big-budget action hit. What makes videos such as "Janie's Got a Gun" or Madonna's "Papa Don't Preach" classic cinematic videos is that they directly illustrate the songs' narratives, stories told through dramatic scenes that are intercut with performance footage.

Strictly cinematic videos seem outdated today, since traditional story videos have become music video's equivalent of representational painting in a modernist, abstract world. Today, this style lives on in country music, R&B and hip-hop, perhaps because those musical genres uphold a tradition of narrative ballad songwriting. In any musical genre, you can probably think of videos that have dramatic scenes supporting the song narrative yet don't employ visual grammar or progress in a linear narrative. Mark Pellington's award-winning Pearl Jam video, "Jeremy," is a perfect example. The video illustrates the story about an alienated suburban kid who shoots himself in front of his high-school classroom. A photographer by trade, Pellington shows us the story in photomontage-like glimpses. It's dramatic, but not in traditional movie form. We would still refer to videos like "Jeremy" as cinematic, because they aspire to narrative even while they reject movie-narrative devices.

Not all cinematic videos are narrative or dramatic, and the category includes those we call "progressive." In a progressive video, there isn't a "story," per se, but a progression in time or space conveyed by shots edited together into a visual story, if not a narrative one, told using basic filmmaking grammar. Spike Jonze is a master of the form. In his "Feel the Pain" for Dinosaur Jr., J. Mascis putts golf balls around unlikely locations in Manhattan. As they soar through the air, we follow J. from point A to point B.

Everyone weaned on television, movies and comic books understands visual grammar without even trying. Even non-filmmakers would know how to cut together the scene that visually translates this sentence: J. Mascis swings the club and the ball flies over the skyscraper. Shots are like words, and a scene makes a complex sentence. Think about it for a minute. Your daydream about that sentence probably includes a close-up of the ball, a medium shot of J. swinging the club, and a wide shot of the ball flying through the air. In your mind's eye, these shots were cut together in an order that follows basic rules of filmmaking grammar. Instinctively, you wouldn't have the wide shot of the ball flying through the air first. The *visual* story would be confused.

Most of us have such an intuitive feel for visual grammar that explaining basic Hollywood editing seems like stating the obvious. But understand that if you deliberately break the rules (which you may want to try sometimes), you will upset your audience's certainty of how the world works. For example, here's a description of the way a cut signifies continuous action. Shot 1: Character A opens a door in a room and exits. Cut. Shot 2: Character A enters another room through a doorway and closes the door behind him. If rules of screen direction (A leaves frame on left in Shot 1 and enters on right in Shot 2) and cam-

WHO DIRECTS WHAT

CINEMATIC DIRECTORS
Adam Bernstein, Phil Morrison, Jesse Peretz, Spike Jonze, F. Gary Gray, Lionel C. Martin, Sophie Mueller, Jake Scott, David Fincher

PHOTOGRAPHIC DIRECTORS
Kevin Kerslake, Matt Mahurin, Sam Bayer, Dean Carr, Anton Corbijn, Melody McDaniels, Mark Romanek

era angle (the camera remains at eye level in Shots 1 and 2) have been followed, and A wears the same clothes in both shots, we're not confused or disoriented. We know that Character A has just walked through a doorway connecting two rooms. We've "read" the cut unconsciously, and it's a conjunction we've seen a million times. The cut creates the illusion of continuous action. We don't think, "I wonder if this is the same day? That's funny, he's wearing the same suit." We get it.

If cinematic videos are narrative, or tell a story visually using the fundamentals of film grammar, photographic videos are overtly non-narrative and rely less on traditional film syntax. Treatments for these videos describe the photography, the color, the motion, the backdrops — the look and feel rather than the story line. Photographic videos gain structure in the editing process, and not necessarily by the director. When making these videos, the director is more concerned with collecting as many startling, lush, provocative images as s/he can within the universe created for the video. If there's performance in the video, shots of the band playing interact with images of vaguely symbolic objects and unusual, often grotesque-looking people. When a pouty model turns to the camera, glares earnestly, then settles into a new pose, the shot functions more like portrait photography. It tells us something about her attitude, her environment, her physical and emotional presence, but it is discrete and only reveals that particular moment. The individual shots do not advance a narrative or even visual story using the grammar we discussed above. These photographic videos are collages or photomontages and derive their impact from the feelings created or the meaning imparted by the juxtaposition of the images.

SHOT
The basic unit of film narrative; the single, unedited slice of visual information, i.e., close-up of golf ball.

SCENE
A succession of shots that comprises a single visual or narrative idea, i.e., close-up of golf ball on city street, J. Mascis hits the golf ball, it flies past skyscraper.

SEQUENCE
A sequential series of scenes that make up a complete dramatic or narrative progression, i.e., close-up of golf ball, J. Mascis hits the golf ball, it flies past skyscraper, the ball lands in a cow pasture, J. hits the ball, the golf ball flies past chewing cow.

CUT
The transition from one shot to the next accomplished in editing, i.e., from the close-up of the golf ball to J. hitting the ball.

In the '80s, non-narrative videos often used graphic backdrops and other visual gimmicks drawn from screen musicals and performance segments on television, but most videos still relied on the performance, narrative model. As the '80s turned into the '90s, videos advanced along with the technology available: the telecine process and new experiments with film cross-processing techniques (using altered chemistry or procedures to develop exposed film stock) allowed filmmakers a bigger vocabulary to create individual looks. Bernstein thinks non-narrative videos are more evocative. "There are only certain aesthetic concerns you can work out in music video," Bernstein says. "I think a music video is most effective in the same way a good pop song is effective: It evokes an idea or emotion like poetry." Director Tryan George, creator of videos for Toto, Sebadoh, and Eric Matthews, would agree, echoing a sentiment heard often from directors. "If you're trying to tell a narrative story in a music video, you're working against the odds right off the bat," he cautions. "You don't have dialogue and you don't have sound effects, and to tell a narrative story in film, that's tying your arms behind your back. I think the proper way to think about video is to start with the song and to say these are the sound effects, this is the mood. You start with the mood and don't try to interpret the song literally. You give a broader interpretation of the song and the mood."

Videos by Matt Mahurin (Metallica, Bush) Sam Bayer (Hole, Nirvana), Dean Carr (Filter, Marilyn Manson), and Kevin Kerslake (Stone Temple Pilots, Nirvana) best exemplify the photographic stream of music videos. All of these directors make cinematic videos as well but generally tend toward videos that feature color studies, rich texture and manipulated image quality. Fine art photographer Mahurin, who had a wide-ranging career in music videos, reintroduced himself to the music-video world a couple of years ago by making a classic photographic video for Bush, "Little Things Kill." With nothing remotely resembling a story, band performance cuts with close-ups of small furry objects, vague grotesquery or band members posing before an assortment of backdrops. The image quality is striking: desaturated colors create a nearly sepia tone, and swing-and-tilt lenses defocus the edges of the image (special swing-and-tilt lenses have a bellows like those used for large format still cameras and make possible selective focus in a frame).

The use of effects like those created by swing-and-tilt lenses change our understanding of visual language. For example, the edges of the screen in soap opera dream sequences were conventionally blurry and out-of-focus. Eventually, if you wanted to ironically scream "dream sequence" in your film-school epic, you smeared Vaseline around the perimeter of the lens. Now this blurred-edge treatment of the image is common, popularized by hugely successful videos by Mahurin and Bayer. By now, when we watch one of these videos we don't sit there thinking, "I guess I'm watching somebody's dream about Bush."

These videos composed solely of evocative images represent the clearest example of the music video as a billboard for the recording artist, as an introduction to musicians that in previous years would have taken place on cardboard sleeves. Clay Tarver, screenwriter, former MTV producer and guitarist with Chavez, aptly compares music videos to the album covers of the vinyl age, finding the genesis of both in the record companies' need to graphically represent the music found on the disk and to differentiate it from the thousands of other releases in a particular week. Both also became other media for recording artists to extend their creative impulses, to present different facets of their talent, establishing or even commenting on their public personas. Ever since the Beatles effectively seized the songwriting function from the Brill Building's professional tunesmiths — making pop a vehicle for the recording artist's personal expression — performers have been tempted to experiment with and control the face that they turn to the public. Television enabled them literally to face their public, and now that album cover art has shrunk to a three-and-a-half inch square CD booklet, music videos are the cloaks in which pop stars are draped.

Product managers and A&R people (or most bands, for that matter) can't always articulate their vision for either a video or a record cover, but they know they need something singular and memorable in order to awaken bored kids. Bayer's bee girl video for Blind Melon's "No Rain" used one iconographic, marketable image to blast the band onto the charts (and to number 13 in MTV's list of all-time great videos). Nick Egan was an album cover designer/photographer long before directing Alanis Morissette in "You Oughta Know" and Oasis in "Champagne Supernova." In fact, a number of music-video directors come from fashion or fine art photography backgrounds. Matthew Ralston (TLC, "Creep"), Melody McDaniels (Cranberries, "Linger"), Matt Mahurin (Metallica, "Unforgiven"), Dan Winters (Hootie and the Blowfish, "Daniel Johnston"), Anton Corbijn (Nirvana, "Heart-Shaped Box"), Jean-Baptiste Mondino (Madonna videos), Mark Pellington (Pearl Jam, "Jeremy") and Kevin Kerslake (Stone Temple Pilots, "Inter-State Love Song") all work with visual ideas that spring from their photography backgrounds. All have made some vaguely narrative videos, but for the most part their work typifies a photographic approach. Cry all you want about the death of visual meaning, these directors aren't concerned with cinematic conventions, with the relationship between shots, with narrative development. Their work is purely about photography.

THE SOUND/IMAGE RELATIONSHIP

Regardless of whether you're going to employ traditional, movielike visual grammar or not, you will be grappling with the nature of sound/image relationships. I'll never forget accosting an old acquaintance, Nina Gordon, who had recently found success with her band, Veruca Salt. Always a vampire, I asked the alt-rock ingenue what they were doing for their first video. "Well, these friends of ours are going to do it," she replied, "and they are really inspired. They keep saying, 'Your song sounds like kitty-cats. When I listen to your song, I see kitty-cats.' "

As nauseating as that response may have been to me at first, I had to admit that they had gone about things the right way. They had come up with a sound and image relationship. Upon reflection, it struck me that there is a "squealing" quality to their guitar sounds that could vaguely sound like a cat's meow. If they think the song sounds like kitty cats, well, then they should shoot kitty cats. I don't really

VERUCA SALT IN THE SPOTLIGHT

remember too many kitty cats in their video. I do remember that MTV played the damned thing fifty times a day.

Though some videos demonstrate sound/image relationships that are more resolved than others, the best show a dedication to images that truly match the music. Perhaps one part of the song sounds to the director like a bulldozer pushing dirt, another part sounds like a bicycle wheel stuck in a pothole. Trying to explain this subconscious phenomenon, even to yourself, is like trying to explain emotional responses to music. You can't account for the endorphin rush you get after a certain chord change in a song any more than you can account for the absolute rightness of a successful sound-image relationship.

Often it relates to movement: Certain objects or images move like a conductor's wand and perfectly match the tempo of the music. Perhaps lampposts whiz by on downbeat intervals, or uneven terrain creates a blurry undulating line outside your window that moves along to the song's melody. In Handel's time, string quartets serenaded royal guests afloat on barges. The slow-moving riverbank provided appropriately flowing imagery, but our music moves at the pace of the superhighway. When the blaring car radio provides a soundtrack for passing scenery, you're having the quintessential modern moment. In your car with the window down and a good song on the radio, you're filled with emotion and music, the music flies by like the trees on the side of the road, and for a moment your life feels like a movie. Jonathan Richman has put the feeling on record for all times with "Radio On" as he describes flying down the dark highway with his AM radio on. Richman recreates the perfect experience of a good sound-image relationship.

Creating a memorable sound-image relationship demonstrates the artistry of a music-video director. The most oft-noted example of sound-image relationship in cinema is the dance of the satellites in *2001: A Space Odyssey* (1968) in which Stanley Kubrick ingeniously accompanies slow-motion, tumbling spacecraft with Strauss waltzes. At first, this relationship between sound and image seems impressive because of the disjunction between 21st-century technology and 18th-century music. Like many other stylistic aspects of the film, this disjunction seemed radical at a time that valued the new or up-to-date, when the obvious choice would have been "modern" or "futuristic" music. Watching *2001* today, you can't help thinking how dated the film would feel if Kubrick had made that choice. The relationship between sound and image works here even if you're not thinking about it in such analytical

THE RHYTHMIC LIZ PHAIR

terms. Perhaps Kubrick chose the music simply because the spaceships moved like people waltzing. In movement and in tone, intellectually and on a physical level, the imagery perfectly matches the music.

Other examples of resonant sound-image relationships, especially in music videos, are harder to deconstruct. Often a sound-image relationship springs from the video's concept: for example, if a song sounds "mechanical," machines might chug or churn on screen. Liz Phair's "Supernova," not an especially impressive video, has a great sound-image relationship, probably because Phair was both the songwriter and director, and instinctively served her own work beautifully. During the main hook of the song, Phair shows men rowing a crew shell. A bold choice, for these athletes have nothing to do with the vaguely narrative concept, and they appear only during the recurring hook. The jaunty, ascending guitar riff just happens to sound like guys dipping their oars in and out of the water. That's not some arty, impressionistic association — it's rhythmic, it's inherently musical, and it works.

Percussive movements make for good sound-image relationships. Not every song warrants a lot of jumpy movement, but there's nothing better than a music video that features on-camera "synch moments" that don't rely on the editing alone. In Spike Jonze's MC 900 Ft. Jesus video, "If I Only Had a Brain," the singer bounces around the inside of a cardboard box for most of the video. When his body hits a side of the box, each bounce creates a percussive action that punctuates downbeats in the song's groove. That's much more effective than relying on cuts made to the beat, a standard way of making images match the music. You want to see conductor's batons. You want to see drummers hitting skins. You want to see feet stomping and hands clapping, because these images are inherently musical. Any footage can be cut in a way that matches the rhythm of the music. What's harder is shooting footage that's inherently musical.

INTERLACING NARRATIVE: THE CLASSIC VIDEO FORM

Aside from pure performance videos in which every shot features an artist performing the song, most videos adhere to the same structural form: a performance element in which the artist performs the song intercut with the other visual material that make up the video. In a cinematic video, it would be a narrative or story element in which actors and/or band members act out a story line. In a photographic video, whatever is not the performance — models pouting, dwarves prancing, looming thunderstorms on the horizon — carries the visual scheme of the video. In either case, the story element and the performance element remain separate, often existing in separate spaces or worlds, but with constant cutting between the two. Video commissioners will often talk about the balance between performance and concept, what we call an interlacing narrative.

This formula comes to mind when most people first think of music videos, and the examples are numerous. Consider Aerosmith's "Crazy," which like "Janie's Got a Gun," is a classic cinematic video, though the narrative doesn't directly apply to the song's story. Liv Tyler and Alicia Silverstone pump gas while a lecherous redneck leers. Cut to Liv's dad rocking an arena stage. Liv does a striptease for an embarrassed Alicia at a strip club amateur night. Her hands slink down the pole; Steven Tyler's hands slip down the mic stand. Alicia's mouth opens wide to express astonishment; Steven's mouth opens wide to sing the chorus.

There's a consistent back-and-forth between story and band, an interlacing of performance and narrative.

The work of director Lionel C. Martin, who cites Alfred Hitchcock as one of his biggest influences, demonstrates quintessential interlacing narratives. Martin's Boyz II Men video, "I'll Make Love to You," is a camp classic and true to form. After installing a security system in a sexy young woman's impossibly palatial house, the handsome hero is smitten. Smiling warmly, the installer hands her his business card and we actually hear him say, "If you have any problems, give me a call . . ." (videos with a dialogue intro are perhaps worthy of their own sub-genre, Michael Jackson's "Thriller" being the archetype). Cut to the Boyz, singing like Men in the back of the house.

For the rest of the video, our young security-system installer tries to pen a love letter to the mansion-dwelling babe, but our attention never strays from the performing Boyz. The hero paces in front of an antique roll-top writing desk. The Boyz sing. Frustrated, he crumples up a piece of paper and throws it into the trash. The Boyz sing on. He finally breaks out the Boyz II Men CD and plagiarizes "I'll Make Love to You" for his love letter.

BOYZ II MEN: THEIR SONG IS THE STORY

He delivers the tome to the girl complete with a classy red wax seal. She reads it while soaking and gloating in her candle-lit bathtub. The Boyz croon once more. This interlacing narrative is a special case, because by showing the song lyrics as love-letter inspiration, Martin has creatively inserted the song into the story. The narrative is a three-minute love story inspired by the lyrics, of which the lyrics themselves are an integral part.

The form no doubt derives from the conventional pop-song structure in which chorus refrains summarize or comment upon the narrative lines of the verse. One could look for, and find, structural ancestry that includes the community singing and solo flights of gospel, the antiphons of sacred music — who knows, maybe even the ancient Greek choruses who chanted asides to the action unfolding in front of the audience. There seems an overall tendency in interlacing narrative clips to feature performers during the chorus, and narrative vignettes during the verse, placing our alternarock gods firmly in the Greek chorus.

A catchy chorus makes the hook, the jingle that's going to occupy the minds of millions of record buyers, so record companies want performer identification during the chorus. TLC's "Waterfalls" clip by F. Gary Gray is a perfect example. While virtually each line of the vignette-laden verses gets illustrated, Left-Eye and company are primarily seen performing in the choruses, knee-deep in a wading pool. We can sing along, because they sing along.

This conventional form could also have its roots in the original conception of how music videos would be used. If music videos replace the experience of being an audience member in the way that renting videocassettes replaces the experience of going to the movie theater, then the presentation of live performance in video is essential. Many of the super-group videos from the '80s offered the experience of being backstage. We wanted to know that "Sometimes when you're alone," as Jon Bon Jovi ponders in "Dead Or Alive," staring at nothing through the tour plane window, that "All you do is think . . ." This interlacing form applies to non-narrative, photographic videos as well, with alternating scenes of performance and textural, conceptual footage.

Maybe you've thought about what type of video, cinematic or photographic, makes the most sense for the song. You've worked out a sound-image relationship and have visualized how the interlacing narrative structure plays out. Now, how are you going to present the performer in your video? There remain some important stylistic issues to resolve before polishing up that treatment.

USE OF THE PERFORMER

On the most basic level, a music video is only as good as the performer. There's a reason why video directors aren't the ones giving acceptance speeches for the little silver spaceman, MTV's version of the Oscar, at its televised awards gala. People identify music videos with the artists, and MTV only started showing director credits on music videos in 1993. Even music-video directors themselves don't refer to music videos by their directors: no one says, "Have you seen the new Sophie Muller video?" They say, "Have you seen the new No Doubt video?" Making the artist look good is really a video director's first job. Would anyone really remember the "Sabotage" video, a paean to '70s-style TV detective shows, if the Beastie Boys weren't in it? One guiding light in making a music video is your artist's rock-star quality.

Many classic film icons achieved star status by transcending the medium. Film hunks Marlon Brando and James Dean make obvious examples, but consider silent-film star Louise Brooks. *Pandora's Box* (1929) pulls out all the German Expressionist stops (the deep shadows, the off-kilter sets that mirror the inner world of the characters), but it's her naturalistic performance that makes it a timeless masterpiece. In her demeanor and the knowing look in her eye, Brooks gives us a modern woman in the midst of an artificial world of stylized sets and melodramatic performances. Whenever she looks at the camera, she seems to be looking through it, right into your heart.

Rumor has it that when Nirvana was faced with the unpalatable prospect of doing a video for "Smells Like Teen Spirit," they chose Sam Bayer because they thought his reel stank. To the avatars of the new punk called grunge, making a video was a compromise anyway. Why not do it with a director whose reel looks the most generic? Watching the video with that in mind gives Cobain's performance a Louise Brooks quality. Even though the video (in which tattooed cheerleaders wear outfits emblazoned with the crossed-A international symbol of anarchy) drips with self-deprecating irony, Cobain seems disdainful of being in a video at all. Kids who think the video itself is cool pick up on Cobain's punk rock, anti-video performance. That we feel Cobain's sneer means the video successfully conveys the artist's intention. Bayer facilitated the creation of Cobain-as-rock-star: He did his job.

At any level of rock-star quality, it must be determined how the performers fit with

KURT COBAIN / LOUISE BROOKS: ROCK STARS

the other elements of the video. Performers in interlacing-narrative videos often function as narrators, standing apart from the story elements. As balladeers, they narrate the song's story; as music-video performers, they narrate the video's story. Sometimes this relationship becomes literal and the performer coexists with the story. Julian Temple's Tom Petty videos "Freefallin'" and "Into the Great Wide Open" exemplify performer-as-narrator videos. Like a Shakespearean actor giving an aside, Petty sings directly to the audience from a fore-ground corner of the frame. He winks at us while story elements fill the background. The notion that a video "illustrates" song narrative is underscored in "Great Wide Open" by the video's fairy-tale book visual scheme. We're the children to whom Petty reads a bedtime story, and his tongue-in-cheek presentation makes it all work.

Rap clips commonly employ the performer-as-narrator structure. Rappers from both coasts, Dre to Nas, have shot videos that feel like travelogues through the 'hood. They stand in the foreground singing about the town they love, while life in the town goes by in the background. When the musical performers themselves appear in the narrative, or they interact with the actors in the narrative, music video verges on opera or musical theater. This occurs when the singer's third-person relationship to the song's narrative shifts to the first person. Madonna exemplifies this shift. Endless discussions highlight the various ways she's presented herself through music video and defined the medium. Though "Borderline" demonstrates a classic interlacing narrative, Madonna herself is the main character in the story. She's subject and object, chorus and tragic hero. In Madonna videos (think of "Material Girl"), "story" and "performance" are one and the same, practically inventing operatic/musical-theater videos.

APPROPRIATION AND GENRE

In "Material Girl," Madonna inserts herself into a recreation of the Technicolor musical *Gentlemen Prefer Blondes* (1953), appropriating a familiar movie tableau, the big-budget song-and-dance sequence. Her singing and dancing as she portrays the character Marilyn Monroe played in the movie connects Madonna to both the character in her song and also to a cultural icon that she seemed destined to emulate. Spike Jonze directed the quintes-sential appropriation video, Weezer's "Buddy Holly," and it won MTV's best video award. In "Buddy Holly," Weezer appears in an old episode of the 1970s feel-good sitcom, *Happy Days*. All of the favorite characters, Fonzie, Richie, even Al the malt shop proprietor, watch as Weezer performs their song for the gang. The song's narrator says he's just like Buddy Holly and the object of his affection is just like Mary Tyler Moore, two pop culture icons that *would* be invoked by an ironically hip, TV-saturated fan of *Happy Days*. The video's success depends on media-savvy shorthand, on the audience having the same ironic, so-uncool-it's-cool response as the band and director. We know immediately that the sneaky fun is snatching media icons for subversive uses.

Similarly, Jesse Peretz won an MTV award for "Big Me" by placing the Foo Fighters in cheesy European Mentos commercials. Music videos appropriate the look and feel of home-shopping channels, talk shows, sports shows, silent movies, foreign movies, *America's Funniest Home Videos* and intros to '70s TV cop shows. In these videos, directors instantly convey an attitude, idea, time or place and stick performers on them like little vinyl Colorforms figures.

Appropriation renders all genre discussion pointless. There's no such thing as a "Western" music video, or a "film noir" music video: Music videos put genres in quotes. If television programs and commercials reference movies, theater, literature, opera, history, art, photography and current events, music videos reference all of the above — and other music videos. Music videos rip off any recognizable art/pop cultural movement that gains more than a moment of the public's attention. Rock-star whims influence this trend. Trent Reznor likes Joel-Peter Witkin photographs, and that's what he gets. Mark Romanek's "Closer" video slaps Reznor right in the middle of an environment that could be called Witkinland, in which the brightest

A TRIP TO THE MOON: **PRE-PUMPKINS**

star of techno-gloom music spins in a sepia-washed gallery of horrors.

The most memorable "concept" videos in recent years appropriate cultural and media imagery. In "Tonight," Jim and Valerie Ferris put the Smashing Pumpkins into a Georges Méliès-like silent film, appropriating not only his whimsical surrealism, but even specific images from his *Trip to the Moon* (1902). Charles Wittenmier puts the Counting Crows in Edward Hopper paintings, Tupac Shakur winds up in a '90s, African American remake of the 1979 Australian Armageddon flick, *Mad Max.* At a certain point, we expect and enjoy a bit of solipsism in our music videos: "Hey, that's the one that makes fun of that Soul Asylum video." We applaud a director's cleverness, and we're suckers for media nostalgia. Music videos can be the film equivalent of Wacky Packs, or skateboarder and hip-hop T-shirts that appropriate and mutate '70s corporate logos. Appropriation in music video emulates sampling in music, creating new forms from the sediment layers of previous eras in musical and cultural life. When a video commissioner says he or she wants a treatment that's something they've never seen before, quite the opposite is often true. They'd love it if you could just think of something that hasn't been retread already.

Big-time directors and ad agency creative directors have assistants who do nothing but amass "tear sheets," clippings from books or magazines that are used to clearly illustrate a certain photographic look or style. As an agency pitches a campaign that has the look of films noir, the creative director shows photographs that use high-contrast lighting, moody dames smoking cigarettes or other recognizable film noir elements. Music-video directors often submit tear sheets along with their treatments. Tear sheets make for quick, visual shorthand: It's easier to show than tell. After years of this practice, it's easy to see how appropriation has become a dominant form. Music video fairly screams "It's all been done before, but who cares. I'll just Xerox it all!" If postmodern art theory places context over meaning, then music videos are one big postmodern medium with recontextualization of meaning every time you hit the clicker. In "Bedtime Stories," Madonna floats around Frida Kahlo–inspired surrealist imagery and the audience of teenagers vaguely registers the images as secondhand. We don't try to infer meaning from the images themselves, for we know that they're an appropriation, that they're merely meant to indicate an affinity with the artist and her work. To the vast majority of the audience, the Kahlo images spring only from Madonna's music, not from any experience of the paintings themselves or the painter's life. They are Madonna's images now because they illustrate her video and she chose them.

Most directors we know feel the same way about appropriating social and political issues or heart on sleeve causes in videos, and that feeling extends to a general bemusement with overwhelming production value. Music video, after all, should be fun. "Commercials and music videos are the last place that I want to see somebody make a serious social statement," says Jesse Peretz, for one. "And I don't want to fucking see gorgeous cinematography in a thirty-second Sprite commercial. To me it's a total misuse of energy and air time. I do not want to see a fucking music video preaching to me about homelessness while its real intent is to sell two million records so that the band become millionaires and the record corporation increases its income by two or three million dollars."

ALL VIDEOS ARE BASED ON THE SONG

The preeminence of the song differentiates all of music video's ancestors from music video itself. Operas follow familiar story lines with multiple arias and recitativo, and musicals set comedy and drama to tuneful song and dance. But a music video depicts the song itself — beginning, middle and end. All of the conceptual thought and aesthetic agendas aside, if you're making a music video, the song is the sacred text you serve. You must know it inside and out. The most useful side effect of going through the pain of treatment writing is that if you've forced yourself to listen to the song a million times, you know every fill, every riff, every little nuance of the vocal performance.

VERSE AND CHORUS AS A NARRATIVE BASE

We've established that the classic music-video form evolved from traditional song structure and that the interlacing narrative form follows the classic verse/chorus pattern of most pop songs. Some directors see each song section as a different entity. "In order to keep a video interesting," says Bernstein, "there needs to be three types of imagery: performance, a story line and abstractions. In my mind, every verse, chorus or song section is a scene. My job is to make those scenes interesting, and in the progression of scenes to have things change. Verses are all going to be similar, so that every time you come back to the verse, it's a similar type of material but you've progressed, you've revealed something, something's different. The same thing with the choruses. Choruses are almost always identical, and it's always a challenge for me to keep the choruses interesting, but if you have a progression of material within the choruses, that's gonna float the boat."

Some directors deconstruct a song down to every musical phrase. You'll figure out as you listen intently to a song what level of detail you need to make your daydream conform to the structure of the song.

HOW TO LISTEN TO A SONG

If years of watching television makes the average citizen visually literate, constant exposure to radio renders most people musically literate. We're not talking about being able to read Stravinsky's scores, but about an innate feel for pop songs. Most people know the difference between a chorus and a verse, for example, or at least sense it intuitively in the repetition of the chorus. We believe that pop songs developed from a natural call-and-response sung in heartbeat rhythm; they simply feel right. Your job is to take your natural understanding of how a pop song operates and apply it to a specific goal. Writing a treatment requires directed, purposeful listening: You need to generate images and narrative suggestions that will coalesce into a treatment.

You'll be mighty familiar with the song by the end of the process. "I listen to the music that I'm given a million times," sighs Nancy Bennett. "Well not a million times. Probably fifty or sixty passes, and in the final phase of listening I usually write down every single lyric, grunt, and moan, and break down the structure of the song. If it's verse, chorus, bridge, development, whatever it is. I think about how structurally the song is repetitive or calls back to the original theme stated. I think part of the process of listening to something so many times is that you get gut reactions that sometimes you heed."

We take a four-step approach to listening to a song for the first time; each can create new possibilities for visualizing your video.

LYRICS

Most non-musician types fixate on the lyrics of a song first. That big, swelling chorus is the hook we sing to ourselves in the shower. Especially if the lyrics are found in a cheesy love song, we can't help trying to relate to the words and make forced connections to our own lives as if we were reading a horoscope. But when listening to a song for treatment inspiration, fixating on the lyrics is a dangerous game. Many alternarockers in the '90s attempt to be vague, absurd and poetic as an affront to traditional songwriting. "What does it mean?" is the worst question you can ask a songwriter because they don't want their songs to be interpreted literally.

Now that music video has matured, direct, literal lyrical interpretations tend to be avoided. Directly illustrating the lyrics seems intentionally campy and musical-theater-esque, as in Judas Priest's "Breakin' the Law," which finds the band robbing a bank. Besides, rock song lyrics function like sound poetry, and lyrics are successful when the phrasing of the words works well with the music. This phrase is Rock 101: "Jumping Jack Flash, it's a gas gas gas." If you're listening to the lyrics for treatment inspiration, you have to be as associative with the lyrics as you would be with the other aspects of the song. Often a creative disjunction works: if the lyrics are dark and gloomy, present "happy" images.

Critics will attack a video first by asking "What does that have to do with the song?" Maybe nothing, but when you're writing a treatment, the lyrics have to be addressed.

If your treatment has nothing to do with the lyrics, video commissioners and rockers still want to hear how your video concept works "against" the lyrics, or to sense that you understood the song. Often, video directors will pick up on one aspect of the lyrics when they're writing their treatments, riffing on one line or phrase to generate images.

RHYTHM

We next respond to rhythm in a song, its tempo, its "groove." By simply tapping our feet or drumming on the desk, we determine the song's tempo, whether a song is fast or slow. Tempo has much to do with conceiving a music video. A fast-paced song immediately makes us think of a faced-paced video with rapid cutting. A slow, dirgelike song conjures up a flowing, elegiac video. Think of Liz Phair's oars clipping through the water, or the landscape evoked by Jonathan Richman's cruise down the highway. The rhythm suggests specific images or places. If the song moves to a dance beat — a tango, for example — we're immediately transported to an exotic locale. Editors love to cut to the beat as it provides them a natural cue to the length of a shot. Given the fast, insistent beat of rock, it's easy to see why MTV's signature style soon became quick cutting.

INSTRUMENTATION

Isolating the various instruments used in a track leads to greater understanding of a song. Rock instrumentation is pretty straightforward, some variation on guitar, bass and drums. We all know what those bedrock instruments sound like. Where they occur in the song and how they're treated in the song's production (fuzzed-out with distortion; clear and bell-like; echoing like gongs) make a rich vein to mine for sound-image relationships. We tend to think of song parts in terms of their instrumental associations, "drum intros" and "guitar breaks." For treatment-writing inspiration, note where a certain instrument or sound recurs in a song and determine whether it could correspond to a recurring visual motif.

STRUCTURE

Most rock songs reflect their twelve-bar-blues heritage in the structure of verse, chorus, verse, chorus, an instrumental break (which is a solo or variation on the verse or chorus), and a bridge that leads into choruses or instrumental breaks. As with lyrics, rockers like to toy with these conventions. Structurally, Nirvana's songs couldn't be more conventional, and it's easy to analyze their songs: the verses are quiet, the choruses are loud. With other bands who are more inventive with their song structure, it's important for us to identify different song parts, even if they are not strictly choruses or breaks, because we'll assign those song parts different duties in the visual scheme.

WRITING THE TREATMENT

For video directors, the frustrating thing about writing treatments is that directors aren't writers. Accustomed to working in a visual medium, writing seems like an unnecessary pain in the ass. "I hate writing treatments," wails Jesse Peretz. "Writing treatments used to be the part of the process that made me fucking crazy and miserable, that whole phase of 'I have a tape, I have a deadline, obsess, what am I going to do,' and listen to the song over and over again and obsess some more about what to do. . . Once I get the idea, I start having a good time." Treatment writing brings Nancy Bennett back to school days. "It's just like homework," she says. "If you've done your homework, it's easy. If you've done the outline and the research, the paper gets written. It's the same thing."

All of those good Strunk-and-Whitey rules you learned in high school apply to treatment writing. Be direct, honest and simple. You're in the awkward position of having to make an impression on the band and to flatter them, but you don't want to clutter your treatment with flowery prose. "The composition, the light, the mood," emphasizes Bennett, who saw many treatments in her previous life as a video commissioner. "Those are the things you need to convey because those are the things that are gonna keep an audience interested, and those will enable you to take an audience on a ride, whether it's narrative or abstract, whatever it is. Those are the things that make someone see, feel, look and ponder. The narrative approach is storytelling, taking somebody through an emotional arc to a conclusion. When you write treatments like that, they need to be pretty specific for your client. When you do something that's more abstract, you can get away with less detail, but you still have to have the punch. I think the directors who work do incredibly detailed homework, even if it's only two paragraphs. That always got my attention [as a commissioner], something well written — which I have to say was the exception to the rule. Ninety-nine percent of the stuff that was submitted to me was torturous butchering of the English language. I think that another really important thing is the presentation of visual references. That can really help quite a bit because once again visuals are subjective and you have to spell them out. Perhaps a little insight as to where the industry is: In the early '80s when I was first starting out, treatments were very free form. There's been an evolution over time of them becoming more like commercials, and with more of a client presence there's more control and people write to sell."

Randy Sosin, a video commissioner for A&M Records, sees much more collaboration happening between artists, labels and directors. "I think the system is being reinvented every day because it gets stale every five years," he observes. "I think the old process was sending the song out and waiting for a director to come back with an idea. So basically you're buying a marketing plan from a director. Now that there's a generation of bands who've grown up actually watching music videos, I think bands come in with a lot more of an idea of what they want. The bands sometimes write songs with the video in mind."

FORMS OF THE TREATMENT

Three modes of treatment writing seem to have evolved, and two approaches dominate. The first, my favorite, is to write an unfolding description, prose that describes what happens on screen as the imaginary video plays in my head. I write this chronologically: A happens, then B happens, then C happens. This works best when the video is like a short dramatic film, when there is some payoff at the end (a surprise or sense of completion in setting, identity, action), because the treatment will truly read like a short story. I've found myself getting into traps, though, when I have to write "As we go back to the chorus, we see more shots of the band" over and over again.

When you're writing a narrative video and describing its events, it's hard to also describe the video's look. If your video concept doesn't depend on a particular look, simply describe the video's action and the reader will assume a basic level of well-exposed, typically lit, normal-speed film.

Breaking down the description into outline form provides the second treatment-writing method. If you're doing a video in which the look is as important as the narrative or conceptual events, then it's useful to make separate mention of how you treat the image. Some directors use headings such as "The Concept," under which they describe the video's events, and then add a heading, "The Look," which details the various camera tricks and film-processing methods. Given that most videos are interlacing narratives, another way of breaking down a treatment is to separately discuss "The Performance" and "The Concept." Though less fun to read and less attention-grabbing, these schematic treatments are more succinct. If the goal of the treatment is to let the person reading it quickly understand the video, then consider a very direct, organized system for presenting your concept.

In addition to narrative, storylike descriptions or outlinelike breakdowns, some directors gamble with a third creative approach that resembles vague babblings, cut-and-paste ransom notes or Japanese poetry. It's not meant to simply make an artistic statement or demonstrate ennui; if a director can crystallize one image that neatly summarizes the song, the effect is like the thunderclap intuition of a Zen koan.

"I strive for the simplest, most direct treatment," advises Sosin. "A one-sentence treatment to me is the best treatment in the world. I just want to know the overall vibe; I want to know that the director has actually listened to the song and has a vision. And you can see that from the treatment. It'll come out on paper. Be simple, really succinct and to the point." Susan Solomon, once a video commissioner at A&M Records, wants more detail. "A good treatment," she says, "is one that walks you through the video. It not only sets the tone, hopefully there's some reference to how the video looks, and it walks you through so you know what's going to happen before you shoot it. I used to get these treatments sometimes, they were so vague, all fucking adjectives. You never knew what it was about. Even someone who's not visual [should be able to] see this thing."

SAMPLE TREATMENTS

Here's some of my treatment-writing. This is an example of the narrative, prose-unfolding style. I open with a paragraph that describes the thematic agenda of the video, though sometimes I use opening paragraphs to summarize the video's look and visual references. The vibe I got from this band, partly from the earnestness of the song, was that I could appeal to them with a proclamation of anti-conformity and alienation. The proposals below are reproduced unedited, exactly as they were presented to the bands and commissioners.

COOL FOR AUGUST
"DON'T WANT TO BE HERE"
WARNER BROTHERS RECORDS
TREATMENT, "SCENES FROM A MALL,"
BY DAVID KLEILER,
ZEITGEIST PRODUCTIONS

Have you ever felt completely alienated in a shopping mall? Have you ever thought, "We're all just consumer-culture slaves," as you watch a gaggle of mall rats line up to buy the exact same beauty product? Have you ever been in a mall and sensed the collective melancholy of so many lone shoppers? For a lot of folks living in So Cal communities, malls substitute for public space. Malls replace parks and main streets. In a shopping mall, I wonder if the old men gathered on benches wouldn't be happier in a less pre-fab environment. I wonder if the struggling young mother wishes she could think of some other way of spending time with her children...

We follow two characters ambling through a typical American shopping mall on a busy afternoon. Our heroine is a high school girl out with her girlfriends. She pretends she's right at home in the mall: she scopes guys, cracks jokes with her girl-posse and does a lot of shopping. Soon she becomes alienated by the environment and her friends - the Winona Ryder to their "Heathers." These Heathers stand in line after line, all buying slight variations on the same clothes, shoes and beauty products. She models a dark-colored dress while the Heathers just laugh and convince her to get one of the light-colored ones that they're all getting. She keeps looking in her wallet, noticing that she's running out of money. Gradually she falls back from them. In the garish food court she sits at a table looking distracted while the boisterous Heathers laugh and have a good time.

If only she knew our hero, a slightly older high school kid who works at one of the fast food joints at the food court. Think Judge Reinhold in Fast Times At Ridgemont High. He's having a similarly alienating experience on this mall afternoon. We follow him from his job flipping hamburgers, through his sad attempt to relax during his lunch break. First he goes outside to have a cigarette by a mall entrance. Before he can light his smoke, he gets accosted by a security guard that motions to a "No Smoking" sign and tells him to step away from the building. Later he winds up in a store that's a parody of The Sharper Image or Brookstones. It's filled with stupid foot-massagers and little black gadgets with blinking lights. Puzzled and bored at the same time, he fiddles with these useless items. He sits in one of the massaging chairs until the sales person at the store shoots him evil looks. He finds solace in a cool, vintage-80s video game that's tucked away in a remote corner of the mall. We see his look of concentration reflected on the screen of the game's glass. Hunched over the game wearing his fast-food uniform, he seems utterly alone.

Throughout these vignettes of our two high-school heroes, we catch glimpses of the Cool For August boys, performing their song with intensity. Light reflected off of some unseen body of water dapples Gordon's face, and we're not initially sure where he and his band mates are. They seem to be on some kind of stage, but they're basically facing each other, and their performance is covered in slowly-dollying close-ups. Within these intimate close-ups, the general vibe of their performance environment is in stark contrast to the garishness of the mall scenarios. However, as the song progresses, wider shots reveal that the band is in fact performing on a stage in middle of the shopping mall. It's adjacent to a fountain/wading pool hence the shimmery light that plays on Gordon's face. This is probably where kids come to sit on Santa's lap during the holidays, but this season it's an oasis of cool...For August. They look out of place here in a good way. They're the honest rockers battling against the tide of shopping mall conformity. Gordon's refrain, "I know I don't want to be here" takes on a more obvious meaning. There's a crowd of folks watching the band, but many shoppers just stroll on by.

Our heroes are two of those shoppers. Each arriving simultaneously at the stage — perhaps pulled by some mystical force of rock — they stop to watch the band for a moment. Their eyes meet. Are they going to introduce themselves, discuss their alienated lives, move to a farm in the Pacific Northwest and bake their own bread? Of course not. This is a mall — no one has any kind of real interaction. She has to go back to her friends, he has to go back to work. They're shoppers passing in the night. By the end of the song, we follow as she continues shopping with her friends, and he goes back to flipping burgers. The Cool For August band plays on....

This would be shot with a "well-exposed" color negative film look, as if it were one of those *teen dramas from the '80s. Ideally the mall would have lots of awesome '80s architectural details as well (remember the Hollywood Galaxy before they put that museum in there?) that the camera would study when we weren't with our heros. Besides, other folks in the mall would be given some activity: a guy in a fast-food mascot-suit, other bubble-gum chewing teens, wannabe gang-bangers and families. These folks would seem like real people, not the usual parade of music video grotesques. Even though there would be some funny business in the stores, the mood here would not be "wacky." There would be an attempt to bring out the mall melancholy. Think Jake Scott's REM, "Everybody Hurts," but much more toned-down, less "slick." Amidst all of these other elements, the band's performance would be given a chance to breathe. Covered from a number of different angles, we would really get an intimate look at Cool For August's rocking abilities.*

Here's another example, Jesse Peretz's treatment for Foo Fighters, "Big Me."

FOO FIGHTERS
"BIG ME"
CAPITOL RECORDS
TREATMENT: JESSE PERETZ
X-RAY PRODUCTIONS
REVISED 3
12-22-95

The video for "Big Me" is a parody of three well known Mentos candy commercials. For our purposes, however, the candy in this clip is the sweet and tasty Footos, "The Fresh Fighter."

The parodies of the actual commercials will be fairly true to their original form, mimicking the key moments, repeating the blessed gestures, and of course always ending with the classic popping in the mouth of the Footos candies, followed by the shrug, smile and grin, with the out-stretched hand victoriously clutching the roll of Footos. The band as a group will be key players in each, as well as having their individual moments at the end of the spots where they pop the candy in their mouths, shrug and grin.

The first commercial lampooned (probably my favorite) is the one where the businessman parks too close to a woman's car so she can't get out. She notices the situation and yells at him as he walks away. Unfortunately, he indicates he can do nothing at this time because he is both important and late (this is suggested in the spot by him pointing to his watch and shrugging). Luckily for the young girl, four workmen happen to be walking by and seeing her predicament, lift her car and move it into the street. In our video those guys are, of course, the Foo Fighters. (We will also extend the build up of them during the earlier portion of the event, so that we see them walking down the street, and get a chance to recognize them). The businessman notices this drama unfolding and is initially confused. The woman then pops a Footos in her mouth, smiles and shrugs, and the businessman's harsh exterior instantly melts and he smiles as well. Then the whole band (the workmen!) pop Footos in their mouth, and repeat the classic gesture with an unbelievable new-found happiness.

The next scenario would be a parody of the Mentos commercial in which the kids (The Foo Fighters) are trying to cross the crosswalk on a busy street. They seem to be in a bit of a hurry. Dave is straggling behind. A limo pulls up into the cross-walk between him and his friends, and comes to a stop. Dave, in a full-on Mentos mood, decides to get back at whoever is in the limo for being so pushy and separating him from his friends. He opens the door to the limo, and the businessman inside is on a cell phone, and boy is he un-amused!– unaware of the forth-coming Footos candy, which will obviously mellow the scene considerably. Sure enough, Dave busts out a package of Footos, pops one in his mouth, with a shrug and a smile, melting the world around him. The business man can't help but smile back. Dave looks outside to his pals and everybody looks back so impressed with his cleverness, popping Footos back in tandem, holding their individual packages with delight. . .

Finally, we find the Foo Fighters on stage two thirds of the way through the video performing the song in a little club. We see them play for a few short shots, and them we cut to a variation of the commercial where a kid tries to sneak in the club through the back door. He comes to the door and a bouncer nods his head "no" at the kid in a very mean way. The kid goes off. A few performance shots, and then we see him tying a bandanna on his head. He comes back to the door with a guitar strapped on. He opens the door and the bouncer is looking somewhere else. The kid sneaks by, and climbs onto the stage and lifts a pack of Footos and drops one in his mouth, then holds the package out in front of his face, and shrugs and smiles. The bouncer stops and smiles, and the kid turns to the band who repeat his action in unison, having suddenly forgiven the boy's inappropriate actions, in true Mentos spirit. The song ends, and a package shot, with a picture of a roll of Footos candy appearing on the screen and a voice (by now, well known to all in the Western world) saying "Footos – The Fresh Fighter!"

Perhaps the examples have reassured you that the treatment need not be timeless literature in order to accomplish its mission: communicating your intention to the band, the record label — and yourself. Now you have to covert your daydream into the dollars and cents necessary to put your vision on film.

chapter two

Somewhere, right now, in the cramped office of a music-video production company, the following scene unfolds:

Carol — a music-video producer in her early thirties, dressed in downtown-camouflage black accented with a chewed pencil threaded through the hair piled on top of her head — glares at a spreadsheet glowing on her computer monitor. Invading her space, Jack, 28, cranes his neck to see the screen, frowning, tapping the toe of his scuffed Pumas and muttering to himself with an occasional "Hmmm." His breath smells like old coffee and stomach acid, because (like too many of the so-called directing geniuses with whom Carol works) numbers stress Jack out so much he can't even eat.

Like a blind Ouija-board reader, Carol's right hand automatically, almost magically, waltzes mouse across trackpad. With a click, she selects a column and frowns. She can't suppress her instinctive need to crunch numbers over and

budgeting >

over in an attempt to please directors and find the means to accomplish their visions. She thinks, "Maybe we don't need the honey wagon," then quickly checks herself. "Wait a minute, that's crazy. I can't do that. If we're going to be in a desert location, there won't be a bathroom for miles. Why must he insist on the desert?"

As if Jack can read her mind, he blurts in her ear, "Yeah, exactly right. Do we really need that honey wagon?"

This is too much to bear. After working on the budget for hours, Jack hasn't come up with one constructive suggestion to keep costs down. Carol hisses: "Okay, so you tell me. Where's my crew going to piss? Can you tell me that? Where are they going to piss?"

"Well, there's got to be a diner out there somewhere. They can piss during lunchtime. I just want the job, Carol, and they're not going to award it to us for, what are we up to, eighty thousand?"

"You're the one who insists we shoot in the middle of nowhere. You're the one married to his little 'birdcage in the desert' on a fifty-thousand-dollar budget, which doesn't begin to cover it."

"Look, it can be done for the money. Did you know I did my first five videos for . . ."

"Under ten thousand dollars. I know, Jack, but now you don't have an insane girlfriend who shoots all your videos for nothing. These are real jobs with real crews and they're not going to piss in a pot. We've got to be able to come up with some real solutions. You've got to be able to compromise."

"Well, I'm not going to change my idea. I see this video. I know in my head how I would shoot it. How can I compromise?"

"I've been thinking. Do we really need to build the cages? I mean, I know this great baseball field in the Valley that has a desert feel, and there are these geodesic jungle gyms nearby that could work as one of your birdcages."

"No, no, no."

"Listen to me, if you shoot it there, we'd save money on art department and the whole nightmare of a company move to the desert. That's the only way you can get that scene and the rest of the video."

Not unlike a four-year-old, Jack springs to his feet, grabs the treatment from Carol's desk and crumples it into a little ball. He throws it in her direction and storms to the door. "If you're not trying to realize my vision for the money, then I'll just have to find a way to produce the video myself." On the threshold, he adds for dramatic effect, "No one at this company gives me the support I need."

Carol slumps in her chair and thinks what she always thinks after Jack's tantrums: there is life after music-video producing. "If I take the LSATs in March, when can I apply to law school again?"

DAYDREAMS VS. REALITY

In an ideal world, writing a music-video budget would be a creative process in which a producer and director work out a plan for executing the treatment for the money allocated. In the real world, writing a budget is often a battle. Even if the money seems plentiful, writing a budget marks the first skirmish in the conflict between real and ideal that rages throughout music-video production.

Directors who live in the world of ideals want their daydreams realized, but, when pasted with a price tag, those daydreams get tempered by reality. "You cannot separate the financial from the creative," says old-school executive producer and rep Jerry Solomon. "They go hand-in-hand. I think a lot of people want to separate the two, but there is no separation. If you want to blow up the city of St. Louis in your video, it's going to cost you a shitload of money. There's no way around it."

KIM CHRISTIANSEN

In the situation above, Jack, the director, wants an unrealistic company move to the desert, so a cheaper alternative must be found. "Directors have almost no idea how much things cost," says producer Kim Christiansen (Fountains of Wayne, Sebadoh, Sublime). Kim is warm and outgoing, and though she is hungry for success in the business, she maintains an ironic distance that shields her from the storms of her occupation. "A concept of time is something that a lot of artistic people lack. They don't know how long it takes for twenty people to walk down the street with the guy who's carrying the light and the guy who's carrying the camera, each person carrying their little box that they need with them for the next shot. And somebody needs to have a cigarette and everybody needs to go to the bathroom. That takes an hour for a company even if you're going around the corner. Directors that are just starting out don't know that. They haven't seen the monster in action and the monster is the whole process, the whole film crew, everybody who is making things slow. Sometimes you get a schedule and you just think, 'Bless his heart.

He's so cute for thinking that he's ever gonna get this fifth shot let alone the twenty-fifth one.' You're both trying to achieve the same thing, and my goal is always to help the director get on film what he wants to get on film. It's like a puzzle you need to solve."

"Well, for me, directing and producing aren't that far apart," demurs producer and director Nancy Bennett. "They really fuse together for me. Before I ever directed anything, I was very much a director's producer. It was always about collaboration and making it possible for the director to get the vision. So if that was my task, I needed to understand their vision almost better than they did. And at times I needed to have the client finesse to be able to explain what they were trying to do. I tried my damnedest to see things the way they were seeing them and leave my ego at home. The goal of the director is getting something gorgeous that shows what they have to say, that's also powerful, emotional and looks beautiful, makes everybody happy and does it within budget. You know, the same goal as the producer, the DP, PAs or the person sweeping the stage."

You often find producer/director teams that have been together over the course of many jobs. They develop a shorthand, an intimate knowledge of what process makes each of them most comfortable and are able to cut through many of the issues that cause conflict. Spike Jonze and Vince Landay have such a relationship. "I've worked with the same producer for four years," Jonze says. "I work with him really closely on the bidding. It makes such a big difference to work with the same guy every time. When you first work with a producer, you spend half the job getting to know each other, feeling each other out. It's the same every time. When that's consistent, it makes everything else easier to judge."

Producers must constantly remind directors what things cost. And producers don't simply sign checks and organize money. Once they agree to do a job, they guarantee the video's completion and delivery to the record company. If Jack wants to shoot one little scene in the desert, money gets taken away from other parts of the video. If too much money gets spent on one part of the video, that scene jeopardizes the whole project and the video might not get completed as described in the treatment. Jack's reputation will be tarnished, but so will the producer's for not being able to rein him in.

The producer knows that the label views the video as just one aspect of the marketing of the artist and has budgeted the video according to the marketability of the artist. "I'm in Creative Services," says video commissioner Randy Sosin, "and the way it works is that Marketing gives me that money. I don't have a budget; they tell me what they've budgeted for the project, and at the end of the day, it is a business. When you allot X-amount of dollars for that particular artist and give that dollar figure to a director and they come back with an idea that's X plus thirty thousand dollars, or X plus ninety, it's a harder process. I'm very much in favor of trying to fight for the extra dollar and I really want the money to go up on screen. I want to give a director tools to make a video, but they've made it harder on record companies. The powers that be at a lot of record companies, and at my record company, feel ripped off a lot of the time."

"The whole point of the video business is costing the record company and the artist as little as possible, and getting the most for their money," says Geffen's Mark Kates. "And for you [as a producer] that's a nightmare."

WHAT A PRODUCER DOES

What does a producer do, exactly, besides the budget? The producer's job description can include multiple functions. On feature-film sets or high-budget commercials and music videos, each of the functions can be embodied by a different person: the executive producer, the line producer, the associate producer, the unit production manager, the post-production supervisor. The music-video producer's role borrows aspects of all these producing functions, including dealing with the financing sources (the labels) and shielding the director from the label like an executive producer, helping the director organize the set like a unit production manager, wrapping out the job's paperwork like an associate producer, and scheduling the postproduction like a post supervisor. But in the music-video world, the producer looks most like the line producer, the person actually in charge of organizing the production, budgeting, hiring the crew and working with the director throughout the shoot.

"It's crazy how many people say they're producers," says Christiansen. "I wish there was another word for it. I would rather not say I'm a producer. It's way too broad and there's a misconception among crew people that somebody's making money and it isn't them. That's not the way it is. Most of the time the director's not making any money. Most of the time the producer's making much less than if they were to do any other job. The sound guy makes more money. The PAs sometimes make more money."

Maybe you had in mind the classic movie image of the cigar-chomping studio producer who makes broad-stroke decisions about what actors to cast or argues with the director about whether he can have his helicopter shot. The closest analogy in music video to the shouting studio producer is the executive producer from a production company. These folks generally represent several directors and oversee their careers like agents. They send their directors' reels to video commissioners, coax the commissioners into considering their stable, oversee and sometimes write first-draft budgets, and hire producers. If a production

MEET THE PRODUCERS

Music-video producers handle multiple tasks that otherwise would be parceled out to several people on feature-film productions. Only on the biggest budget shoots do the producers have assistants, most typically a production manager who works with the producer in the way an associate producer might on a feature. PMs deal with purchase orders and some unit production manager jobs: transportation, location managing, and the mountains of paperwork. If there's a production manager on the job, the production coordinator is his or her assistant. They'll be the ones to type up the schedules and call sheets and handle the bulk of the office work. There might be a couple of coordinators, and some extra office PAs, but for videos with budgets up to half a million bucks, you won't have more than this. So that you can appreciate how many roles a music-video producer fills, we've listed decriptions of the producers who would be found on features and commercials.

executive producer

Responsible for the business affairs of production, yet also must be able to recognize potentially profitable material and talented artists, find funding for that material and, with a producer, assemble the creative team.

producer (line producer)

Responsible for the planning, scheduling, budgeting, hiring, and overall management of the production. A producer's creative influence can be great or little depending on their personality or relation-

>>>

company supports a director, production fees get cut and budgets get embellished. A powerful production company that has faith in an up-and-coming director will chip in company money as an investment. By adding to the video's production value, they're hoping their new genius will impress potential clients.

Line producers, freelance workers hired by the production company to budget and oversee the spending of those funds on the shoot, don't have the power to say yes to a production, they can't approve spending extra money, and they sometimes get in awkward situations when directors go over their heads and ask for help from nurturing executive producers. Executive producers encourage directors to think they think only of them and will do anything for them. They also want line producers to be their watchdogs, keeping a tight grip on those budgetary reins. The person in the middle? The line producer, a bad guy to the executive producer if the shoot runs over budget and a snarling, snapping killjoy to the director who wants to spend more money realizing her vision.

"The role of the producer is to say no," John Owen, Adam Bernstein's producer, maintains. "At some point you're a courier of bad news to the production company. At that point, producing is just bean counting and cell phoning." Christiansen disagrees. "I hate to be the one that has to say no all the time, where I'm kind of like the enemy. I don't ever want to be in that position. I want to always be a part of the team with the director and the DP, and I don't want to have animosity between the three of us. When you have to say no, you can pull the director aside and say, 'Listen, if we get this extra light that your friend the DP here wants, you're not gonna have any more film, any more time, any more anything else. It's either this light or maybe an hour of overtime or maybe another hour of telecine and another can of film. These are the choices you have to make. It's often the first time that the director has ever worked with an art director or a DP. They don't know why these people want certain things or why they want their crew around them, why they need to have three grips and three electrics. They get pissed: 'Why are these guys all standing on my set doing nothing all day long? Why do we have to pay for them?' And you turn to them and say, 'Honey, do you know how to spark up the genny [a portable generator], because I kind of do but not really, you know. When I learn, then maybe we can not have these people around. But right now it's one or the other.'"

As a low-budget videomaker, you function as both director and producer, embodying two opposing jobs, the realist and the idealist. For maximum daydreaming, creative genius, you shouldn't worry about money, but someone with an eye on the bottom line needs to set limits. With the devil in one ear and an angel in the other, you must constantly shift between a practical approach to your job and a creative approach to your job: "What a great room, only I wish it was painted red."/ "Shut up and live with it, unless you pay the folks who own it, you can't paint it." "Wow, I know my rock starlet would be great if I just gave her another take."/ "If you blow any more film on this set-up, we'll never be able to shoot anything else."

"You know, I can give one other piece of advice," offers Bennett. "In my own experience being a producer/director, you can't divorce one from the other. It's important as a director to give up the financial controls to somebody you trust. There's a mutiny and it's inside your own head. When you take on both roles, you're preventing yourself from thinking artistically because you're thinking in a management sense. It's a conflict that I have to fight all the time. But in making low-budget videos, you have to produce

ship with the director. In any case, they influence the success of the production by how they allocate resources.

associate/assistant producer)
The producer's assistants. The titles are ill-defined and sometimes given for extraordinary effort and sometimes as a political gesture, but they typically handle many of the adminstrative tasks associated with the production.

unit production manager (production manager; UPM)
Develops a detailed shooting budget, works with the assistant director on a shooting schedule, hires the crew, guides the production through the day-to-day logistics of the shoot and makes out the daily production report for the production book.

postproduction supervisor
Responsible for the details of post-production activity, for example, scheduling labs and recording studios, coordinating the director's and editor's schedules, and monitoring postproduction expenses with the production accountant. The UPM (and, less frequently, the assistant editor) often moves to this function when shooting stops.

production accountant
Supervises expenses by preparing cost reports, holds cost report meetings with UPMs and producers, is responsible for bank accounts, payroll and accounts payable, and prepares the final audit at the end of production.

<<<

as much as you have to direct, and the two are pretty much self-defeating. So, just think about your shot and take the time you need to render the concept the way you envision it."

This inner struggle makes life hell for the low-budget videomaker. Embrace the schizophrenia. Understanding the essential duties of a producer, what things cost and how long things take, will make you a director who comes to a producer with a firm grasp of how to make a vision a reality. It will also make you more sensitive to the hell of music-video producing, making you a better person when you get a chance to work with producers.

BUDGETING IS THE PRODUCER'S CONCEPTUAL WORK

If treatment writing is a director's conceptual work, budget writing is a producer's. Directors must visualize the video before they can write the treatment and producers must visualize how the scenes in that treatment will be shot before they can write a budget. From experience, they know how long a scene will take to shoot, what special crew people need to be hired, what rental equipment to round up, and, most importantly, how much everything costs. Now, obviously, these are all aspects of the production that the director should be familiar with as well, and talented directors come to producers already knowing how much their video will cost and with clear explanations of how they intend to shoot.

John Owen takes a hard-headed but practical approach to budgeting. "The first thought is usually that there's never enough money to do this right. From the first conversation you learn that the record company wants to spend seventy grand. I figure, well, how hard is that. It's chimp. You know, you take seventy grand and you divide it up into twelve categories, it's a no-brainer. And then I look at it completely negatively, looking at the treatment purely for trouble spots. I see forty extras and that jumps off the page. I see night shoot, it jumps off the page. I see big art department, you know, an 'angel comes down in the middle of the surgery' scene. Trouble. Then you set up a kind of Chinese menu in which you get only one from column A. You can have two from column B and C, but you can only have one from column A. So you go with your first-draft budget to the executive producer who tells the label, 'You get the angel but you can't have the forty extras.' You just immediately start giving them choices and say otherwise it can't be done." A Chinese restaurant menu is a funny analogy, but understand what John is saying: If you add a more elaborate lighting set-up, you can't have as much film. If you have to have the film and the more elaborate lighting, you can't have the props to dress the set. It's like ordering from a Chinese menu when you know you only have twenty bucks in your pocket.

Producers usually draft a music-video budget before the job gets assigned. A record label proposes a ball park figure for a video and, once they see treatments they like, a new round of competition begins. Directors with the chosen treatments submit a budget as part of a package with the treatment — the treatment describes what the director wants to shoot and the budget demonstrates how it can be done for the money. Record companies typically don't simply seek the lowest bottom line; they seek budgets that make sense. If two different treatments call for state-of-the-art postproduction effects, and one of the corresponding budgets comes in much lower than the other, video commissioners will distrust the capabilities of those submitting the lower budget. A more realistic budget will often work in favor of a potential producer and director than one that seems unrealistically low. As with any work-for-hire, however, producers often try to underbid the competition.

HOW TO BREAK DOWN A TREATMENT FOR A BUDGET

No set formulas tell you how to read a treatment and then draft a budget, but most producers address the following issues first: What are the locations? Are there sets to be built? Are there special effects? Does the concept need props and other production design?

Christiansen looks at shooting days and crew first. "I start with whether it's a one- or two-day thing, and if there's any notable equipment, like a crane shot or a Steadicam. Any extra equipment like that costs $1,500 more and has to be budgeted. I just have a standard, one-day, you-stand-there-and-we're-gonna-shoot-your-music-video budget. You need a crew, you need food, you need some lights maybe. And the least you can do that for, in my opinion, is twenty thousand, because if there's a production company that wants to take a fee, if the director wants to get paid and the producer wants to get paid, then you're at that magic number. And post-production is always seven to ten thousand dollars. So, if you do it the traditional way and you're not getting anything for free, then you're stuck with that twenty thousand number."

Especially with music video, many approaches suggest themselves for a particular production circumstance: "Do we remake specific aspects of *Attack of the Fifty-Foot Woman*, or do we simply suggest the low-budget, B-movie quality of it all?" When using special effects or a particular set-design "gag," producers use common sense and ask the specialists about costs. Then there are bids within the production company's bid. If an art director underbids the competition, then the production company agrees to hire that art director's crew for the job, if the production company gets the job.

When you're doing a low-budget video, put in your hard costs first, then figure out

WISE GUYS

A dialogue that could have been lifted from a screwball comedy starring Rachel Weissman and John Owen, partners in life as well as producing, illustrates different ways producers deal with directors.

John: "Well, I don't give a shit what the director's shot list says. As long as they know on day one they only have nine hours budgeted out of the twelve needed for the shot list."

Rachel: "We have such a different approach. It's hilarious."

John: "You do whatever you want in nine hours. You have nine hours. You had better get your video in nine hours."

Rachel: "John and I are complete opposites. I almost approach the job as if I'm the director, you know, but not making creative decisions. I want to know how you're gonna get that shot. I want to know how that shot's gonna cut with that shot. I need to make it real for me. John couldn't give a shit."

John: "I just want to know when this fucking job's gonna be over so I can go home."

Rachel: "Yeah, we have a completely different approach. There's definitely a role-playing situation with producing. Even if directors are aware of it and say, 'I don't want to have a mother figure as a producer,' they buy into it. We're the responsible ones. It has always been that way and will continue to be that way. There's the child who is the director, the mother who is the line producer and this sort of auntie, the executive producer, who plays both sides, wanting to please the director but also

>>>

how much you have left to spend on crew rates and food. Here's a rough sketch of a $5,000 video budget.

Film Stock	2,400' @ $100/400ft.	$600.00
Processing	2,400 @ $00.15/ft.	$360.00
Telecine	3 hours @ $300/hr.	$900.00
Online	2.5 hours @ $300/hr.	$750.00
Offline/Online prep	5 days/$100/day	$500.00
Dubs/Tape Stock		$150.00
Crew	8 folks/$50/day	$400.00
Equipment/Lights/Camera/Lenses		$500.00
Petty Cash/Meals/Expendables		$200.00
Art Department/Props		$300.00
Location Fees		$100.00
Transportation/Car/Van rentals		$150.00
Miscellaneous/Insurance		$90.00

This budget assumes a lot. It assumes that your friends live on a commune and are willing to work for $50 per day. The online editing fee here is totally academic and assumes that some community center with an RM440 will rent it to you that cheaply. There's a remote possibility that someone with an Avid will let you on their system for two days for $250/day. I used to use this fee as a director's fee and try to spend $100 to $200 for my offline expenses and pocket the rest of the money. Then there's the cost of generating an edit decision list, which requires getting onto somebody's computer editing system and typing up a list. This usually costs money. There was a woman who did it for me in New York who charged $1.00/cut. Most videos have anywhere from 150 to 350 cuts, so this would cost $150 to $350. I used to curb the number of cuts I allowed myself just to keep this cost down.

LIVING LOW-BUDGET

My low-budget production mentor, George Spyros, was at one time a badly exploited, frustrated karaoke-video director at the bottom of an evil karaoke food chain. Jobs came indirectly from a New York University professor who wrangled them from a Japanese karaoke concern. This professor got $10,000 for each video he delivered, but subcontracted the work to two of his students, who in turn subcontracted the work out to George, leaving him only a $2,600 budget for each video. To make it worth his while, he tried to keep $1,000 for himself. Needless to say, $1,600 doesn't promise much production value.

These financial constraints meant George took a guerilla approach: He spent money on nothing and was an inspiration and a resource for how to get things done cheaply. Every location was "stolen," meaning that they all were places where one didn't need permission to shoot or could shoot illegally and not get arrested. Many of the videos that George made were shot on Hi8 video, and he always knew cheap processes to make the video footage come out looking something like film. He would edit the karaoke videos on an old tape-to-tape system that he owned and, since he knew all the out-of-the-way vendors in New York, he found astonishingly cheap post-production facilities. He remained a firm proponent of the unsupervised transfer to video and the unsupervised online edit for only $35 an hour — one tenth of normal cost. The first few videos I did I cut on George's editing system, and working around him opened my eyes to how production could be done cheaply. But remember, it's not a simple formula of "cheap is good so do it cheap."

Adam Bernstein has some practical advice for low-budget planning. "Do everything you can with in-camera effects," he says. "There's a ton of age-old special effects that can be done for nothing. For example, in the They Might

wanting respect from the producer. There is an emotional attachment to wanting to please the director. And, if a director's really good, they seduce you and make you feel as though they can't do anything without you and if you could just help them it would be so awesome . . . and you fall into that trap."

<<<

GETTING STARTED:
DARREN DOANE

Darren looks slightly older than his 24 years, perhaps because he has the competent, confident air of a savvy businessman even though his office is staffed by high-school-aged skate kids and decorated with Star Wars paraphernalia and Pennywise posters.

"I got involved with music videos basically because I loved comic books. I was a comic-book fan, a comic-book dork, geek completely. My goal was to be a comic-book artist. I always had a video camera because I grew up surfing and skiing, so I was always videotaping. I struck up a friendship in junior high with a guy who was shooting super-8 since he

DARREN DOANE

was like ten years old. So we hooked up making films. Eventually my interest in film got bigger, and the day after my friend Dave graduated high school in 1990, we decided to make a fake résumé saying that we were UCLA film-school graduates. We made a bunch up at Kinko's and sent them out to every record label that we had an address for with a fake, BS resume with Brian DiPalma as a reference and phone numbers that we knew would be out of service. Then a company calls and says, 'We got your stuff right here in front of us and we have to have a video shot in three days. Can you be in New York? The budget's five thousand dollars.' I said, 'Yeah, sure. Let's do it.' So, now I had to make a real video. I thought very clearly: I'm gonna do what I've been doing. I'm gonna go find someone on

the college campus who's a cinematographer who has access to a 16mm camera. I knew a guy who was always filming. I called him and he said, 'Hey, I've got access to a camera.' I said I would buy the film. I don't know what I'm going to do with it when we shoot it but I'll figure it out. In the meantime, I'm gonna shoot my super-8 cause super-8 was just coming back into videos with David Fincher's Paula Abdul video. So we went out, we shot, we came back and I just started making phone calls. I've shot some film. What do I do? You need to get it to video. How do I transfer it to video? And I figured out telecine. Okay, once I had it on VHS, I called a few places. I've got 3/4-inch masters. Went in, edited it. Called the record label. What needs to be in front? Gotta have a slate. I just asked the questions. There's always someone who can answer a question, so that excuse you gotta throw out. Sent it to the label and three weeks later it's on MTV. I think my parents had planned to spend about forty thousand on me in film school, but I asked my dad if he would just give me ten thousand in cash. I would go down to Hollywood and find bands that are on labels but didn't have budgets in their contracts to do videos. I approached them and said I would do a video for them knowing that their label's gonna service it. Any label that gets a free video is gonna service the video to MTV and hope it gets accepted. I found two bands like that. I did Video Spore, they got it to MTV and, within the course of about a year, I now had three videos, two of which had been on MTV. And I was just about to begin learning the ropes."

Be Giants video 'Don't Let's Start,' John Linnel is singing as the whole world moves behind him. We stuck him on his back with a tripod over his chest and wheeled him around. It looks great and it's a no-budget effect. Also, try to shoot where you don't have to light, and plan so that you don't shoot a lot of film. Be aggressive about where you do post. There's always going to be facilities that are less expensive. Locate crew members on their way up who have a career or personal reason to work with you for cheap. Don't go after anything you're not going to be able to pull off effectively."

Finding cheap or free facilities is an essential low-budget strategy. Director David Roth (Soul Asylum, Boss Hog, Jayhawks), a laid-back luminary on the Minneapolis scene who published a local fanzine before getting behind the camera, suggests that "Every city has a media access center, and most places have two or three. Join them and use their equipment, their lights, their cameras, editing suites. It's almost like going to school. Tell post facilities your situation and ask if they have an editor who works after hours or who'd be interested in music videos. A lot of editors will work cheaper if it's something that's more fun. If you're comfortable with it, tell Kodak you're a student to get a deal on film."

Even the most successful video directors take on low-budget work if they love the band or want to explore an inspiration. "With the low–budget stuff, I know I'm going out alone," says Kevin Kerslake. "The higher-end low-budget stuff I usually don't do. I end up doing the really low-budget stuff for ten or twenty grand where you just barely cover costs if it's you and a couple of other people. That's more like reportage, or what kind of situation you can create. It's a good form to explore a scene or shoot a band. I've done that a couple times with Mazzy Star. The band lends itself to something stripped down and sort of lazy. That's the area that I feel comfortable with, in terms of the lower-budget stuff, because you can sort of meander, discover things with the camera and basically work off of completely different inspirations."

Sets, props and other art direction can be the biggest bulge in your budget. A clever art director can help trim the fat. "Hollywood has a very inflated price tag," says art director Jonathan Wellerstein. "Everything's very expensive here. You ask for something and it's three thousand dollars, and I know it can be done for three hundred. You just have to be willing to go that route, to recycle materials, use flats more than once, save a lot of things. If there's a half gallon of paint, I'll save it to use the next time. The Cardigans video, "Lovefool," for example, was a real tight budget. People bid in the range of fifty thousand dollars for art department, and I said I could do it for twenty. We don't mind putting in an eighteen-hour day, if that's what we have to do, and using stuff that's already been used."

Low-budget work requires a state of mind, a state in which any cool house or apartment you've been in and met the owner is a potential location. A mindset in which you buy a piece of equipment on your credit card, use it for the shoot, then return it after the shoot. In this mode, any slacker friend of the band becomes a potential crew member. Their parents make potential extras, and their parents' houses make perfect locations. You can find a college near most any town in America, and every college represents a wealth of free labor and equipment. The low-budget director is Tom Sawyer painting the fence, getting everyone to join in the fun: You don't have to be a con man, you just need never be afraid to ask anyone for anything, for any freebie. For help in decoding the above and descriptions of camera and lighting packages, turn to Chapter 4.

FILM FORMATS

Your choice of which film format to use — super-8, 16mm, 35mm or even video — dramatically effects your budgeting. Super-low-budget filmmakers enthusiastically embrace super-8 (see the Norwood Cheek sidebar), low-budget ($2,000 to $20,000) videos rely on 16mm, and high-end, major-label videos use the bright colors and tight grain of 35mm, the stock on which most feature films are shot.

If you're not up for the next Celine Dion or Spice Girls video, you can make 16mm look like you should be. DP Mott Hupfel has some thoughts on 16mm vs. 35mm, advice for saving money while making a beautiful image, and the cost advantages of black-and-white stock. "There's a lot of difference between 16mm and 35mm. If you're going to compete in the music-video world today, and make your video look like the ones that everyone's seeing on TV, you have to make it look like 35mm. The tricks to do that are: One, don't use a super-fast film stock because 35mm film does not get as grainy as 16mm. The grainier everything gets, the more muddy it is, the less sharp it looks. If you use a slow 16mm film [an under-200 ASA film], you'll get less grain. Two, if you use a longer lens, in either 16mm or 35mm, you get shorter depth of field, which means less in the frame is in focus. Thirty-five millimeter has less depth of field at every focal length than 16mm does, so that's what people are used to seeing in both feature films and music videos that have higher budgets. So when using 16mm, use longer lenses to get less depth of field. Not only does it make the image look more like 35mm, but it also draws attention to whatever is the center point of the frame.

"Three, in 16mm, if you have things that are really, really dark, they tend to get muddy, too, because of the grain. When things are dark in the frame, they use the larger grains in the film. If you keep things a little bit brighter, you get a crisper image, and that's paramount for production value. If the image is soft, blurry, a little bit dark, all of those things tear away production value, and make your video look more like a student film.

"Four, if you don't have a lot of money and you want to shoot interiors, shoot in black and white because it doesn't matter what kind of light you use. You don't have to worry about skin tones, you can shoot under fluorescent lights, you can shoot at night, you can shoot anywhere, and everything looks fine. You don't have the skin tone issues of color film, which I think is the major thing you have to worry about with color film. Every kind of light will effect the way skin looks, and unless skin tone looks totally natural, the image looks bad to most people."

HI-8 VIDEO

The Hi8 video format has put near–pro level video quality in the hands of the consumer, namely you. The key to shooting in Hi8 is that the footage needs to be transferred tape-to-tape, so that one can create a more filmic look essentially by degrading the video quality with the transfer. Tom Surgal, for his John Spencer Blues Explosion "Afro" video, transferred all of his Hi8 footage to beta, and from those tapes struck sub-masters which he used for the offline edit. In this respect, he treated Hi8 just like it was a film negative. To make it look more filmic, he shot the footage using the "digitizing" effect on the camera, used very contrasty lighting, and made everything just slightly out of focus. This was by far the most successful video Matador Records has ever produced — it was on MTV in regular rotation — and no one can tell that it's shot on Hi8 video.

> **REVERSAL FILM**
> Film that produces a positive image when processed rather than a negative image that requires a print to be struck. Originally developed so that the amateur wouldn't have to make a print.

WHY DOES A $5,000 MUSIC VIDEO LOOK LIKE A $20,000 MUSIC VIDEO?

If budgets vary over a wide range, why do music videos look substantially the same? Even a casual observer recognizes the truly expensive production value in the Smashing Pumpkins' "Tonight" video or the sleek styling of Toni Braxton's "Unbreak My Heart." But the nearly invisible difference in production value between a music video made for $5,000 and one for $20,000 generally astonishes the non-production person. Darren Doane laughs as he makes the point that the difference between a $5,000 video and a $20,000 video is the crafts service table that feeds the crew.

INSIDE DARREN DOANE

Let's listen in on low-budget director Darren Doane's stream-of conciousness dialogue as he approaches a budget in his dual roles as producer and director:

"Okay, if I'm shooting 35mm, my camera package is gonna cost me a thousand bucks. I've been to Birns & Sawyer [a Los Angeles film rental company] for seven years. I'm gonna buy their insurance so I don't have to have an insurance policy. So it's eleven hundred dollars. Plus tax, I'm at twelve hundred bucks out the door. If you don't know the rental houses you don't know the industry. You gotta know these people. They're the ones who save you when you need a favor. Next, I look at my lights: I'm gonna spend about four hundred. I'm gonna use four lights, two 1Ks that can plug into any household outlet and two 1200 pars. The pars are a different light from the 1Ks, a more powerful light, a white light. So you've got four lights and plenty of extension cords, five hundred feet of extension chords. With those four lights, you can light anything, truly anything. I've shot my last thirty videos on that package and no one would know. I know that I'm gonna call Reel Good, a film dealer in Hollywood. It's like buying drugs: He weighs out the film for you. It's the greatest thing in the whole world. For 35mm, I pay twenty cents a foot, so if I shoot about five thousand feet of film, that's about fifty minutes of raw footage. That's a lot of film. I know that I'm going to pay ten cents a foot to develop it at RGB. Then I gotta go transfer. My transfer is where I don't skimp, and I put a lot of money into telecine. I go to Pacific Ocean Post and use a guy named P.J., a phenomenal colorist. I'm gonna spend three hours in there at three hundred bucks an hour plus tape stock and now I'm at about fifteen hundred bucks. Now I gotta edit. My edit's for free because I got my own system and do my rough cut here. I transfer all my film to Betacam, half-inch window burns of my Betacam. I do my direct VHS to VHS. I handwrite my list. I take that list into an Avid that takes the Betacam. It's assembled in less than an hour. Add my opening slate and I'm done. Now it's just a matter of where I put my money into my crew and how extensive my shoot is. Now maybe I need to pull in a favor. It's not brain surgery. You just have to know five things. Then it becomes how much better a director do you want to be? And I think that's what directors should be focusing on. They shouldn't be focusing on budget."

<<<

NORWOOD CHEEK ON SUPER-8

Think in this day of palm-size video camcorders that super-8 cameras are just for retired tourists with white socks and sandals? Think again. Super-8 has long been a workhorse for super-low-budget filmmakers and videomakers. It's relatively inexpensive and can be transferred to video or blown-up to larger format film with gorgeous results (Bob even worked on a feature documentary that had regular-8 and super-8 elements blown to 35mm film). Grainy? Yes, but not disturbingly so in video format. We would describe it more as a pleasing overall softness in the image. And that softness is accentuated by the wonderful, pastel-y colors super-8 delivers.

Norwood Cheek, a director from Chapel Hill, North Carolina, who has made hundreds of videos for bands such as Superchunk, Squirrel Nut Zippers, and Ben Folds Five, has crowned himself the Southern Prince of Super-8. His enthusiastic advocacy of super-8 deserves special attention from low-budget videomakers, especially those just starting out. Like many in music video, Cheek likes using in-camera, "analog" processes. His latest Ben Folds Five video features elaborate rear-screen projection — actual projected 35mm film, instead of a post-production/video effect. Norwood's super-low-budget strategies:

"I think shooting with super-8 is one of the most liberating video- and filmmaking experiences anyone can ever have. To me, video's not even an option because with super-8 you really get the look of film. It's a great-looking format with even an okay camera. That's the great thing. People could be sitting at home right now and potentially there's a great old super-8 camera sitting in the attic that their father or their grandfather had. Even regular-8 has come into this kind of renaissance. Regular-8 was discontinued by Kodak in 1992, but this guy, John Schwind, is importing them from England and selling them at Yale Labs [213-464-6181].

The exciting thing to me about super-8 is that you could be in a band and make a video yourself. If there are three or four guys in a band, one of their parents or aunts of uncles has a super-8 camera — guaranteed. They could get a free camera, buy five or six rolls of film, film each other playing, and have it transferred. The trick is editing, but there are so many colleges, even high schools, that have VHS editing systems. And Kodak gives students deals. You could do it all on super-8 for under $100. For $200, you could have a great video.

And I think it's pretty easy to pull off a super-8 video. You get used to watching MTV and seeing these kind of super-pristine-looking videos, when all of a sudden you notice that Veruca Salt video that was shot on super-8 ["Seether"], or maybe that Beck video ["Loser"]. That's the advantage of using super-8: It does have this cool, unique look to it. The first video of mine that was on MTV, Superchunk's "Precision Auto," was all super-8. I shot about twenty-five minutes' worth of footage, which ends up being almost nine rolls of film. Nothing. I did all my own editing, cuts-only, on borrowed 3/4" equipment on the campus here in Chapel Hill. I had just gotten this super-8 camera for $200, a Chinon 208 XL. It can take the 200' magazine and do a lap-dissolve. I knew I couldn't do the dissolves later on in post-production, so I did in-camera dissolves, which is kind of crazy. But there's nothing like that originating-on-film dissolve, or those originating-on-film special effects. It has this certain look that you can't imitate electronically.

With super-8 you can do really fun things that might normally cost a lot of money. Some super-8 cameras run at nine frames per second, so you can shoot at nine frames and then have it transferred at nine frames, and it will give you this cool 'jagged' look. Because of the cost of 16mm or 35mm film, you have one or maybe two days of shooting and that's it. With super-8, usually you own the camera, so you can take a week or two weeks and do whatever you want, wait until you've got the perfect light, for example. If you have to build a set, you can do that. If it starts raining, it's no big deal. You can come back another day. In a lot of ways, it takes the pressure off.

For me, being both a director and cinematographer, it's much more relaxing because you really feel in control of the camera. You can throw it up in the air, strap it onto the front of a car. If it falls off, well, it's not that big a deal. You're able to take a lot more chances. Throw it off of the top of a building if you want to. Put it on the train tracks and let a train go over it. No company is ever going to let you do that with a 16 or a 35. It allows you to really explore all the potential of what's out there. With other formats, larger formats, the camera's too big. Super-8 allows you to tie the camera to the end of someone's guitar and they can still play their guitar without any effort. And you have this amazing shot where the camera's following all the movement of the guitar.

Super-8 can save you from having to spend the extra money on doing a supervised telecine. All the super-8 videos I did in the beginning, like the first twenty videos, I didn't even supervise the transfer. It was just a straight transfer. Super-8 is a cool-looking and super-forgiving film. You can do bad lighting and everything still turns out great. With 16mm or 35mm, all the imperfections of makeup or the lighting or the set, are really exaggerated. Super-8 allows you to produce something on a total shoestring, with very limited funds for set and lighting, and make it really cool. My favorite super-8 lab is called Yale Labs out in Los Angeles. It's pretty much a full-service lab for super-8. They process my film, and they transfer it, too.

If the budget was a couple of thousand dollars, I'd probably shoot about 15 rolls of super-8, have those processed and transferred to Beta-format video at Yale, unsupervised. Edit on Beta — I get rates of $75 an hour, which is really nice. With the finished product, I would then go into a telecine place and do a tape-to-tape transfer and tweak the colors if I felt like it was necessary. That way it would just be this three- or four-minute tape I'm refining instead of all of the footage.

<<<

If you made your video for $5,000, you're a miracle worker and that you shot a video at all qualifies as heroic. Since you approached the job like a starving artist, nobody got paid, including yourself. When you're making a video for four times $5,000, you're making the same video and everyone on your crew, maybe even you, gets paid.

Let's look at a broad-stroke budget breakdown. A director's fee (10 percent of the budget) for a $20,000 video is $2,000. A producer's fee (five percent of the budget) is $1,000. Note that a director on a $20,000 video rarely gets his or her full 10 percent because it seems outrageous for one person to eat up so much of the budget. A producer in this situation often takes more than five percent, and they should because they have to work alone: a $20,000 budget doesn't have room for a production manager or a production coordinator (sometimes a wannabe production coordinator PA fills these jobs). Considering all the days the producer has to work alone, they'd more than likely make less than the PAs. A production-company fee (generally 20 percent), equalling $4,000 in this example, includes insurance and overhead costs like office rent, phones and messengers. This production company figure tends to vary greatly in budgets this size. If the production company in question does multimillion-dollar commercials or high-end music videos, they don't need a piddly little $4,000. They want to "develop" younger directors, so they'll often donate their support. The fee definitely gets paid to lower-echelon companies, and many production companies have a no-exceptions fee policy. Look at the figures again. After only three fees, your $20,000 video budget yields only $13,000 for production. Wait. It gets worse.

Assuming you get reasonable deals on rental equipment and that the director edits the video her-self, processing and all editorial and post-production fees amount to approximately $4,000. In addition, the film stock will cost roughly $1,000 if you shoot 4,000 feet of standard 16mm stock. (On an extremely low-budget video, you would shoot half that amount and try to get re-canned film.) Added to the fees above, you've now spent $12,000. With a nine-person crew consisting of six keys and three seconds paid an average day rate of $300, an art director/props person at an equivalent rate for the shoot day and two days of prep, and three PAs making $100 a day for three days' work, you've now spent $16,000. You haven't rented a camera or put anything in front of it, and you only have a little less than $4,000 left. You haven't rented any lenses, miscellaneous camera stuff, grip equipment, generators, lights or audio playback, and a multitude of other expenses large and small. You haven't

WHERE TO ORDER COMPUTER PROGRAMS

Writers' Computer Store
(800) 272-8927

built any sets, paid for a location, bought anything for the band to wear, fed your crew or rented any trucks.

The budget analysis above spells out the paradox of shooting $20,000 or even $30,000 videos. Most in the industry agree that these low-end "real"-budget videos — and they do consider a video in the $20,000–$30,000 range a low-budget job — challenge producers and directors more than a $5,000 video. Also, with twenty or thirty thousand dollars, you have to spend the money. You're less likely go begging your old high-school drama teacher to shoot in the school's black-box theater. Besides, you're working with a producer now (it's too much money to produce yourself) and people in a position to dole out favors aren't as sympathetic to producers. When you only have $5,000, you're pathetic and people pity you, including the record company. When they pay $20,000 for a video, they expect certain industry standards. They want you to shoot brand-new film stock and expect you to hire an assistant camera person and a stylist. Also, when you're working with a real crew with its fees and schedules, suddenly you become tied to a one-day shoot. When making low-budget videos, I would shoot over the course of three or four days: Since no one was getting paid, anyone who worked with me helped whenever they could.

RECANS
You can find recanned film stock at: The Raw Stock Exchange in New York, (212) 255-0445

Duncan Sharp came of age during Seattle's grunge reign and has worked with budgets large and small for the quintessential Seattle label Sub Pop among others. He runs his own company in Seattle that feels more like a kind of film and video community center than it does a music-video production company. I remember visiting him while he played computer games with his business partner, who was seated at the other end of the room at another desk/computer. There was lots of super-8 equipment lying around. "The biggest difference between a $5,000 video and a $25,000 video is that on the $25,000 video you're probably gonna get paid," Duncan says. "On an artistic level, you're just gonna be able to shoot more film and you'll be able to spend more time editing it. With a $5,000 budget, you're really challenged to make things concise, simple, and visually legible."

"What I find really interesting in the difference between a $5,000 video and a $20,000 video," says Jesse Peretz, "is that [the $20,000 budget] tends to make people feel like 'Oh, my God, I have so much to work with' if they're used to $4,000 or $5,000. They think it will really change the way they work and suddenly they're fucked because it quickly becomes no different. If I were going to make an $20,000 video right now, I would think, 'Okay, I'm going to make a $5,000 video, get three friends to help me out, maybe rent a camera. I would try to spend as little money as possible on the crew and up-front costs and put all the money in front of the camera in location and art direction and having enough film to shoot."

Julie Hermelin points to increasing pressure from the record companies as being the main difference as she moved up the budgetary ladder. Two-thousand-dollar videos weren't a big deal after the first $10,000 video. "Then I did a $50,000 video and the $25,000 videos weren't pressure anymore. Those were easy. Now I just did an $80,000 video. And that's not pressure. Why? Because I did a $280,000 video where the record company was breathing down my neck, where I didn't sleep for a month and a half. I lost like 15 pounds. I thought I was going to kill myself or kill someone else. Now if somebody calls me up and they've got a $10,000 project, I say, 'Cool. I can just go out and shoot some film of the band.' The record company's going to be happy if they get anything, and I know that I can do something that looks good for $10,000. Record companies increase the pressure with the amount of money they give you. And if you feel that type of pressure, then it'll have an effect on you."

Phil Morrison explains the difference in relation to his experience with commercials. "I think that the commercial process is a whole, whole lot easier than mid-level music video making, the twenty to fifty grand, newish band or second-record band hoping to break out of *120 Minutes*. For me, making commercials is equivalent to making low-budget videos for indie-label bands. It all comes down to expectation. On a low-budget video, the expectation and the means are balanced. In a commercial, the expectations and the means are balanced: Agencies only do what they can do for the money. If they can't afford it, then they just do something else. They don't say, 'Can't you get people to work for free?' They don't say, 'Don't you love the product?' the way video commissioners say, 'Don't you love the song?' So, the people making commercials are modest in a way that the people making music videos would never conceive of being. But there is a modesty about the low-budget videos: 'We want to do a video, we have this much money, what can you do and when can you do it?' And you say, 'Well, I can do this, and it'll take a month to edit because we're dancing around somebody's Avid schedule.' Everyone is happy. On commercials they expect a whole lot, but they pay for it. I've come to find that I can do commercials that are really fulfilling. The Little Penny commercials and the Energizer commercials or the Nike Ice Man Cooketh were as fulfilling to me as any of my favorite videos have been."

To me, the disillusionment of the low-budget director most distinguishes a $5,000

GETTING STARTED:
NORWOOD CHEEK

"When I was first doing videos, I wasn't trying to make any money at all. I was just trying to do something with my time, really. I wanted to work with film, but I didn't have any ideas for a short film. So I decided that I was just going to do videos for a while. For my first twenty videos, I would tell the bands, which were mostly Chapel Hill bands, that I could do a video for them for like two or three hundred dollars. With that amount I knew I could shoot a certain amount of super-8 film and I could afford to tranfer to 3/4" videotapes. I did anything to cut corners: splicing all the film together so you could save that dollar-per-reel splicing fee, for example. There's something really great about that because, when you only have two hundred dollars to make a video, the ideas become really important. There's not this great-looking 16mm or 35mm film to make a lame idea look great. You've got this super-8 film that has a cool look to it, but it's not anything spectacular. Your ideas have to be pretty striking.

<<<

video from a $20,000 video. Two kinds of directors take jobs like this. One, established directors who like the band, work so often that they wouldn't even consider taking the measly two-thousand-dollar director's fee, and approach the project with simplicity in mind because they usually have so much more money in their budgets. Two, directors who come from super-low-budget video backgrounds, land $20,000 gigs, and suddenly think they have bundles of money to play with when they don't. Maybe it's the first time they've ever worked with a producer, or the first time they've ever considered paying a crew. These directors think that they can make *Apocalypse Now* when they're actually making another $5,000 video just like they've always done and, in fact, a $5,000 video with more constraints and less shooting time.

When I shot the second Helium video, I experienced precisely that kind of disillusion. Everyone got excited about the first Helium video's success on a $6,000 budget, but I failed to realize that, with all of the deals I got on equipment and labor, it had the production value of a $20,000 video. When I actually had $20,000 to do their second video, I had grand designs for a much more elaborate production, and I became a bad parody of an over-ambitious director. As in the first video, I wanted Helium to play in a dark, dingy environment during the verses, then in a bright, colorful world during the choruses. That chorus world occupied a gallery where pastel plastic flowers twirl around singer Mary Timony's head, each of which had a motor to make it spin. Way too labor intensive. If I had hired a more experienced producer, I would have been reined in right from the start.

The worst part of the video, though, was the verse world. I had fallen in love with a dilapitated former mental hospital in Waltham, Massachusetts. But it was January and there was no heat. Outside, the temperature never rose above 20 degrees and, since the buildings were boarded up, inside it was easily 20 degrees colder. There was no electricity, and, as always when you rely on anything too heavily, our generators didn't work at first. The producer, executing my desires, made the asylum day a "real day" with full crew. The band was grumpy and the freezing, resentful company moved in slow motion, lug-

HELIUM IN THE CHORUS WORLD

ging lights up and down three flights of stairs. If it had been just Mott, Mary and I, as during the extra shooting days of the first Helium video, then working in the mental hospital wouldn't have been as terrible. This shoot day, however, was one of the worst of my life and we got about half the shots we had planned.

Except that I felt the need to keep shooting, even after sunset. Because we needed one more shot, the producer became the scapegoat. I remember standing around in the pitch black arguing with Mott. Sarcastically, Mott barked, "And I'll bet she [the producer] wasn't smart enough to bring flashlights for when we wrap." Of course, she was standing next to us in the gloom and we didn't even know. My heart sank because I knew that my own insanity had created this situation. If I had thought of shooting something simple and reasonable for the money we had, I would've spared everyone a lot of misery. The paradox to remember is that you have to curb your ambitions when you jump to the bigger budgets.

THE ESSENTIAL INGREDIENTS REMAIN THE SAME

The essential ingredients of a video never change. You need a camera, lighting, a place to shoot, things to put in front of the camera in addition to the rock band, and some way to do playback if you shoot the band performing. Then you need to process your film, transfer it to videotape, offline edit (the rough cut), then online (the final edit). Only the amount of money you spend on each ingredient changes.

As with treatment writing, go through the budget-writing process yourself to learn about the larger creative process. "As a producer looking at a project for the first time, it's the same thing a director does," says Bennett. "You think about how many set-ups you have. The alleyway. I need the dream sequence. I need the in-home, in-bed sequence. I need the bathroom sequence. You think, 'How many locations is that? Can I do three of these in one location?' Okay, we know who the DP is and how much that will cost and we know where the locations are — how many shots can you do here? Oh, shoot, you still left out scene number 10. Is there a place within this context where we can do that? You have to say, 'Okay, I know with a fast director I can do maybe five set-ups in a day at one location, and with a slow director maybe two and a half set-ups. You think about the personalities involved. You start thinking about the look that's been described and you know immediately that, if the concept calls for available light, you won't be needing a lot of lighting equipment and maybe you'll be able to avoid a generator. I break out how many scenes, how many characters, how many parts to the story need to be there for it to be told. You have to think about what's really essential, especially when you're trying to trim a budget, but you also have to think about what the director really needs to get her point across, to get her promise to the client across." Even if you have $200 to spend, it's worth figuring out exactly how you're going to spend it. Don't focus on how little money you have; there's never enough money in any budget.

I had a revelation while watching Jake Scott's slickly compelling "Fake Plastic Trees" video for Radiohead. The video vaguely emulates the pharmacy scene in Oliver Stone's *Natural Born Killers,* with harsh fluorescent lighting revealing an endless store aisle. After seeing the video many times, I noticed that there were two mirrors placed at an angle that created the illusion of the aisle continuing into infinity. This beautiful video, with a budget no doubt well in the six figures, depends for its major visual appeal on mirrors that must have cost well into the two figures.

Even on big-budget jobs like the Radiohead video, the short prep time endemic to the form (the video commissioner has a say, the band has a say, the management has a say, and, ohmygod, the single comes out next Tuesday) means money gets thrown at problems created by the scheduling and doesn't end up on screen. Studio space gets rented at the last minute and large crews get hired to do what could have taken fewer people with more time. "What I find is that with $150,000, everything expands to fit the budget: It's harder to drive bargains, everyone's working retail," says Adam Bernstein. "No matter what the budget, you're scraping around trying to figure out how to make it work." This doesn't mean if given all the time in the world the art director of the Radiohead video would build a half-mile-long aisle, but music video makers always scramble to make do with what they have. Relative to Hollywood movies or commercials, music videos are cheap. Unless it's a seven-million-dollar Mark Romanek video such as Janet and Michael Jackson's "Scream," even big-budget videos take cost-cutting measures. They always put mirrors at the end of the aisle.

Directors will tell you that their creative process is the same no matter the size of the budget, but be aware that budgetary concerns will prevail as you concieve your music video: Don't propose helicopter shots or shooting in the south of France for a $10,000 video. And the production objectives for the director are also the same regardless of budget: You want the most for your money, the most shooting time and the most film for the best coverage. You work with what you have, and always opt for low-budget alternatives, for example exterior locations with natural light instead of interiors that need to be lit, and in-camera effects instead of post-production effects. Use friends instead of actors and unpaid interns for your crew. Director David Roth told me he's done a video shooting at 16 frames per second, and not just for a cool effect but to save one-third of the film cost.

The most significant practical difference between low-budget and mid-level videos can be seen in who handles production chores. "My advice is to fire the producer," recommends producer Christiansen. "Right away. And do it yourself. You have to." Low-budget video directors generally produce their own videos, and that can be a terrific learning experience. When you make a low-budget video, you thrust yourself into the role of producer as well as director. You have to be the person calling in all the favors and organizing the shoot — precisely what a producer does.

chapter three

Once the treatment and budget are approved, you stand in the open doorway to a wedding, a wedding that you've planned, worried over, scheduled, and organized. The key members of the party have to be pleased with the result: The band becomes your fiancee, the record company your in-laws. The wedding's details drive you insane, but the wedding day itself must be well scheduled; folks need to know where to be and when. They need to be kept busy and fed. The activities have to move at the proper pace and conclude when planned. Your in-laws must be pleased with the festivities without burdening the planning with their unwelcome involvement. Your bride? Well, with luck it will be one of the most memorable days of her life, but, while the last-minute details pile up, you think, "I'll be satisfied if she doesn't storm off the altar." Music videos come together quickly, often with only days between final approval and the shoot. Getting organized is not always an **planning >**

organized process, and it's a scramble to get all the necessary elements together. As producer, you must assemble location, equipment and crew.

Producer Kim Christiansen gives a breathless description of her days before the shooting begins: "It's crazy. It's so ugly." The highlights:

"You're faxing everyone all day long.

"This person needs an insurance certificate and everybody needs a P.O.

"Put up Post-it notes with how long you can spend doing things.

"Order the equipment.

"Stay until ten o'clock at night and do the call sheet and the production book and the schedule.

"Sit on the phone all day and order walkies [walkie-talkies], food, the director's chairs and the lights.

"Finding a location, that's the nightmare because you can't be sitting in the office making phone calls and location scouting at the same time unless you think of somewhere and say, 'What about that place?'

"After five, you start to call the crew that you're probably gonna work with in two days and wait for them to call you back because they're all working. You page them and they call you back, sometimes. You leave a message with the key grip's wife. He's gonna be home at midnight or whatever and you miss people for a day or so. Then, the next day, they call you and you start to talk to them about their rates, how low they are and how upset they are about it. You wish you could do something about it but you can't because you really can't. It's either do it or don't do it."

Whew.

"Location is the biggest headache from the beginning," she continues. "It means talking to civilians who may be used to people coming in and giving them ten thousand dollars for one day to use their place. You call and have four hundred dollars or whatever, so you want to shoot for free. And you're calling this person and for twenty or thirty minutes they want to tell you about the time that Bette Midler was there, and between nine A.M. and five P.M., you've got three hundred phone calls to make. But you're on the phone with this person who wants to talk about the last time they got paid ten thousand dollars and how many stars were there and how fabulous it was. What you really want to know is whether there's any chance in hell that we can possibly shoot at your place for, you know, a tenth of that?"

As director, you have to get your storyboards, song breakdowns, and shot lists together, then work with the producer and the key members of the crew (or get your own thoughts together) to develop the video's visual strategy. Ideally, you want to use this pre-production time to let your vision develop and grow. A successful shoot depends on thorough, detailed pre-production, and, as Adam Bernstein says, "If you've done your homework, things are never going to go that wrong."

Many producers say that during the pre-production process their job is simply to give the director enough space to work on the things s/he needs to do. They maintain that the directors need space to be creative and calm so that — like an athlete preparing for the big competition — they can focus on the shoot. Watch for bad patterns in the producer-director dynamic here. When the director is a man and the producer a woman, too often you see a playing out of age-old gender roles, the woman as nurturer and provider for the man's creative vision, the woman behind the man, doing the grunt but getting none of the credit. Believe it: There are many codependent director/producer teams.

During pre-production, while the producer wrangles details, the director has end-less meetings with the artist, the label and the band's management. Directors need to bond with the artist or band because they need to feel like the artist trusts them enough to per-form well. That involves hearing the band's ideas but also checking in with the record label's video commissioners and A&R people, and the band's management, to reassure them and coddle them.

Though different producers have different ideas about the priority order of pre-pro-duction tasks, nearly all agree that deciding on the location tops the list.

LOCATION

The question of where to shoot affects more than the audience simply appreciating the cool alleyway you found to display your singer. If your treatment calls for extensive art direction or elaborate sets, and you have the budget for it, you'll be shooting in the controlled envi-ronment of a sound stage. Much of what you see on film and television was shot on a set because shooting on a stage is easier — moving to a new camera set-up means moving to a different area of the stage, not packing up and moving the entire crew and equipment across town. Also, directors and DPs feel like they have more control over lighting and camera movement when they shoot on a set. But even if money is no object, you may decide for aes-thetic reasons (or because the band wants to go to Hawaii) to shoot on location.

For a low-budget video, location shooting is generally the only practical alternative. Studio time has become increasingly more difficult to come by and more expensive if you can get it. Even if the action in a typical low-budget video takes place in a non-specific location that could be created in a studio, the budget limitations often require finding an inexpensive space to act as a studio substitute. "In the first three years I was doing videos, every video I did was location-dependent," recalls Bernstein. "If you're doing a low-budget video, location is the most important thing you can possibly come across because you can't afford anything else. You can't really get into building [sets] until you're well over the hundred-thousand-dollar mark, so you depend on the strength of the idea and the location."

Darren Doane agrees. "Location is everything," he says. "You walk into a nice house, there's a million-dollar set. Even if you don't have a lot of money, well, the beach is still the beach. You know what I mean? You can't put a price on that."

Location is a primary element of the treatment. While you were dreaming your video, you may have conjured up images of palm trees and sand, or gritty streets in the shadow of the Berlin Wall (don't worry, we all have). What would U2's "Mysterious Ways," directed by Anton Corbijn, be without what amounts to a *National Geographic* special on Morocco as the backdrop? The title line gets neatly summed up by how we feel about the Middle East, the customs as veiled to Westerners as the gauzy face covering of the dancer who makes the song's chorus literal. Consider Kevin Kerslake's videos and his use of the intricate architecture found in dilapidated industrial buildings, "Unsung," the groundbreaking video for Helmet, for example.

But the very things that make a location creatively appealing sometimes make for dysfunctional production. So, though you want to shoot in a visually exciting location, consider the practical concerns:

WHAT IS IT GOING TO COST?

No guidebook records how much a donut shop or a house costs to rent as a location. You always have to wheel, deal and barter. Obviously, a commercial or movie can afford to shut down a supermarket for ten hours so they can shoot there — you can't. Locations often add to the cost of shooting in indirect ways. Difficult access to shooting areas — long hallways, stairs — means that you need more folks to help you lug equipment around, which means more people you need to pay and more mouths to feed. Fancy locations with nice furniture mean more expensive items that you have to replace if you break something, and you will break something.

CAN IT BE INSURED?

The only way you can insure a location is to have a blanket production insurance policy from a production company. You are not insured if all you have is a rental company's insurance policy on its equipment. This is the most compelling reason to attach yourself to a production company's policy, to get insurance any way you can. When you shoot in a space owned and run by a city or a state municipal agency — many cool old buildings are in the hands of the state — you absolutely need to have an insurance policy or the local government won't even talk to you.

WILL THE NOISE YOU MAKE (AND YOU *WILL* MAKE NOISE) AND THE ALL-NIGHT LIGHTS EFFECT OTHERS WHO LIVE AND WORK IN THE AREA?

It's a rock video, right? The neighbors will feel the noize.

IS THERE ENOUGH ELECTRICITY AND CAN YOU SAFELY ACCESS IT?

Yes, we suggest some risky behavior in this book; being unprofessional with electricity is not one of them. If you're working in any kind of commerical space that's properly wired, you can "tie in," or have an electric (an electrician who works for the gaffer) attach boxes to the main trunk cable in the building. Only do this if you have a union electrician on the shoot. You could blow the power for a whole city block, or worse, someone might die.

CAN YOU GET LEGAL PERMITTING OR AN OWNER'S PERMISSION TO SHOOT?

"Stealing a shot," or "stealing a location," the terms for shooting in a place where you have no permission at all, is an addictive high for a low-budget videomaker. To shoot without permission is an initiation into the world of low-budget production. But understand that stealing locations is accompanied by anxiety and stress. If you ever get thrown off of a location before you're done shooting, it feels like the end, and not just of the video. I've been incredibly lucky stealing locations and I know that the karmic location-stealing wheel is going to turn against me at some point.

The moment you start thinking about how to find or use a location, you've begun thinking like a filmmaker, marrying your daydreams to your project's planning. Once a location is selected, all the key crew members — the assistant director, the director of photography, the director and producer — do a scout to figure out the logistics of the shoot. When the space appears in front of you, the director in you starts composing shots. Then you must begin thinking like a producer, looking for ways to consolidate the camera set-ups. For example, say your video has a narrative element that takes place in a store, and you've found one that looks great and the owner's really cool. Great. But in your treatment, you also need to shoot the band in a space that looks like a basement. Can the stockroom in the store be dressed to look like a basement? Decisions about shots, how many set-ups can be accomplished in a day, props, set dressing, other nearby locations all cascade from finding that first location. Only when a location is chosen can the real work of preparing for the shoot begin.

The first challenge is to find that perfect location. On a big-budget job, the director sits in a hotel room or production office and peruses photographs of potential sites, maybe venturing out in a Land Rover with assistants, DP and location scout. This is almost never the case for a low-budget video. Of the many hats a low-budget director wears, location scout is among the most prominent.

Being a location scout seems like a fun job. What wouldn't be fun about driving around, searching for cool spaces and getting paid upwards of $350 a day. In fact, if you were given a big-time budget, location scouting is one of the many jobs that you wouldn't do yourself, but you're happy to do it for a low-budget video. It's most fun if you can recreate a particular kind of Hardy Boys feeling. Remember those fantastic after-school afternoons exploring the creepy, old, "off limits" abandoned house? Making that kind of energy useful in your adult life is one of the pleasures of the job. Often when Mott and I were looking for a location, it would hit me. As he was widening the hole in a chain-link fence under a "No Trespassing" sign ("Come on, Dave, just climb through here before anybody sees us."), I would look down at my watch, read 5:00 P.M., and think, "Wait a minute. Don't I have to be home for supper?" I was 27 years old and I was out joyfully rummaging around abandoned buildings like a fifth-grader while most of my friends labored in fluorescent-lit offices.

For a DP, like Mott, the perfect location means usable light, easy access for crew and equipment and an interesting texture against which to set the band. "A great location would have good light that already exists," he says, "because that way you save money, and you have natural lighting, which looks good. Anything that's visually interesting or different that you can put the band in so it won't be them standing in front of a blank wall. It has to have colors or depth or large, open spaces. I like dilapidated things, broken-down buildings, both for access and because they tend to look cool. It's pretty clichéd, but they're useful."

Jesse Peretz found just such a perfect location for the Shudder To Think video, "Hit Liquor." "There's a boat in the Hudson River in New York called the *Frying Pan*. It's an old, three-story ship that had been sunk for years. The people that owned it brought it up and cleaned it, but they left the aging and barnacles. They created different bedrooms with creepy little pictures — a fully art-directed boat with lots of different spaces on it. We got the whole boat for $700 for as long a day as we wanted; we had a sixteen-hour day and shot the whole video in one day. We were able to shoot a video that had six different rooms plus the big performance space all on one boat. I think that's definitely the key to low-budget videomaking."

Let's say you've found a perfect location like the *Frying Pan*. Now how do you secure permission to use it? Telling people that you want to shoot a music video in their home or business is like showing up at their front door with a wrecking ball and saying "We're here to do a little remodeling." There's nothing in it for them but pain and sorrow. No one living within a fifty-mile radius of either New York or Los Angeles remains charmed by film production.

Only in cities like Dayton, Ohio, where the presence of our very unimpressive production for "Motor Away," a Guided By Voices video, made all the local nightly newscasts, do people get excited by the glamour of television. In Dayton, some of the folks we encountered were charmingly guileless when it came to film production. For example, I wanted six tow trucks for the final shot of the video. Becoming desperate the night before the shoot

because we had secured only five tow trucks, we made a rather extravagant offer to a local tow truck owner, who didn't quite understand. "You mean, I pay you $400 for my tow truck to be in the video?" We were tempted not to set him straight.

The *You Stand There* philosophy demands shamelessness when securing a location. It takes a certain bravado to impose a production on someone's property. If a space is privately owned, obviously you need the owner's permission. You should always offer some payment

THE PRIDE OF DAYTON: GUIDED BY VOICES

for a location, no matter how little you can spend. If you paid for one million dollars' worth of production insurance, use it as a bargaining chip. "We're insured for one million dollars!" makes an important-sounding gambit when you're telling a suspicious businessman that you want to spend fourteen hours vibrating his building's foundation with a rock band. But you have other bargaining chips. Offer footage to small-business owners, shots of the property without the band that can be used for commercials or an industrial film — it won't take you any time to shoot. If the band wants a performance scene shot on the stage of their hometown club, tell them that they have to offer the club a free gig.

Also, you can't be bashful about asking the band if they know cool places to shoot. Have them drive you around if you're shooting in their city. Some of their regular haunts might be perfect places to shoot. One of their dads might work at a gorgeously smudgy factory, or one of them might have a job in some awesome store full of colorful junk. One of them might be an alum of a school that has terrifically stuffy-looking buildings on campus.

Shooting at any institution — schools, colleges, hospitals, government buildings — is particularly difficult, though. Alec Kashishian (director of *Truth or Dare* and Madonna videos), for example, wasn't allowed access to his alma mater, Harvard, when he shot the multimillion-dollar feature, *With Honors*. Here's the way in: Loiter around campus and introduce yourself to some film students, then offer them the priceless opportunity to work on your video for free — if they sign out the campus television production studio. I've even asked film-production professors if we could shoot at the campus studios for free in return for offering unpaid internships to students who could be our crew. Mind you, this doesn't always work, but it's worth a shot.

If you're shooting on city streets, you're supposed to have permits. Permits take at least forty-eight hours to secure in most cities, and can cost you hundreds of dollars, depending on the city. The major cities have film-production offices that make this relatively easy for professional productions. Production companies get permits all the time and have relationships with the people at the office. On the other hand, it's hellish for the low-budget director without an impressive-sounding company name.

Aside from the fact that it's the legal, sane thing to do, a permit is absolutely necessary only when getting thrown off the location would bring the entire production to a standstill. What happens if you get stopped on the street and asked what precisely you're doing blocking traffic and lighting up the neighborhood? You're probably not going to be thrown in jail. Usually when the cops drop by and see the ragtag state of the production, they walk off convinced that you're too pathetic to shut down.

If you want to proceed properly and not risk embarrassment, investigate the film-production office's files filled with potential locations. Some cities, such as Boston, have special files for "free" locations: state-owned properties for which you donate a nominal fee to charity in order to shoot in the space. These locations tend to be abandoned hospitals and institutions, and they make good, generic — if sometimes a little creepy — music-video locations.

For many directors, location scouting — with a Polaroid camera at the ready in the glovebox, always scouting even when they're not working — is a way of life. Julie Hermelin finds locations everywhere she travels and captures them on a small-format camera for later use. "Keep your eyes peeled for anything unique in the world, especially if it's cheap and unique," she advises. "Shoot your vacations in super-8. If you're going to an interesting location, bring your camera along. You can put it in a video during telecine. If you're friends with the band, shoot the vacation you take together. It's footage with the lead singer. You can spend hundreds of thousands of dollars on locations you find when you backpack some-where for no money." Even if you don't carry a camera around your neck like a tourist, keep your eyes peeled for space and architecture that inspires you. You will need to be as resourceful as possible and have a mental file of locations at the ready.

I had the importance of location impressed upon me during only my second video. Matador Records needed a video made immediately to placate grumpy New Zealand post-punk noise-rockers, Bailter Space. They didn't even care about getting a treatment. They just wanted to spend $5,000 or less and needed to shoot something before the band left four days later for a tour. The only instructions: shoot "something cool" and make it appropriate for Bailter Space's droney opus "EIP" in which the singer endlessly whispers "Things are falling apart, things are coming together . . ." The only thing the band wanted to see in the video was (read the following in the thickest New Zealand accent imaginable) "ahwt-a-focus smahll medahl ohbjects." Since this was the band's first video, Matador wanted to show the band playing. Now it's really not too hard to shoot small metal objects out of focus. The dilemma was where to shoot the band. The location needed to be visually exciting, and, to make me feel like I'd done my job of conceptualizing the video, somehow appropriate for cut-aways of small metal objects and in tune with the band's vaguely techno aesthetic.

The main problem: We lived in New York. I can die peacefully if I never see anoth-er video in which a bunch of rockers sullenly roam New York's streets. Band-walking-around-city videos are so tired at this point that they are nearly invisible. Using urban loca-tions for gratuitous ambiance, especially if it reads as an attempt to make a bunch of white rockers look bad-ass, smells inevitably of cheese. For Bailter Space, I wanted a background that looked modern and otherworldly but that wasn't easily identifiable as urban. And, need it be said, we had to shoot somewhere for free.

Luckily, a friend who was staying with me had a major brainstorm (classic situa-tion: the out-of-towner shows you a cool place to shoot in New York). Near the FDR Drive, which runs alongside the East River, near 125th Street in Harlem, large piles of rock salt loom over obsolete refineries like mountains of snow. What makes this location different from any old generic industrial backdrop is that, viewed from the right angle, you'd think you were on the lunar surface rather than in Manhattan. The moment I saw it I knew I had to shoot there.

Unfortunately, the city sanitation department owned the rock-salt desert mountains. Since we had less than forty-eight hours before our shoot day, there was no way we were going to get a permit, and, at the time, I was too clueless to get insurance. We had to shoot there with no permit. On the fateful day, I constantly looked over my shoulder, expecting to be shut down every ten minutes. Our crew was tiny, but conspicuous as hell against the saline-white backdrop. Thousands of people saw us: We were shooting next to eight lanes

BAILTER SPACE: ROCK SALT MINERS

of traffic on the FDR Drive. We had no lights, so we were working with large pieces of mylar and mirror boards, which reflected intense light beams that I was certain would blind an unsuspecting driver and cause a massive, multicar accident. Baking in the harsh sunlight, there was no way that Bailter Space was going to perform without heavy doses of imported beer and weed, which added to my distress as the police came by a number of times throughout the day. But, instead of asking for a permit, they wanted to know where the band was from. The cops evidently assumed that we wouldn't be crazy enough to shoot in such an obviously out-of-bounds location without a permit, so they didn't even ask for one.

I think I used the old standby, "We're NYU students," with some of the cops that came by that day. Always tell them you're in school. While shooting the first Helium video, "XXX," completely permitless in Boston, Mott and I got harassed by a security cop. As if on cue, Mott said, "We're Mass Art students," while I simultaneously barked, "We're

Museum School students." Needless to say, it didn't work that time. Even music-video producers who work on real-budget jobs use the film-students ruse. On top of a parking garage in Hollywood, I heard Tara Fitzpatrick, my producer on the "Alanis Morrissette" shoot for Wesley Willis, explain to the location's owner, who was confronting her about a discrepancy in the permit, that we were film students. When the owner saw the permit, issued by a city agency, which described the production as a music video, the owner was confused. "Well, it is a student film," the thinking-on-her-feet producer explained. "It's a student film called *Music Video*."

By the end of the day on the Bailter Space shoot, we were all so relaxed about shooting on the rock salt that our PA (Evan Bernard, who later found success directing videos for the Fun Lovin' Criminals and the Beastie Boys) was pissing into the East River and I wasn't even uptight about it. I knew I'd made a good decision when the footage screened in the film-to-tape transfer and the colorist kept asking, "Where the hell is that?" In the Bailter Space video, location was literally the entire video: Weird shots featured band members in the foreground, framed by what looked like a snow-covered mountain ridge with bits and pieces of the Triboro Bridge and ramps of the FDR behind it all, just barely suggesting the New York location.

After that experience, I began to think that an unusual location was the key to a great low-budget video. Perhaps too much, as I began to waste valuable preproduction days looking for the ultimate location. Since we never had any money to make the videos, I thought that we started at a disadvantage, so I would spend as much time as possible looking for cool places to shoot, sometimes to the detriment of the production.

"HELLO, I'M AN . . . "
ART DIRECTOR

"Basically my job is the realization of the director's vision. I take his ideas and make them a reality, make them doable. Basically I'm a set builder. I design and fabricate sets so that there's a look. I add a look and a style to the video. I take the director's ideas and make them happen, adding my own little flavor to it."
— *Jonathan Wellerstein, art director*

<<<

THE ART DEPARTMENT

Before working as an art-department PA on a network television series, I never realized how much of what I saw on television and in the movies was shot on a set. Assume that nearly every interior you see on television is a set. When you wonder how movie budgets can exceed $100 million, consider the sets. On a beach in Mexico, a crew shooting another movie version of the *Titanic* story worked on a full-scale replica of the ocean liner. Entire interiors of hospitals get built, restaurants are re-created, apartments furnished. Not unlike actors, production designers, working with set decorators, depict the characters' psychology. Every alarm clock or refrigerator magnet in a character's apartment set should reflect the character. Not unlike a director of photography, a production designer works with the director to establish what colors will be used and what details appear in the frame.

This is why an art director can claim, "Basically, my job is the realization of the director's vision," as does art director Jonathan Wellerstein, a displaced New Yorker now living in Los Angeles who started doing art department work only in the last couple of years, he has already worked on videos for the Cardigans, Tricky and Sebadoh. He's also a drummer and generally wears low-slung, paint-splattered jeans. "Basically I'm a set builder. I design and fabricate sets to create a look. I take the director's ideas and make them happen, adding my own little flavor to it."

Sometimes you can't find an ideal location: Your daydreams call for a space that doesn't exist. Now you need to build a set, or dress a preexisting location to match your imagination. In other words, you need an art department. Hiring an art director is one aspect of production that doesn't reward skimping, even if you have no money. Think of it like this and you'll sense the importance of the job: The art director puts everything in front of the camera except the talent.

The art department employs dozens of people on a feature-film production. The production designer works with the director and DP to establish color schemes for lighting, sets and costuming, and design elements such as the particular period of furniture and props to be seen. They sketch sets, costumes and props, and those drawings serve as the direction for those who actually transform the concepts into lumber and cloth. The art director prepares building plans and detailed instructions for propmasters, set decorators and builders, and set painters. The art director, as lead art-department person, often has draftspeople skilled in architectural drawing preparing building plans for the scenic carpenters. They also oversee the set decorators, construction workers, scenic painters, and the props department as they make the production design materialize.

As with the producers you met in the last chapter, music-video production creates hybrid art department roles that combine several functions into one all-purpose person. The result looks more like the art department on a photo shoot than a feature film.

On a music-video shoot, you often have someone called an art director who does the job of both production designer and art director. (Sometimes this person is simply called the stylist, in keeping with how the term is used on photo shoots.) Generally, a stylist, not a costume designer, is the person who works with wardrobe: most bands appear in current, hipster clothes, and if there are any special costume needs, they are dealt with by the art director. The art director, and maybe, on a big-budget set, a set decorator, each have their own crews. There might also be a makeup person and a hair person. For big-budget videos, these people are at the top of their field and are paid $3,000 a day. Again, so that you can understand the range of activities in the art department, we've described traditional art department functions:

production designer

Working closely with both the director (on creative elements) and producer (on budget), the production designer is responsible for all design elements of a film, from sets to costuming to props, and managing the staff that executes his or her plan.

art director

The art director translates the production designer's plan into drawings and building plans and assembles and directly supervises the crew of painters, carpenters, costumers, props people and set dressers.

propmaster (property master; lead prop)

The person responsible for acquiring, preparing and having available on set anything handled by the band or actors, for example, that pen and paper in the Boyz II Men video. On big-budget jobs, the lead prop works with an assistant, also known as an outside prop or shopper.

scenic artist

Under the supervision of the art director, the scenic paints any surface on the set; ages (gives the appearance of age or use) costumes, sets or props; and produces signage or lettering or even copies of old-master paintings. These folks have an in-depth knowledge of historical periods and their decorative styles and are accomplished artists with contemporary and historic materials.

carpenter

The builders of sets and flats, they have special skills in building structures that are safe, sturdy, and sound, yet can be assembled and broken down quickly.

set decorator

The person responsible for the furnishings and the objects placed on the set. Working under the art director, the set decorator plans the placement of the furnishings with the director and the DP and works mostly off the set acquiring the material for the next day's shooting.

set dresser

Working for the art director and coordinating closely with the propmaster, the set dresser is responsible for the actual placement and moving of the furnishings on the set. The set dresser also maintains and repairs the furnishings on set and keeps track of the items' continuity.

costume designer

The person who develops, with the director and production designer, the character's personality through their clothing and accessories whether through original designs or costumes acquired or rented from a costume shop.

<<<

Music videos seldom boast the budget to support this legion of workers. Even on a real-budget music video, the person called the art director wears all of the hats described in the box. Often, though, a props person will be hired to deal with specialty props, outfitting the entire band in period baseball uniforms or with marching-band instruments, for example. On a rock video budgeted between $3,000 and $30,000, the art director designs and executes everything prop- or set-related. "As someone who works on low-budget videos," confirms Wellerstein, "I do everything: I design the set, I buy the props, I think about the fabrics, sometimes I get down and do scenic painting. All my crew members do a little of everything, and I just kind of like it like that. A production designer should be responsible for the wardrobe and the look, and they should be hiring the people making the clothes so that it all sort of holds together. I dress the sets, I buy the props, I decorate, I do everything."

Some directors rely more heavily on the art department than others. Certainly directors of the photographic school, Sam Bayer and Matt Mahurin, for example, rely on art department to create worlds filled with carefully aged surfaces and surreal little objects. Such directors take elaborate care to use objects not simply because they look cool, but for their symbolism. Though this sounds pretentious, the repeated appearance of an object or objects becomes part of a visual landscape and can create meaning in the video. Showing an object that simply illustrates a line in a song is sometimes less embarrassing than having actors act out a lyric-illustrating scenario.

Using a set or props isn't impossible with a low budget, and art direction can actually be another money-saving creative solution. Videomakers sometimes resort to the age-old tricks of cinema pioneers like George Méliès. If you can't shoot in a grand ballroom, for example, you can create a frame that you place in front of the camera that makes it look like you're shooting in a ballroom. Michel Gondry's videos (his brilliant video for Cibo Matto's "Sugarwater" rivals calculus in its complexity) — even though they have huge budgets — employ such visual tricks. Lots of videos use sets built in "forced perspective," rooms that look larger to the camera than to the eye. A forced-perspective room looks like a huge 30'x 50' room, but is in fact only 15' wide and 10' deep. Like German Expressionist sets in the '20s, these rooms are actually painted backdrops with exaggerated angles that make them look like huge rooms. Instead of shooting on one set and moving the camera around to get different perspectives on the room, these early German filmmakers would build different sets for each perspective and leave the camera in one basic area. (Talk about a non-low-budget approach to solving the problem. . .) A room with nothing in it is a room with nothing in it. A room you fill with easily obtained, bright orange safety cones, for an obvious example, suddenly projects a strong color and a bold shape that can be distributed in an eye-pleasing arrangement or scattered randomly, worn by the performers, and shoved near the lens to play with perspective. Your orange cones provide some sense of graphic unity and design to a once-bare room.

In many great videos, the visual hook is simply a design element. If the search for a visually arresting location makes you look at your surroundings in a new way, art direction should make you look at objects in a new way: their color, their size, their shape, their materials. The director should work out necessary props or design elements such as painted backdrops in the treatment-writing process, but it's also the stuff of collaboration with an art director.

During preproduction, the art director works furiously. While directors shop for locations, art directors shop for materials and props. Armed with Polariod cameras — just like location scouts — art-department crew members take pictures of potential props and furniture to get the okay from producers and directors before spending money. The art department always faces a minibudget struggle within the project's larger budget struggle. Just as the producers complained in the last chapter that there is never a large enough budget, art directors can count on not having enough money to properly execute the director's dreams. They contract for all materials and the services of carpenters and painters, etc., based on the treatment and the budget. For example, if they plan for one "build" day to create and paint the sets and the director changes the color scheme or dimensions of the set at the last minute, the set builders and painters work overtime to finish in time for the DP to light the set the next day. Those expensive hours come out of other line items in the art department budget — props, usually. But the art director will have spent the last two days of preproduction sourcing and bargaining for props. Now he/she has to go back to his or her sources and either strike a better deal, find another source, eliminate it, or come up with an ingenious way of faking the prop. As Wellerstein describes his process, you'll see the pressures. "The first stage: They call me, send me a treatment, I read it, I put together a bid," he says. "If it's awarded, I start lining up a crew and figuring out where the bulk of my time and money is going to be spent. The time is usually really crunched. They'll call me up and I'll start work the next morning. The shoot will be five days from the day they call me and they want a ton of stuff built. Sometimes, I'll get fifteen guys working last minute. That's basically what I do: I have to figure out what needs to be made and get guys making it, and what needs to be bought and get guys taking pictures of it so I can choose what I want. If there are specialty items, I design those. If they want a stage, we'll custom-make that and

I have to design it. We meet at the site, which is either a location or a stage, and we have a build day when we put everything together. That's when the carpenters do their thing, the scenics paint it and the set-dressing department comes in and decorates it. I give it the thumbs up and we shoot it."

The next best thing to a pre-art-directed location is an easily art-directable one. If you're shooting in an abandoned factory — a not-improbable example — there might be movable props around like hand tools or greasy machinery. Luckily the antiquey, sepia-drenched aesthetic in much of '90s art direction works in favor of a low-budget videomaker. Jeff Plansker's videos for the Jayhawks and Belly, to choose one example, scatter rusted-out little toys and old, oxidized pieces of metal throughout. Not expensive items, but they create a truly signature look for his videos.

Objects, just as location, can sometimes determine your video's direction. Go to junk yards and architectural salvage dealers. Go to wholesale suppliers of foam, paper or metal grates. If one of these folks has a group of, say, old school desks that look really cool, then you may make a video that features the band and friends sitting in a classroom. All the rules of low-budget shamelessness apply when aquiring art department materials. If you need something for your video and can only buy it new, buy it at a store that allows returns. Back it goes right after the shoot, and you retrieve your money. Many things — furniture, antiques, used appliances, used clothes, office paperwork — can be rented. Use your shooting insurance to convince a retailer that you'll cover the cost of any damage done to one of their items, then rent it for a fraction of what it costs to buy it. Plead for furniture and household goods from your friends, and throw them in the back of the pickup truck you borrowed.

LISTS

Each and every day, my father wakes up and spends hours working on his lists. On the surface they're innocuous enough: a schedule or goals for the day. But Dad's lists go far beyond incoming and outgoing phone calls and "things to do." A numbers obsession plus some serious control issues made for life-dominating lists, and the lists were always something of an issue with my family. For example, which film to see on any of the three or four nights a week Mom, Dad and I would go to the movies could only be determined after he'd completed his lists. "There's a 7:50 show at the Hearthstone Plaza, or the 8:15 show at the Brattle, or the 9:45 at the Circle." If the film wasn't on the list, we wouldn't see it. In fact, we wouldn't do anything if it wasn't on his list. Dad's lists' mathematical formulas produced seemingly random answers for his son. "Well, David, perhaps I could meet you at 2:43," or, after poring over the illegible figures bleeding through napkins attacked by chewed-up ball-point pens, "Um, why don't we say that you'll pay me $208.47 of the money you owe me."

I stumble along denying and repressing the list-making behavior that has jumped generations and into my life. Clearly list-making can be neurotic/compulsive behavior. Why do anything when you can just write a list and schedule what you'd potentially do? Why write anything when much more immediate pleasure can be had from an endlessly revisable outline? But now I am going to free myself — and you — of guilt. In order to successfully produce or direct any film or video production, you must tap into latent list-making compulsions and embrace your inner list-maker.

Preproduction is one giant exercise in list-making. The best lists comprise an outpouring and indexing of all of your thoughts on a given subject, and that's what you should be doing during preproduction: thinking of everything. The list of everything you could possibly imagine shooting marks the beginning of your shot list. The list of phone numbers of everyone you've conned into working on the video makes a beginning for your production book. From call sheets to purchase-order logs, there is endless list-making attached to any kind of production.

I have a theory that the film business is filled with neurotic, disorganized people whose work defines their only sphere of control and order. But no matter how personally disorganized you are, you have to be organized for a shoot. You're under scrutiny when you direct, usually by a jury of peers, and there's a certain performance anxiety associated with being a director. My biggest fear before any shoot day, and it's shared with other directors I've known, is that I will look like I don't know what I'm doing. My worst fear on a shoot day is that people will be sitting around waiting for me to figure out what to do next. The rockers will get restless, then there will be a mutiny, resulting in emasculation in front of everyone on the set. But when you have good lists, a shoot day becomes nothing more than a series of tasks that you check off one by one. This is the only way to alleviate director performance anxiety.

STORYBOARDS

When I did my first video, "Sunday," for the band Wider, I thought to myself, "What do directors really do unless its making a storyboard? If I'm not the one actually operating the camera, if I'm not lighting the set, or a thousand other tasks on the set, what am I really doing here?" Since I didn't feel confident about my ability to manage the shoot, the only way I could feel in control was to crudely plot every shot so that I would be telling the DP exactly what to do at all times.

Here's what I did, and, though it was time-consuming, I think it makes a totally useful way to prepare for your first video. I used a single 3" x 5" index card for each shot I envisioned in the video. I drew each card according to the order of the treatment, then separated and grouped them by camera set-ups, following the logical shooting order. The best part was that after I finished each shot I could cross it out and put it away, making my disappearing deck of cards a gauge of my progress.

CALL SHEETS

The list of performers and crew, and where they need to be when. Some computer programs for production scheduling will automatically generate the thin strips used on boards that keep track of who's in what scene, what kind of scene it is, and what crew is necessary.

PRODUCTION BOOK

The producer's bible that lists phone (and fax and cell phone and E-mail and beeper number and so on) for everyone on camera and off. It includes the shooting schedule, locations, contacts at locations, and any other detail that the producer and their assistants needs to have at his or her fingertips.

PURCHASE-ORDER LOG

Generally a ring binder (or, in smaller productions, part of the production book) that contains a copy of all purchase orders for the production so that the accountant or producer can keep track of daily expenses and manage the reimbursements.

On the lined backs of the cards I wrote a thorough description of each shot, detailing camera moves. On the bottoms of the "frames," right beneath the drawing of the shot (this is the truly insane micromanagement element), I wrote the "timings," or the durations of each of the shots. Given that the song was over four minutes long, this was a little ludicrous. I had quite a stack of cards, some corresponding to shots that were only a few seconds long. For example, I would determine that a particular shot should run from 1:32 to 1:36 in the song's duration in order to correspond to a particular guitar riff. This painstaking storyboard was as thorough a deconstruction of a song as I've ever done, just because I thought that's what I needed to do. It took me a week. And with fourth-grade drawing skills, it gets tiresome drawing a drum kit.

The first video I did, then, was the very opposite of "Let's go out and shoot a bunch of shit, see what we get and edit it later." My first storyboard represented total ignorance of the video-making process, specifically the director/DP dynamic and the director/editor dynamic. I've subsequently learned that, even though it's always useful to draw some pictures, one doesn't really need to draw such an extensive storyboard. But this first storyboard got me thinking very specifically about "breaking down" the song.

Most people in production will tell you that it's useful to storyboard, and they say they do it even when they don't. "When I do a video, low-budget or high-budget, I storyboard the whole video," says Bernstein. "Obviously, sometimes you show up and something wonderful happens that you didn't expect or something you wanted doesn't happen because you run out of time or whatever. But for a lot of videos, I'll show you the storyboard sketch and the video pretty much follows shot for shot." Peretz claims his inability to sketch keeps him from using storyboards, but technology may come to the rescue. "I use shot lists but not storyboards," he says. "Although I have a new storyboard program for my computer because I can't draw."

Some directors let the job dictate their preproduction routine. Spike Jonze lets the idea — and Spike almost always refers to his videos as "ideas," a clue to his belief that the single great idea is the key to a great video — dictate his preproduction preparation. "On some ideas," he tells me, "it's just a shot list, and on some ideas I'll storyboard it real specifically. On the Bjork video ["It's Oh So Quiet"], I found the location first, then went and videotaped the whole thing and blocked it out, so we knew exactly what every shot was (except the bathroom scene was freeform a little bit). Other ones, like 'Sabotage,' we just ran around with a camera for two days. I had little scenarios worked out, and the stuff we needed for those, and beyond that, it was very loose. It was real freeform, and that was great because that idea lent itself to just running around with the camera. There was a crew of maybe, like, seven people but most of it was the four of us [Spike and the Beastie Boys] taking off in the car, going around and grabbing stuff and coming back to base camp."

Having a storyboard undoubtedly makes communicating with everyone much easier, and it helps you work out your control issues. Even if it's just to draw floor plans for lighting or set dressing, there's always some point where I'm forced to try my hand as a draftsman. After the Wider video, with its comic book–like storyboard, I had a liberating and crucial realization. Storyboards shouldn't illustrate

---

GETTING STARTED: TRYAN GEORGE

[Tryan made his first video for $200.] "I knew I wanted to make a film. I figured music video was probably the thing that I had the resources for and the easiest format. I got a super-8 camera, went to Boston, and shot this thing. To save money, I transferred all the stuff myself. I projected it on the wall and shot it with my video camera, which produced some really amazing funky effects with gels in front of the projector. I was making something to have a reel and I knew that shooting it on video wasn't gonna get me anywhere. I think at that point music videos were getting into this really texturey sort of thing, so super-8 was kind of appropriate. I have this theory that your first video is gonna be your best video for a while because you're so unindustry at that point. You've got so much energy and you make things happen. You go against the rules."

<<<

---

the entire video. People bang on and on about the most detailed storyboard ever, and a surprising number of music-video directors cite Alfred Hitchcock, who painstakingly storyboarded, and claim that they like to plan every moment of the video. They're lying. Videos are not like commercial productions in which every moment of a thirty-second spot can be found when you look at the boards. This is not because the director is lazy and didn't have strong ideas about what s/he wanted. It's simply because even big-budget videos are subject to change. It's the nature of the medium and the speed of production.

Though storyboards make essential tools, beginning directors should forget their dreams of planning every second of the video before it's shot. Videos evolve as they're being made. No matter how controlling the director, the video's outcome can be quite different from the director or band's original intent. First of all, music video is as much an editor's medium as it is a director's, and there are plenty of decisions made in the editing room. Music videos developed around the notion of "cutting to music." Even when the director is also the editor, there are many approaches to cutting a video. If the director has done a good job, the editor will have as many options for which shot to use as possible.

> **STORYBOARD**
>
> A sequential series of drawings that illustrate key moments in your production. They generally provide reference to or suggest characters, actions, costumes, locations, props. Think comic strips. You can get special pads of paper made for storyboarding, and now there are computer programs that relieve the pain and embarrassment of drawing.

The editor needs options, because the artist has input during the editing process. Rockers don't often know much about filmmaking, but they know what they don't like when they see it. They know when they think they look bad, and, inevitably, they will want to see changes and they'll want to see the editor use as many shots as possible in which they think they look cool. A knowledgeable director will allow the piece to evolve through the editing process. Rarely does an editor sit with a storyboard and cut together something that looks exactly like the director's rendering. Maybe this all sounds like rationalization for not doing the work of storyboarding, but just to assure the neurotic novice who thinks s/he needs to painstakingly storyboard every second of their first video: If you draft most of the major shots, you'll be in good shape.

You can get by without doing a storyboard, but there are two lists that you must make that form the backbone of your project: the song breakdown and the shot list. Every director has their own method, but most have a variation on this two-list system. These lists make up the bulk of the director's work during the preproduction process.

If a director listens to the song a million times while writing the treatment, they listen two million times while planning the shoot, resulting in a detailed chart of the song — the song breakdown. Then there is the most important list, the chapter and verse of every shoot: the shot list, which describes all possible shots in the video. Getting a shot list from a director marks the starting line on every shoot and its reception is whispered about, anticipated, welcomed with near-ritualistic fervor. "She hasn't written her shot list yet," or, "Well, I can't do anything until I get the shot list," are overheard constantly in the days before a shoot.

FREE FORM: THE BEASTIE BOYS

THE SONG BREAKDOWN

The song breakdown is the director's method of deconstructing a song and presenting it in a way that can be understood by everyone working on the video (it's also known to directors of live-performance, multicamera shoots as the "tick sheet").

There are no rules for writing a song breakdown, but it must represent every moment in the song. This is how I do it: In the far left corner I put a column labeled "Time." These times are based either on CD-counter numbers or a stopwatch and a tape recorder. CDs are more accurate and, if you've got a CD player with a remote, it's easy to push Pause and then write down what's happening in the song (I know that these jottings are not time-code accurate and that I'll have to change them later). There's no money in a $5,000 video for time-code playback or, more precisely, there's never enough to rent a smart slate, the thing with the rapidly changing red digits that gets waved around in front of the camera (it has actually appeared in some videos, such as Guns and Roses' "Sweet Child o' Mine," or, more recently, Spike Jonze's "Sure Shot" for the Beastie Boys).

Sometimes a rocker will have a DAT player that you can borrow, which generally has better sound quality for playback and provides more accurate timings, but you'll have to rewrite the time numbers on your breakdown if you didn't already plot it out with the DAT counter numbers. Invariably, I use the band's reference CD — a CD that the band's given by the record company before their record is released — to write the breakdown, and the CD counter numbers help us cue up when we shoot. If possible, try to make a DAT copy of the CD, or dub the CD to a master editing tape before you shoot, so you never lose this valuable piece of audio. You'll need it to lay down the audio track before editing.

The intervals of time that appear in this far left column correspond to the next two columns, "Song Part," and "Instrument/Lyric." These are the basic components of the song that we discussed when we talked about treatment writing. If you're uptight about what to call a certain part of the song ("Is that the 'chorus,' the 'verse,' or the 'jam section?' "), just ask the rocker who wrote the piece: "What do you call that part when the bass drops out and the guitars go *chunka-chunka-chunka-chunka-chunk*?" Since your average alterna-indie rocker is concerned with redefining rock and shattering age-old song structure conventions, they'll often answer with something like, "Oh, that's the 'bicycle section' cuz it reminds me of when my older sister took me out in the driveway and . . ." Feel free to create your own terms, call what you think sounds like the chorus the chorus, and what you think is the verse the verse, even though the band thinks it's the other way around.

Most rockers will happily give you their lyric sheet. Record companies will also give you a lyric sheet, often before you've written the treatment, because they need to include it with the MTV submission forms accompanying the video. (MTV wants to make sure the song isn't preaching suicide or condoning child pornography.) However, as with defining your own song part terms, it's often more fun to figure out what the lyrics are by yourself. My interpretation of the line in the Fall's "15 Ways" that declares "You've got to be cheerful heart-ed" as "You've got to be tough, old harlot," made crusty post-punker Mark E. Smith wryly confess, "I actually quite like your version better." A bonding moment. Yo La Tengo found my mutilated lyric transcription of their opus "From a Motel Six" so amusing they published it in their band's fanzine — the only thing they found amusing about our shoot.

Not only do I write down every line of the lyric, with the corresponding times for each of the lines in the time column, I also note every instrumental event in the Instrument/Lyric column. For example, if the song starts with nothing but the bass, the Time column will read "0:00," the Song Part column will read "Intro," and the Instrument/Lyric column will read "Bass Only." When the lyrics come in, I usually italicize or underline them so I know they're lyrics and I don't have to write "vocals start." When there's a notable guitar line, bass part or drum fill, I cram in phrases that say something like "cool guitar part" in the same column. Every song dictates different terms. Every song has different notable moments and it's up to you how far you want to go mapping them out.

The method you use to deconstruct a song doesn't matter as much as simply doing it. During preproduction, directors pace back and forth listening to the song, conjuring images for every moment, making sure they can see the song from beginning to end. I don't know how many times, while facing a looming shoot, I've suffered a panic attack that I've tried to calm — but that I've made worse — by listening to the song. While listening to the song, you should be constantly asking yourself the question "What am I looking at now?" at every section, with every beat. Only with experience will you know what 10 seconds in a song feels like, as well as how much screen time a certain activity needs and how you will edit shots together for each section.

When defining your terms for the "Song Part" column, it helps to borrow from the nearly universal terms of music: Intro; Verse I, II, III; Chorus I, II, III; Solo, if there is one; Instrumental Section (sometimes I call this simply the "C" section, and the verses and choruses "A" and "B" respectively); Outro, or Fade-Out; and End.

Adam Bernstein has his own method to address these issues. He creates a timeline of the song, horizontally along the bottom of the page. He attaches his storyboard above the timeline, with each shot drawn on Post-it notes. "I basically block the song out by section and then actually do a giant chart of what images are going to play in what part of the song. I shift it around until I think it progresses in the right way, until it's unfolding in an interesting way. Then I storyboard from the chart. I place a vertical line that goes: open, verse one, chorus one, verse two, chorus two, bridge — however it breaks down. Then, on the horizontal line, I'll have performance, story line, and perhaps one other category. I get these little sticky pieces of paper and write down everything that's going to happen in the video: 'Fred sings from a fountain,' 'Fred sings from behind the wheel of a car,' 'Girl smashes TV set,' 'Girl in lace bikini dances in front of funeral pyre.' You can predetermine what's going to happen in the clip and how much of every shot or section you need. You know what part of the song it's going to play in and what amount of time the action has to fit into."

The last column in my song breakdown is for "Shots." I almost never type anything in this column but leave it as a margin that I write on during the shoot to note which shots covered what parts of the song. Like the script/continuity person on a movie, I make lines down the side of the page as I shoot that give me an immediate visual sense of how much I've shot to cover a particular part of the song. Ideally, my shot list would be numbered and organized in such a way that each shot would have numbers that I could then neatly fill in to this final column of the song breakdown. But it never works that way. I don't attempt a numbering system with my shot list, I just write it. On some level, a shot list should be nothing more than a compilation of every possible image or activity that you could imagine included in your rock video.

THE SHOT LIST

If you haven't written a shot list, you'll not only have a harder time getting the work done and communicating with the crew, you'll be consumed by guilt — especially if you're working with a bunch of people you aren't paying. You didn't do your homework. If you can't write what you want to see in the video, even in the most basic way, then you're not ready for the shoot. There can be no writer's block when it comes to writing the shot list.

The glorious thing about writing a shot list is that there *needn't* be any writer's block. As a skilled producer can extrapolate a budget from a treatment, a director should have no problem generating a shot list from it. The phrase, "the band performs on a roof," could mean dozens of shots, and you should just write them down and never worry about stating the obvious. There is nothing wrong with writing "shot of whole band," because once you've written that sentence, you've created what is potentially a twenty-minute task for your shoot day. You've committed everyone on your crew to an activity. That phrase, "shot of whole band," becomes part of your command.

No matter how banal the shot list might seem — "Isn't it obvious that we would shoot a close-up of each bandmember" — everything needs to be included or you will almost certainly forget something. And the people working with you will respect you for writing it. No matter how primitive your ability to describe images in prose, the only way that anyone — primarily your DP — will pin down how you really want a shot to look begins by writing the shot on the page. Even if your shot list is cryptic, the DP will get a sense of what you want to see in each shot, and from there s/he will brainstorm with you about composition, lensing and camera movement. "For me," says Mott, "I would like to have a director that had not just the narrative idea for the film but a distinct idea about very specific shots, because then a little bit of the pressure's off. Because once the decision — 'it's going to be a tight shot of her in front of the window' — is made, I can be making other, more detailed decisions. You have to have directors explain what they're talking about because usually it's incredibly vague. They have a distinct idea for anywhere from five to twenty shots. Since shots are generally only two seconds long, that's less than a minute, and songs are around three minutes. There's always a major amount of the video to be filled up."

Anything mentioned in your treatment probably translates into a number of shots.

Knowing that you want a shot of the singer singing eliminates only one of the seven elements of any shot that need to be described in your shot list: 1) Distance; 2) Angle; 3) Lensing; 4) Camera Movement; 5) Subject/Action; 6) Location; 7) Props. Think about the coverage of a dramatic scene in a conventional Hollywood movie. If we imagine a scene between two people, there might be a "master shot" in which you see the whole bodies of both performers and the entire set. Then there are "two shots," or "medium shots" in which we still see both performers within the frame, but less of their environment. It is generally understood that medium shots that are "singles," or shots of a single performer, show that person from the chest up. Then there are "close-ups," in which we see the face of only one performer.

I want to define the camera's relationship to the subject right off the bat. When I write "wide shot," it refers to how much of the set we see in the frame. It describes the perceived "distance" of the camera from the subject. Perceived distance varies greatly depending the focal length of the lens. Remember that "wide shot," which describes what is seen in the shot, is very different from "wide angle," which describes the focal length of the lens. You can shoot a "wide shot, wide angle" in which the camera is not far from the subject, but in which you see the whole set. You can do a "close up, wide angle" in which the camera will be super-close to the subject, which will appear distorted. "Extreme wide shots," "wide shots," "medium shots," "medium close ups," "extreme close ups" — I use these terms to specify shot composition, not focal length, because I first want to get a sense of what will be included in the frame.

Then I try to give a general sense of camera angle. If we're shooting from below, it's a "low angle." If we're

---

TAKE YOUR BEST SHOT

close-up

a tight shot that probably reveals only a single face or detail of an object; an extreme close-up might only reveal an eye or a mouth

medium shot

reveals the upper body and some of the physical surroundings of the subject; can be a single, with just one subject or a two-shot, with two subjects

long shot or wide shot

includes the entire body of the subject or subjects and includes much of the background

reverse angle

a shot, generally medium to close, from the opposite point of view from the shot that preceded it, most clearly seen in dialogues that switch angles depending on who is speaking, or crowd shots that follow performance close-ups of a singer singing

tracking shot

a shot that moves in the same direction and speed as its subject

dolly shot

a moving shot taken with a dolly or a wheeled, movable camera mount or a Steadicam device that mounts on the camera operator

---

overhead, it's an "overhead angle." I've described angles with self-explanatory terms as "frontal," "side," or, if it's in the opposite direction of the previous shot on the list, "reverse." Then I specify the focal length of the lens, if it's important for the shot, "wide angle," for example, or if it's a telephoto lens zoomed-in, "long lens." If I don't specify, it means that the focal length should be normal lensing with reasonable depth-of-field and no distortion.

ELEMENTS OF THE SHOT DESCRIBED IN THE SHOT LIST:

1) Distance
2) Angle
3) Lensing
4) Camera Movement
5) Subject/Action;
6) Location
7) Props

Next I note the camera's movement. If the camera's not moving, it's "static." If the camera rolls by the subject, it's a "dolly left-to-right." If it rolls toward the subject, it "dollies in," or "dollies out." If there are "pans left or right," "whip pans," "tilts up-and-down," "zoom ins or outs," "whip zooms," or "tracking shots," all must be specified in the shot description. Remember the old 180 rule about keeping your subject on one side of a line and only moving in a 180-degree arc from that line in order to keep screen direction and eye lines simple. And then feel free to break it.

Only after I've described the camera's location in relation to the subject, lenses used and how the camera moves, do I talk about what's in front of it: subject/action, location and props. "Extreme close-up, overhead, wide angle, static: Jim sings in laundromat holding a dog on a leash" would be an adequate shot description. It addresses the seven elements of a shot: 1) distance — extreme close-up; 2) angle — overhead; 3) lensing — wide angle; 4) camera movement — static; 5) subject/action — Jim sings; 6) location — in laundromat; 7) props — dog on a leash. Once you've had a conversation about shots with your DP (or yourself), the shots take on a life of their own. Sometimes a shot will come to be known as "that cool overhead shot from the rafters," or the "rack-focus shot from the mirror." The fact that these shots have taken on a life of their own should be reflected in the shot list. Every job creates its own shorthand, its own lexicon; use it in your shot list.

HELIUM IN THE GLOW OF THE DUKANE 3000

When Mott and I were shooting the first Helium video, "XXX," we lit the band with an overhead projector. To acknowledge the dinkiness of our operation, and to mock over-earnest film technicians in general, we kept referring to the overhead projector by its important-sounding brand name, The Dukane 3000, as if this outmoded light box made for high-school AV labs was a vital piece of filmmaking technology. Our other bit of shorthand was to refer to the classic psychedelic oil and water effect that was projected by the (imagine this intoned by a booming voice) The Dukane 3000, as "Strawberry Alarm Clock," in reference to the '60s psychedelic band. These shorthand jokes became serious business when we were on the set discussing shots, saying, "Well, if we do Strawberry Alarm Clock/Dukane 3000 now, then we can cover her with another Strawberry Alarm Clock close-up and save the rest of the Dukane 3000 shots for later." The crew thought we were insane, but we knew exactly what we were talking about. I don't think my shot list said, "shots with the Dukane 3000," but it could have, and should have.

You psyched up the band with your storyboard, and you have your shot list in hand. Your producer has the location, crew, and props lined up. Here comes the bride . . .

chapter four

We're reaching those final few, fleeting moments of sunlight commonly known in production circles as "magic hour," the coveted window of opportunity when the setting sun gives the last light a lustrous golden quality. But as the sun lowers over the outdoor location of my $5,000 Goops video, I'm feeling less than magical.

Of course, lights are prohibitively expensive, so sunset threatens to shut us down in about ten minutes. And since nobody wants to spend another day at an abandoned chemical plant in Linden, New Jersey, ten minutes is all I have left to shoot the performance for the final anthemic refrain of "Booze Cabana." A lot of rock video can be made in ten minutes, so we keep the camera rolling as the neo-punkers pantomime-rock to a barely audible playback. Eleanor Goop feels the need to interrupt one of these crucial takes. She's got a problem.

"David, I don't mean to be a bitch," says the imposing, tattooed

shooting >

blonde, "but I really feel the need to say something."

"Um, what's that Eleanor?" replies the unimposing, trying-to-keep-his-cool director.

"Well, I just feel like you have to get some shots of us jumping."

"Jumping?"

"Yeah, you don't have any shots of us jumping when we play, and, well, we're the Goops. That's what we do: We jump."

Supressing my urge to giggle in her face amid a resounding Goop chorus of "That's fucking right, man. We jump," I realize that this jumping thing is an issue not to be taken lightly. So while the sun sets over Linden, Eleanor and I quickly choreograph a Goops unison scissor-kick that they execute with Goopish abandon and verve.

ELEANOR GOOP PREPARES TO JUMP

LET THEM JUMP

Though the Goops didn't hire me to do their next video (with a budget fifteen times that of "Booze Cabana" — but I'm not bitter), their jumping abilities figured prominently on *Beavis and Butt-head* for a while. I'll always remember that moment of on-the-spot choreography fondly. I learned that you let the Goops jump, and not just to psych them up for their video or bond with you. You need to have them jump in front of the camera so they look good, so they feel Goop-like. Aside from being able to make decisions on the spot, coaxing a good performance out of the artist, bringing out the essential qualities of the band is the director's primary role during a shoot. A director has to set aside his/her mini-identity crises and be the person responsible for running the shoot. On a low-budget video production, this often means bringing order to chaos.

HOW TO FEEL LIKE A DIRECTOR

Before I started actually directing, I imagined that a director directs, as an actor acts, or a dancer dances. I thought that directing amounted to a kind of performance, a combination of skills that a person could turn on or off: "Don't bother me, I'm directing now." There's a throw-away moment from the movie *Guilty By Suspicion* (1991) in which an unemployed director is asked to fill in for another director at a moment's notice. Without ever having seen the script, this guy has to take command of the crew. We watch as he simultaneously reads the script for the first time and figures out how to cover the scene: "Where's my AD? Okay, let's see, 'camera comes out of a bar.' All right, people, let's put the camera on the dolly right here." This insignificant moment is intended

THE ULTIMATE DIRECTORS: *GUILTY BY SUSPICION*

only to indicate that this character is a talented director, and it's movieish and unreal. As an idealized vision of how a director should be able to direct without a moment's preparation, however, it resonated with me. I used to think that, ideally, directors should have "chops," as musicians have chops. If the jazz soloist can play with any pickup band, I thought, the director should be able to walk onto any set and start directing. It's this kind of romantic vision of a director that fills the first-timer with fear and dread.

If professional, working film technicians are helping out with your low-budget project, they add to the anxiety of not feeling experienced enough to be able to work with them. Guess what? All directors feel that way. After directing for a couple of years, I started to work with freelance professional crews who also worked on commercials and movies. At that point, I had been a director on fifteen jobs, while many of these technicians — even if they were nonunion — had probably done their respective jobs hundreds of times. In two years I had been a director fifteen times. They had been key grips two hundred and fifty times.

GETTING STARTED:
SPIKE JONZE

"I was doing photography down in Texas, where there was this organization called PAL, Photography Against Land. It was photography of agriculture and things like that. I was working on farms for a while, so I got into photography from photographing agriculture. I was getting free film from Kodak because the organization had a deal with them. So, I was just shooting photos all the time. Mostly I'd do agricultural stuff, but I'd shoot a roll a day, which is the way I learned. I'd shoot a roll, and ninety percent of it wouldn't turn out. Then you figured out, that didn't work because of this, or this didn't work because of that.' Then I'd look at another one of my favorite agriculture photographs and try to figure out how they were done, what the techniques, the lenses or the film were, or how they got that lighting. I also learned about strobes and lenses, apertures and shutter speeds. Then when I started shooting stuff on movie film, I already knew that stuff. I shot some skateboarding for this Sonic Youth video Tamra Davis was directing ["100%"]. I think that was the first time I shot with a movie camera."

<<<

Fifteen. Two hundred and fifty. There's no way you can compare. They've been on more sets doing their jobs than I could ever hope to be on doing mine.

Jesse Peretz has been experiencing this anxiety from the time he got his first "real budget" video, and he still feels it today, even though he has already directed a feature film and now books multimillion-dollar commercials. "From the earliest jobs that I did, I would have an incredibly bad night's sleep the night before a shoot. I had so much fear. I used to call this the *Wizard of Oz* syndrome where I always felt ridiculous, like I'm going to walk out there and pretend that I'm the director. I always felt like it was this weird lie in which I would say I was the director, and everyone treated me like this ultimate authority and I was just pulling the wool over people's eyes.

"And slowly, once you get through enough jobs — and this is the most important thing that you can get out of the experience of being a music-video director that's helpful for feature films — you just gain the confidence that you really can be the director of the film set. Just by being the director and the most significant creative person on the set does not mean that people expect you to be the most experienced, the most knowledgeable or the person with all the answers. It's okay not to know everything, and it's excellent when you have a gaffer who's gaffed fifteen features and a hundred music videos and commercials and seen way more difficult situations that you have. If you're a respectful person, you can get a lot out of the experience of working with really experienced people."

The truth is, all directors feel the *Wizard of Oz* syndrome. Adam Bernstein makes clear that in terms of specific skills, the director has the fewest on the set. "Let's face it," he says, "you don't have to be a rocket scientist to be a music-video director. I had this concept that you could actually train chimps to be music-video directors. All you really need is a good cinematograph-er, a good art director, a great producer and all the video director would have to do is say yes or no. So you could have a chimp, with yes or no buttons, and then you could have all these highly trained people asking the chimp questions, and he could be pressing the yes or no buttons. I actually wanted to start a company called Chimpaganda at which a staff of chimps would be doing the videos. You would have one chimp that does heavy metal videos, another that does R&B, and the other one's alternative. I think for people who want to do interesting music videos, though, you have to move beyond the chimp stage and actually think about it a little bit. The position of director, not just in music videos, but anywhere, is weird because often the least-skilled person on the set, the person who actually knows how to do the least, is the director."

Even when I've been completely prepared for a shoot, I've felt a different kind of anxiety. With everything planned to the last detail, you begin to feel more like some weird party-host-cum-administrator than the guy who jumps into action on the set and starts mak-ing decisions at the snap of a finger. That's the problem with the *Guilty By Suspicion* model. Directing, in most cases, consists of overseeing a plan that has been laid out for days. You're not spontaneously figuring out what to do. Tryan George figures managing the "machine" makes a director. "You end up having less control [than doing everything yourself] until you start mastering the process. When you first start out, you don't know how to operate. You don't know how to get the most out of people. There's a skill to doing that and what you learn in becoming a director is learning how to use the machine."

Then the question that nags all novice low-budget videomakers creeps into your consciousness: "What am I doing here? The DP knows how to light. It would be one thing if I was directing actors, but the band knows how to play their instruments. Why do they need me?" It's important not to be defeated by these anxieties because you're the person who has to run the shoot. Even though you might not feel like a director, you have to rise to the occasion and act like one. Experienced technicians know that most directors aren't as set-savvy as they could be. The old adage "half of doing the job is getting the job" is espe-cially applicable for music video directors. In some cases, especially when you've cajoled the band into doing a video, you're the reason there is a job in the first place.

Directing is a big bluff, and in order to pull it off, you have to embrace the many reasons that you are more qualified than any other person on your set to do your job. First of all, though this might seem obvious, you wrote the treatment, which means — no matter how simple it may be — you're the reason that everyone happens to be standing at this par-

MEET THE CREW

gaffer

The chief electrician, the gaffer supervises lighting and reports to the DP from whom he receives the lighting plans for each day's set-ups.

best boy

You won't actually have one on your low-budget video set, but, since everyone always asks, the best boy is a skilled electrician and chief assistant to the gaffer, who often works ahead on the next lighting set-up to keep the shooting day on schedule. There are also best boy grips and best boy electrics. They manage the equipment inventory for both departments, and are the first people to pull things off their respective trucks.

electrician

Works under the direction of the gaffer and the best boy setting lights and handling all electrical cables and electricity.

key grip

The king of the grips, the key reports to the DP and works closely with the lighting and camera crews solving on-set problems.

grip

Works under the direction of the key grip, handling all heavy equipment, loading and unloading equipment, moving sets, camera, erecting scaffolding, setting lighting filters, gels, flags, silks, (see lighting kit description).

rigger

A grip who specializes in building scaffolding and rigging electrical cables for more difficult camera shots.

>>>

ticular abandoned building at this particular ungodly hour of the morning shooting a video. It's your concept. That grip who thinks you're stupid wasn't bold enough to say, "For this video, I see wind-up mechanical toys shot on super-8."

If you've been hired to do the job simply because you're a fan of the band, you're there to protect the band from the unfamiliar machinery of film production. This might sound silly when you're working with a tiny crew, but on a bigger-budget job, this dynamic becomes more obvious. You're hired to run interference between the band and that grip over there with the mustache, wrap-around Oakleys and pleated Dockers. This guy drives a fully-loaded GMC 4x4 extended-cab pick-up with a license plate that says DAS GRIP, and had to get up at 3:30 in the morning because he lives in the hinterlands. (L.A. producers sardonically compare area codes while writing phone numbers on a call sheet, "Well, there are no 909s on this job. There aren't even any 805s.") Even though these were the guys that beat you up in grade school, some of them have turned out to be incredibly sweet. However, crews alienate the band either because the band members are snobs and won't deal with real people or because they are genuine introverts and can't deal with real people. In either case, crew members remind them of all the terrible, bored soundmen and roadies they've encountered their entire careers, and they're glad you're the one who has to talk to these folks.

"Why is it that it takes two or three major videos for an artist to get one right?" asks A&R man Mark Kates. "I think that when you're an artist and you show up at a two-day shoot for the first time and there's fifty people there of whom you only know three personally, I think that's a little bit intimidating. Somebody like a DP or a director will say 'You can't do this,' or, 'We have to do it this way,' and artists take their word for it. It's only when the video doesn't end up the way they want it do they realize they compromised on a point that was important to them. I think about Beck. He was happy with 'Devil's Haircut,' but 'New Pollution' is the first video he's totally happy with, and, lo and behold, he directed it. It doesn't mean he wasn't happy with previous ones, but there's a point reached where the artist feels like they've nailed it, and it doesn't happen very often. You can have a great video, you can win awards, and it can still be not that artistically satisfying for the artist."

Aside from superficial alienation, bands are truly afraid of looking ridiculous, or, more importantly, they're afraid of being represented in a way that they think is wrong, that doesn't suit their music or their audience's expectations of them. They need somebody on set to protect their sensibilities, and you're the one they trust to understand their aesthetic. No matter how much you think you've ironed out these issues during the treatment-writing process, once the camera starts turning, that's when a band's real anxiety surfaces. For them, it feels like being camera-shy for a family snapshot . . . times a million. They're putting all of their vanity in your hands, and if they feel that you "get" what's good about them, then they will trust you not to let them look bad. It's your job as a director to tap into that part of you that is a fan, to dig down to what you think is cool about the band, and translate that onto film. And that's something the grip over there who just wants to go home can't do.

Remember, that grip over there does want to go home eventually. The shoot is really only fun for you, sometimes the DP and maybe even the band. This is not an exaggeration, it's the honest truth. Even if the crew are all your friends and they think that the band is cool and the song is cool, they still want to go home. This means that you have to be the one running the shoot. Nobody else will. Julie

production assistant (PA)

Production assistant and general helper, whose job description can range from running for coffee to pitching in with the grips to being personal secretary to the director or producer.

Hermelin suggests that you treat people nicely, too. "Your friends are your biggest asset," she reminds us. "You shouldn't exploit your friends because they are doing favors for you and you should show that you appreciate it. Take them out to dinner. It seems like a little thing, but if you do a shoot where no one gets paid, feed them. If you feed people that are working for free, they'll be happier. After you finish the shoot, send them a thank you note: They've done a favor for you, it's a nice thing to do, and you'll more than likely be able to get them to work for you again in the future. Try to pay them, and as soon as you can. Get other things for free in order to give your friends $25 or $50. They'll appreciate the effort and you'll need them again. And, otherwise, you'll not have anyone talking to you."

You, the nice director, are ultimately responsible for forward motion on a shoot day. If it's a low-budget video, it's even more obviously your responsibility. If it's a big-budget video, you can't expect the assistant director (AD) to be truly invested in getting things to move quickly. Sure, the best do, but ADs are not directors. Their job — running around making sure everyone and everything is available to you at just the moment you need them — is absolutely no fun, and they want to go home as badly as everyone else except you. The moment you show weakness, a doubt or a moment of hesitation over what to do next, everyone sees it as an opportunity to go home, the shoot will end prematurely and you won't get the shots you need to complete your shot list. You must create constant forward motion on the set. AD Mike Dignum finds the difference between videos and features in that kinetic energy. Dignum's in his late 30's, British, avuncular, calm and levelheaded — all the attributes of a good AD. Though he's lived in this country for at least a dozen years, he addresses crew and performers with a whisper of a British accent. "Music videos really want to do a lot more than they can in one day, and usually, no matter how big the budget is, it's still underbudgeted," he says. "It's a lot more run-and-gun, not as beat-to-death as a commercial for which you shoot your plate of eggs and bacon for fifty takes until you get it right. Music videos, it's one take, boom, move on. You're on your feet more, you're thinking fast, you're always planning ahead, you never rest. You never say, 'We're going to be in this set-up for two hours.' You know you're only going to be there for ten minutes. The next set-up better be getting ready or it's not going to be ready. I think that music video is basically more demanding, but quite often more rewarding. They're not as safe as commercials. They're a little bit more edgy, the directors have a little bit more of an artistic freedom, and it's nice to work on something like that."

The ultimate moment of horror on any shoot comes when no one knows what to do and nothing is being shot. "There's something to be learned every time you shoot," says

Nancy Bennett. "And I learned this the first time I directed a music video. Everything was lit and set up, but we were standing around and I couldn't figure out why we were standing around. It was because I wasn't telling anybody what to do. Everything may be set up and perfect but, until you're the instigator, you're the midwife or you seize the day, nothing will happen. So you can't be afraid of your own voice." Avoid the shock of inactivity at all costs. Fear that moment of painful embarrassment when everyone on a set turns, looks at you and says, "Ok, now what do we do?" Let the fear motivate you to write your shot list.

YOU HAVE TO GET A GOOD PERFORMANCE FROM THE BAND

No one wants to watch a performance video in which the band doesn't visibly rock out. Period. Darren Doane gets it just right when he says, "All bands tell you that they don't want to look like Metallica, but after they've seen the footage and they look like Metallica, they're so relieved." No matter what the band says, if it's a performance video, it's your first job to make the band look good. Again, you're the one who supposedly knows the band's sensitivities and they trust you. The funny thing is that many of the elements and people you've assembled for the shoot work against you as you try to make the band look cool. For example, the DP who's shooting the video for free may have his own aesthetic agenda and press for slick lighting so it will look impressive on his reel. You, as the representative of the band's heart, must prevail.

So here it is, the most commonsensical advice for playing music-video director on shoot day: Watch the band. Never take your eyes off of them as they perform. Do they look comfortable? Make sure that they're wearing the clothing that feels most natural. Make sure that the sound

MEET THE . . . ASSISTANT DIRECTOR (AD)

More than simply a director's helper, the AD translates the director's needs to the crew and performers; responsible for creating the shooting schedule, call sheets and making sure that everyone needed appears on the set, manages the movement of extras, animals, and vehicles.

"HELLO, I'M AN . . . " ASSISTANT DIRECTOR:

"The job of the assistant director is to make sense of the nonsense. To plan out your day, figure out the best way of running the show, the best order, the way to attack the show. You're the ringmaster, master of ceremonies so to speak, you tell everybody what's going on and what's coming up. That's your job, making sure everybody is safe and nobody gets hurt."
— *Mike Dignum, assistant director*

<<<

and lighting on the set inspires rocking out. A tip: You'll demonstrate your concern if you've happened to place a light that's bothering the singer. A bit of strategic but showy direction — "Get that thing out of his eyes, he needs to concentrate!" — though totally obnoxious can make the band feel like you're on their side.

"You have to turn a performer's discomfort in front of the camera into a virtue," advises Kevin Kerslake. "Sometimes it's the tone of their performance, sometimes it's an angle that turns their coldness into a strength. There are a couple of different ways to do that: you can over-cover the shot so you'll have as much choice of angles in the edit as possible. But I'd rather nurture a performer into a comfort zone. It's a funny medium for them, simply because they're not built for it. The dynamic of their performances has been in a completely different venue. More and more, I feel that the performance aspect of videos is sort of dry. I did this thing for Filter ["Hey Man Nice Shot"] a year ago. It was really pretty invigorating for me, but all these people want me to do that again. A really amazing performance only comes once in a while. I'd just rather spend my energy in a different direction because I'm tired of seeing a guy with a guitar flopping his hair around. I don't think I'm alone in that."

After making the band comfortable, there's an essential technique that helps ensure a good performance. Sometimes singers don't realize that they really have to sing along to the playback, that lip-synching is more than simply moving your mouth along to the song. Always tell the singer to "vocalize," to put out like they're on stage, which, of course, feels natural to them. I like being able to tell the singer that. It makes me feel like I'm really giving the band some direction. But make sure that the playback is loud enough. If you don't have enough money to rent a location playback system and operator, convince the band that the video will be ten times better if the playback system is loud so they need to bring extra amps. Because the singer won't feel as if he's holding center stage all by himself, he won't feel self-conscious about singing in front of the whole crew. Prepare to modulate your playback volume, however, because sometimes the singer is a narcissistic showoff and he wants to let the cute makeup artist know how well he can sing. In that case, you're going to want to dial down the playback in order to dial down the histrionics.

"The first problem I always have with every band is that they want to plug in and play along with the playback because they think to just lip synch is fake," says Darren Doane. "The first thing I say is 'You know what? A: I need all the power in the room for my lights. B: you're making a video. Understand that if you've gotten to this point and we're here, you're fooling nobody. No one says, 'Wow, I can't believe they actually recorded that song right there.' So I say just accept that. When they say, 'I feel stupid just lip synching,' I say, 'Hey, when you guys are in the studio, you do a million tracks. This is one more track. Just look at this as another day in the studio. Welcome to it. Now, let's have a good time."

All directors say that a band or singer's performance is much better if the prerequisite director-band bonding has taken place before the big day. The director has to perform a delicate balancing act of being at once flattering to the band but not so obviously kiss-ass that they alienate everyone else. "The most important thing is to get to know the band and try to hang out with them before the shoot so you don't just show up on the set trying to build a relationship while you're telling them what to do," advises Spike Jonze. "You're trying to build trust as you're directing them. It's much better if you can go hang out with them for a few days, or go out to dinner with them or whatever."

Strategically, you might want to have the band rock out a little bit, even if they're not playing the song of the day, just so they feel comfortable. Remember, this is how they loosen up at sound checks and backstage before performances; make the moments before the shoot as much like a performance as you can and you'll more than likely get a real performance.

Peretz has an interesting theory, a philosophy really, about a band's performance that makes sense in our postmodern, referential rock age. Many of the alternarock bands that Jesse works with think it's embarrassing to "rock out" too hard while they're on the set. They're self-conscious, and in the post-punk world of "We don't want to be rock stars," they think it's too cheesy to put out for the camera. David Roth also sees the pressure on a band to be someone they're not. "I see the cringing they do when the label people keep pushing them," Roth says. "A lot of front men are kind of introverted or meek and they have to pretend that they're not. They feel really dumb lip-synching, for example. About eighty percent of the time bands come to me and say, 'I feel really dumb,' and I don't know what to tell them. Well, yeah, you're pretending to play, to rock out in this big, empty space. I understand."

Jesse has a metarock solution to this problem. He tries to get the band to think of themselves as a "rock band" — with full quotation marks. "The biggest issue you run into," he maintains, "is the band's feeling that they don't want to appear uncool in their video and that there's something uncool about trying, that the more you try, the stupider you seem. And if you wear flashy clothes or somehow go for it, then that means you're a sell-out. To me that's the death of video. It's like, what's the point? Who wants to fucking see a bored band? It's boring to see people who claim to have been brought up on Kiss not know how to rock out like Kiss. I try to sell it to them by coming up with ideas that — using Ash as an example — make them so much the rock band in the video that they get to step out of being

PHIL MORRISON CATCHES A WAVE

Ash. They're just the band in the video. The ideal for me was the Foo Fighters who, in the Mentos video, totally went for it in a warlike way, wearing retarded Dutch-style jogging suits like soccer players. And in the end, they seem cooler than any band I've ever made a video for." In this way, Jesse gets to have his cake and eat it, too: The band gets to think of their work as if it were performance art while they still rock out enough to make his video successful.

Working in the same rock universe, Phil Morrison also finds reluctant video stars. "It's very, very, very hard [to get bands to perform for the camera]. Evan Dando was not interested in being in front of the camera, believe it or not. Juliana Hatfield has these super-intellectual ideas about how she wants to present herself, and they're really well conceived, but then she freezes up. It's such a cliché, but it works: the 'This is your video, after all' approach when someone is just kind of frozen and feels like, 'I'm not an actor,' which they're not, or 'Lip-synching is stupid.' A band has legitimate reasons to feel all of those things, but the problem is that they don't realize it until they're on the set. Often, if it's a low-budget video, it's because their friends are around. Their friends are starting to question how cool it is that this band is doing a video, anyway. I have fallen back on that cliché, saying, 'You might feel stupid right now, but we're going to be gone after today, and hopefully this is going to be on TV forever, and you're going to look stupider on TV if you're only halfway doing something.' I've also said, 'If you feel dumb doing this, then make it clear that you feel dumb doing this. It's your video, you are welcome to indicate that.' One of the great, great low-budget videos ever is 'The Ledge,' The Replacements video. I believe that Randy Skinner from Warner Bros. — and here's a tribute to a video commissioner — directed that video. It's set in a warehouse, and it's basically the band sitting on a couch. Now it would probably seem very obvious, but it really was perfect because, at the time, a video of a band sitting around doing nothing was really radical. What makes that video better than most videos of bands sitting around and doing nothing — which has now become treatment D — is that it expressed a point of view about the video. The other one that does that really well is Sophie Mueller's Weezer video ["Say It Ain't So"]. It's more than just anti-video. What the Replacements' video did, and what good Pavement videos do, and what the best 'quotation mark' videos do is to say, 'I actually care a whole lot about saying I don't care about videos,' as opposed to just, 'I don't care about videos.' It still requires an artist to perform. Kim and Thurston [of Sonic Youth] seem so smart about videos just because they're smart. They were really particular, as they continue to be, about what the video was going to be like in advance. Once we were doing it, they knew they had nothing to gain by going halfway. I wanted them to make out in their apartment in the video, because the song, 'Titanium Expose,' had a very domestic feeling, and there were other things that happened in the video, like Thurston reading *TV Guide,* wearing pajamas. At that point, they had an aloofness toward the public about their relationship. They seemed really nervous about it, kind of giggling about it. They were also smart enough to know that I was going to be left with a huge hole in the video if they didn't do it, and that

if they didn't mind the idea of it when they were removed from the set that they should trust that instinct on the set. I have to remind bands that they have final cut so there's nothing to be gained by not trying something. If they saw something in the video and didn't like it, they could bury it. "

Sometimes you have to trick an artist into a good performance. If someone always jumps left when you tell them to jump right, then maybe you should try telling them to . . . you get the idea. Jesse has a classic story about how he got his ex-bandmate/rock-star friend Evan Dando to perform in a Lemonheads video. At one point during the "It's a Shame about Ray" production in Australia, Evan became evasive, grumpy and uninterested every time he was

EVAN DANDO LEARNS QUICKLY

in front of the camera, and Jesse wasn't getting the kind of performance he needed to make the video work. "A lot of times, people in bands get to the point where they start getting bored or thinking it's a stupid idea and just stop trying," he says. In an inspired moment of director manipulation, he started shooting close-ups of the other members of the band — much more than he ever would have needed — to unnerve Evan. "I would have the whole band playing, but the camera would just go between Dave Ryan and Nick Dalton and pan right by Evan." It worked. After a while of feeling left out, Evan was eager to get in front of the camera and perform. "It wasn't even a matter of him saying, 'Hey, when are you going to shoot me?' But when I said, 'We'll do a pass of you now,' it was like magic. He was total- ly on again."

One tremendous advantage to directing rockers and actors in a music video instead of a feature film is that you're shooting MOS (the old Hollywood film-production term mean- ing filming "without sound"). You can shout at the subjects while the camera rolls just as a fashion photographer cajoles constantly repositioning models. In front of a rolling camera, most people feel so on-the-spot that they'll do whatever you say if you bark orders at them. This works especially well during performance takes. If the guitar player puts on a goofy grin in the middle of a take, you don't need to yell "cut" and start all over again. Just yell at the guy, loudly enough so that you're audible over the music: "You there! Stop grinning like a goofball!" It helps me sometimes to think of music-video performers as guinea pigs in some grand Pavlovian experiment. You yell at them, they jump, and hopefully they jump in just the way you want. Well, it works for me, anyway.

My favorite Pavlovian experiment was the "15 Ways" video for the Fall. The Fall loomed large in my personal rock-star pantheon. Other directors might be intimidated if they had to do a video for the Rolling Stones or Sonic Youth, for example, but, since I was weaned on art punk, directing the Fall meant directing a band that I had worshipped from the time I was a child. This daunting proposition was made more daunting by the band's legendary front-man Mark E. Smith — a notorious drunken speed freak who had recently gotten arrested for smoking on a transcontinental flight — and his ill-concealed hatred for shoot- ing rock videos. During the the Fall's previous video shoot, Smith so despised the video- makers that he only agreed to be on the set for 45 minutes. Total. The result included almost no shots of Smith, and, in the few shots meant to capture him singing, his lips weren't remotely in synch. For "15 Ways," I was given a mandate from Matador Records: "Dave, go to Manchester, bond with Mark as much as possible, and bring us back a $15,000 video in which we have shots of his face actually singing the song."

Now, knowing that Smith would be temperamental and disagreeable and reject almost anything I suggested, I wrote a treatment in which he had very little to do. Playing off his trademark speaking-singing vocal style, I proposed that he spend the entire video posed as an anchorman for a vaguely '60s-style surreal newscast. I thought that if the concept kept him bound to a chair behind a desk, and if it could justify having the lyrics on a piece of paper in front of him, there was no way that I wouldn't get shots of his face singing. Besides, if we were prelit, three takes meant taking only fifteen minutes of an acerbic rocker's life. Of course, I wanted much more.

The treatment called for shots of the other band members roaming through Manchester dragging their amps like convicts dragging a ball and chain. I also wanted Smith out on the streets singing the song into a microphone like a crazed field reporter reporting back to himself. Finally, I wanted the whole band to converge and perform the final choruses. I knew that if I shot each band member individually, I would have an easier time of it: they'd be trapped with me. I also knew that, at worst, I would at least have Smith sitting behind that newscaster's desk singing. I had created a world in which even if he was struggling to remember the lyrics, it made sense for him to look down at the paper.

CAUGHT: MARK E. SMITH

This whole set-up would have worked perfectly had Smith not shown up five hours late to the newscaster's set. I was so utterly freaked out that I just told Mott to start running the camera the moment Smith walked into the room. I had less than an hour to get all the Smith shots in the video.

I had done no better than my predecessors, and I thought I had a watertight plan. My role had nothing to do with direction at this point because I didn't have time to explain what I wanted him to do. I needed shots of him primping for the "broadcast," just as a real newscaster might. So I lied. I shouted to him from behind the camera, "Mark, your tie looks

DIRECTING TIPS

A tip from Tryan George: Direct singers by giving them an "eye line," a spot on which to focus that also focuses their performance. "Giving a performer an eye line that gives them a place to look and just a brief idea of what their demeanor should be is gonna make a performer feel more directed," he maintains. "A lot of them will have intuition about how to play to the camera but some of them won't and they'll just sort of stand there like they're recording or incredibly bored. You've got to remind them that we're trying to get a visual representation of them playing, and just giving them a point to focus on often gives them a little more intensity. Otherwise they're looking all over the place."

Here's another Darren Doane tip for directing rockers: Don't let the singer use the microphone. "When you stand up there with a mike we can't see your face and have to shoot from the side." And a rocker-scheduling tip from AD Mike Dignum: "Basic rule of thumb —rock bands want to stay up late and sleep in late, so always schedule your day to start a little later, not six o'clock in the morning. If there's something you can shoot first without the band, then do that earlier and then bring the band in."

<<<

crooked . . . Fix it . . . Fix it!" Since he was also tragically drunk, this resembled working with a recalcitrant child. Also, since I was appealing to his vanity by saying such things as, "You want to look good for the video, don't you?" he was following my directions perfectly, not knowing that they were directions. Most of the shots of Mark "acting" we took when he had no idea we were rolling.

"My tie's wot?" slurred Smith, tugging at his clothes.

"Mark, could you fix your hair?"

"We're not shooting this, are we Dave?"

The set fell hushed, the tension crackled and the crew and the producer were amazed that we were shooting the belligerent Smith without his knowledge.

"Of course not," I said, lying unshamefacedly. "I just want you to look good for the video."

Certainly, what Smith was doing that day had nothing to do with acting. It was more like a perverse game of Simon Says. In my experience, this is the model for directing rockers, or anyone for that matter, in a music video. You roll the camera and tell them what to do while the camera is rolling. Again, always capitalize on the MOS aspect of your shoot. Don't try to make the rockers act like actors. They're not, so make the best of their proven talents for spontaneity and improvisation. Remember that they never know what's going to happen when they step out on a stage and have long ago gotten used to rolling with whatever. If you rehearse activities with them, you're running the risk of making them feel self-conscious. It's an unfailingly bad idea to propose a video in which the band has to act. It can be the most painful experience of all time. Unless, of course, the band happens to have been born for the camera.

Another problem with having dramatic sequences that incorporate the band or actors is that there is never enough time during a music-video shoot day to properly rehearse actors or cover a dramatic scene. That's why so many of the actors in music videos are merely "types" and their activity in front of the camera gets reduced to what is essentially posing. The pretty girl looks longingly out the window to indicate that she misses her lover. She looks up, she looks down, she turns her head to look out of the window in synch with the song. Is that acting? Of course not. But imagine shooting the sequence above in the middle of the night after the band was already wrapped, with the director standing next to the camera saying, "Okay . . . Look up, look down. Okay, now look out the window."

That's no different from what I was doing with Mark E. Smith, except for substituting a trained, professional actor. Remember that "acting" in a music video is merely movement. But this demonstrates another circumstance in which the ridiculous budgeting and scheduling of music-video production work in your favor. Actors can't overact in music videos because they don't have the time to act at all. When they have to be talked through every movement while they're on camera, actors expend so much energy listening to you and your weird game of Simon Says that they don't fall back on any bad actor's habits. As a first-time video director, you should never be intimidated by working with real actors. They often get a kick out of the job and assume that you possess a special knowledge about how to make a music video that must include a whole different set of skills than the wannabe dramatic film directors with whom they usually work.

YOU HAVE TO KNOW WHERE TO PLACE THE CAMERA

This might sound obvious, but your other major task on the shoot day is to direct the camera placement. Even if you've storyboarded extensively, shots have to be composed, and no matter how prepared you are, you can never really predict how things are going to look through the lens.

Helping to compose the shots is the ultimate way for you to engage in the shoot and feel like a director. Isn't this what everybody thinks of a director doing? Holding out two hands, forefingers and thumbs extended to form two right angles that frame the world, a director scurries around the set saying, "Hmmm . . . I see the camera looking at them from here. No, wait a minute, I see the camera over here." This is the first thing any director wants to do, but be forewarned. When you're shooting the video yourself, you can put the camera wherever you want. But when you're working with a DP, there has to be a real collaboration, otherwise, by the end of the afternoon, the DP will lose interest and won't want to contribute. You don't want your exasperated DP to turn to you and say, "Well, now where does the camera go?" Collaborate on the compositions with the DP because s/he is truly your partner on the set. "Inexperienced directors," Mott says, "don't know what you need and what you don't need for a shoot, so you [the DP] have to make a lot of those decisions, like what kind of lights you want, what colors are good, what materials are good, things like that. The director usually has no eyes at all [because they can't look through the camera], with all that's going on because, rarely, in low-budget shooting, are there video taps. So when it comes down to the actually shooting, they have no idea what they're doing."

The sad truth is that not all of directing a music video is commonsensical and bluffable. "If a person's an inexperienced filmmaker," Mott maintains, "they have no idea what the different millimeters on the lens are. If you tell them the lens, they have no idea what that means at all. Then you tell them that you're on a wide shot, a medium shot or a close-up, they still have no idea what you're talking about. Are you talking about a medium shot of a building, or a medium shot of a rock star, which could include the guitar or not include the guitar? If they don't take the time to look — and they often don't take the time to look because they're in a major hurry for one reason or another — how can they have any idea what you're shooting? When I'm shooting, I feel like I get more creative in the moment, under the pressure, just doing whatever I want to do, unless the director tells me to do something specific."

A good, experienced director knows where to put the camera from years of experience, and the best directors are those who can see "dynamic angles" on the spot. What makes a camera angle dynamic? If you shoot a building looking directly at it from eye-level, you're going to get a two-dimensional representation of that building. If you move the camera in toward the building, down to the ground and shoot it with a wide-angle lens in a way that maximizes the three-dimensionality of the building, and that makes all of its lines converge in the distance, then that's a dynamic angle. The best place to go looking for examples of dyamic angles: comic books. Every frame of a superhero comic book demonstrates the use of dynamic angles. Comic books are a medium, like film, that desperately tries to transcend two-dimensionality, and lots of filmmaking folks study them.

Julie Hermelin has a favorite angle for performance sequences. "A good, important view is the one looking at the band when they're on stage, when you see them from a low angle. I like that, because it's how I see bands when I go to clubs. I think it creates a live-performance feel." Tryan George reminded me that covering a different angle can save a bad location. "If you're in a bad location," he says, "if you shoot low angles and you get the sky in the shot, you can get a feeling of grandeur from the back of a Chevron station." Remember also that the wide-angle lens, which keeps more of what is in front of it in focus because it allows more light in, is the low-budget videomaker's friend.

So, though aesthetic pronouncements stimulate endless debate, I will make this statement: When I'm looking at a location and trying to figure out where to put the camera, I'm always looking for dynamic angles. Unless you've worked out a visual motif to the contrary, shooting dynamic angles makes the best default approach for your low-budget music video. Dynamic camera angles — angles that capitalize on the depth and three-dimensionality of the image — raise your production value.

In the same way that I always opt for dynamic angles, I always put the camera in the most flattering place for the band. Search for an angle at which they look the best, period. This might sound obvious, but it isn't. Say you're shooting a lead singer in front of a really cool building that you want to frame looming behind him and above his head. You're married to the shot. You love it and you have to have the building in your video. So, you put the camera way down low so it's looking up at him, and you can see the building. The problem is that this guy carries around an extra twenty pounds that he picked up from the road food on the band's last tour, so while he's looking down at the camera he displays a most unattractive double chin. Walk away, cry, but don't shoot it. Lose the building you fell in love with. Make yourself do the exact opposite of what you had in mind and place the camera on a high angle looking down at him, so that when he looks up at the camera, he extends his neck, eliminating the double chin.

It's not cheesy or selling-out to place the camera in such a way that double chins disappear and potbellies thin out. Hermelin agrees that she likes bands to look good, "And that doesn't mean they have to look pretty, but they've gotta look cool. You want to see the singer looking good performing for the camera and you want to capture him at his most physically and emotionally intense." Mott advises that you can help the band look good by lighting with a soft white light. "I think that the lead band member should have soft light on him, and his face should be lit pretty well," he says. "People want to see that one person. I try to light the lead person normally, like you would in a movie, then experiment everywhere else."

"Sometimes you set up a shot and it just looks like hell," Nancy Bennett says. "You get into a room and that wide-angle lens doesn't give you the room that you thought you were gonna have or people look really distorted and unattractive. Cut your losses and get the hell out, but do it in a way that doesn't ruin all the schmoozing you've been doing with your artist. Another thing is stamina. I think one of the things that protects stamina and the quality of what you're doing is to not dwell on stuff, not to beat it to death. Move as quickly as you can because most really good actors have probably three really good takes in them.

MOTT'S DP ADVICE

Choosing dynamic lighting can be as important as dynamic angles, and, if you can't see the band, you don't have a video. DP Mott Hupfel passes along some specific advice about light packages and lighting techniques.

"Having two HMI par lights is a very good thing on any job, wherever you go. They're huge lights, they can work inside or outside, they throw a major amount of light. I just shot a job where all we got was one HMI. The band had a big rehearsal space with windows all around it. I needed some kind of light to balance with the outdoors. You take a 1200 par light and when you're shooting from the left, you put it next to you and bounce it off the right wall. It's such a bright light that when it's bounced off of a white wall, it's like having a giant Soft Light, like a 5K through some kind of diffusion. When you shoot in the other direction, you move it to the other side and bounce it off the other wall.

I would say you need two 1200 pars, and a 2K open-face tungsten light, because if you put a colored gel in front of a 1K, you'll lose the light. But if you put a colored gel over a 2K open-face, it's a really, really strong light. If you need to put a band member in front of a colored background, and you have two 1Ks, you have a very small shot. It's only going to light up a color in about a six-foot-square area. If you have someone standing in front of it, you can only get a medium shot. If you have a 2K open face, then you have a large area, a large area of background lit, and it doesn't take that much more electricity. If I were to take other lights besides two 1200 pars, I would take one 1K and one 2K open-face.

I think that bouncing a really small light like a 1K isn't strong enough and you end up getting a muddy, murky light. I would just put it through diffusion. In general, especially for music video, if you can go with direct light, even if it's through some kind of diffusion, it's a stronger image. I think more contrast is better, and often it makes rock stars, who are trying in their own personal hygiene to not always look so beautiful, look more exciting and radical.

If I had a 1K and a 2K and those two 1200 pars, if I was in an interior location and I was just doing a single, I would put the 1K through some 216 or something, onto the lead singer just off center from frontal, then the 2K, shining one way or another, all over the background. Then you could maybe use one of the 1200s as a backlight, raked against the band members.

I wrote some little commandments: Always order many more lights than you can imagine using. You're not doing yourself any good as a DP to save the production money and say, 'No, I can do it with two lights.' You should always demand twice as many lights as you want, and you should always demand twice as much money as you want. Unless you ask for both of those things, you're never going to get them, and without the lights, you'll never make a good video, and without the money, you'll never be able to afford doing what they want doing. You gotta remember to get everything you need. I always forgot to get clothespins and extension cords. Check what they give you at the rental house. Unless you order them, they won't give you the stands for the lights. So you get there, and there's four lights sitting in the truck, no extensions cords. Some places won't even give you the bulbs unless you order them. "

<<<

So why would you do twelve takes of the same set-up with a singer? They're just going to stop giving you variety and start giving you mush. Get what you need and push the envelope of camera angle, emotion, lighting and everything else, but there's only so much you can get out of a situation."

But the director and the band might have different notions of what makes them look best, and that's where problems arise. After doing many videos featuring bands with a "no sell-out" attitude and a determination not to look slick, my rule of thumb is this: If you're grappling with an on-set decision that boils down to an artistic choice and the band looking good, always opt for the band looking good. Always. If the band says they want to look ugly, they're lying. Trust me. You won't use bad-looking shots of the band when you edit the video, so don't waste time shooting them.

THE DP

You've encountered my friend Mott throughout the book. Mott Hupfel has the energy of a 12-year-old and brings an enormous sense of play to his work. He speaks in sing-songy phrases as if he was your second-grade art teacher. He loves what he does and is constantly torn between doing everything on the set himself and delegating to other people. He completely personifies the *You Stand There* philosophy because, while other DPs are anal-retentive

PETER PRESCOTT OF KUSTOMIZED IN MOTT'S LENS

types, Mott's main concern is getting things done. His presence at virtually every step as we've gone through the production process reflects the deep attachment directors have to their DPs, if only for the duration of the shoot. You will often encounter, though, director/DP teams that stick together for years or entire careers, a dependence that gets exaggerated by low budgets. This the classic model: A wannabe director needs someone to shoot a no-budget video for free. A wannabe DP needs to shoot for his or her reel, and is willing to work for free. If this director landed a super-low-budget gig, but the film and processing are going to get paid for, the job becomes worthwhile for the DP. Some lights will get rented and there will be some equipment to experiment with. Also, the director might become a "real" director and help the DP make the transition to becoming "real" as well.

Shared learning makes the relationship between low-budget DPs and directors more than just symbiosis. When a director and a DP are at the same stage in their careers — figuring out how to shoot, how to cover scenes, how to light, what effects to use — real collaboration takes place. This is why a shot list, rather than a storyboard, can be sufficient prep for a director. Though it should be very specific, a shot list is open to interpretation. It becomes a springboard from which the DP can contribute.

Also, although videos can certainly be shot, directed, produced and edited by one person, a good, super-low-budget model is the two-person crew. The director tends to work as producer, art director, grip, playback sound person, stylist and, of course, PA, as well as director. The DP tends to work as gaffer/electric, assistant camera person, grip and PA as well as DP. However primitive this division of labor, it teaches you how to work with at least one other person, an essential lesson for any filmmaker. It might seem like a silly role-playing game to say, "Now I'm the electric and you're the grip," but it's important to understand all of those jobs.

"Often, on a low-budget video, directors end up producing," claims Mott, "so that [the DP] has to take charge of the more creative ends because they're so busy trying to figure out where the donuts are coming from, where the van is parked or someone telling them that they're not allowed to shoot there. It's a little bit easier for a director to deal with those kinds of things, rather than what color the light should be or what shirt the rocker should wear. Those things are more serious in the end, but it's easier [for the director] to say, 'I'm dealing with the lunch right now, you just answer that question.'"

The DP, especially on low budgets that cannot support a video tap, becomes the director's eyes. While the director plays her game of Simon Says with the band, while they're making decisions on where to set up the donut table and whether to cough up the cash for a playback machine to replace the malfunctioning borrowed bass cabinet, the DP makes the images that are, after all, the point of all this activity. The DP frames the shot, meters the light for proper exposure, and moves the camera. Sure, as director you've communicated exactly what you want to see (you have, haven't you?), but the DP assumes the responsibility of putting the action on film. If you're not the DP yourself, you have to place your trust in someone else to have loaded the camera properly, provided enough light, framed the shot as you described, and covered the scene from the right angle and direction.

Most DPs relish the responsibility, though, and if the directors are often the least technically skilled people on the set, the DPs are often the most skilled. They have a complete familiarity with their own tools — the camera, lenses, film stocks, lighting instruments, viewfinders, dollies, cranes and camera mounts — and have a good working knowledge of electricity, rigging and processing chemistry. They work with ACs, grips and gaffers to get electricity to the set and hang lighting instruments. Because it affects exposures and camera movements, they work with art directors to choose colors and materials for the set.

The most important advice from DPs to new directors is to talk to the DP, talk constantly and talk specifically about what needs to be accomplished. "Working with a director who has no experience, you just have to communicate more with them, and make them look through the camera," Mott says. "It's good to have the director show you pictures of things they like. If they show you a magazine and say, 'Oh, I like this color,' or a photograph, 'I like this location,' or, 'I like the way that this person is standing here.' That way you can be very specific."

INFO: CAMERA PACKAGE

A TYPICAL CAMERA PACKAGE:
- camera body
- a couple of film magazines
- one lens
- a matte box for mounting filters
- batteries, or a battery belt
- accessories, such as a pistol grip for hand-holding, focus wheels for pulling and marking focus, and the filters themselves are all separate. Some fancy camera packages come with filter packages and a tripod

Though DPs tend to be confident individuals, they want the director's input and look to the director for, well, direction. "What you want from the director on the shoot is someone actually taking charge and not leaving everything up to the DP," Mott continues. "You need someone else to be in charge because there's too much pressure and too many decisions to be made, and it's better if you can focus on what you're doing. It's good if the director takes charge and says, 'Okay, this is going to be next.' It's good if the director has a really good idea of what's going on inside the camera, even if that means he has to look through the camera a lot. It's good if the director has a very good relationship with the band, so that the band will do what he or she says. It's good if the director has a visual style, knows everything from the band's hair to their clothes to the colors of their skin. A lot of times, directors are thinking about what they're editing already, and they tend to miss what's going on in front of them and how to make it better."

Wannabe DPs will often have their own camera package, which will be cheaper to rent than from a rental house. The director pays for the camera package rental, but then the DP will work for free. This way the DP makes some money, while the director gets to rent a 16mm camera for very little money. But, as you can see in the box listing a typical camera package, the camera is just the beginning of your equipment needs.

LIGHTS, ETC.

HMI

a lamp that mimics sunlight, used for outdoor shooting, for lighting a room for daylight through a window, and for bright natural daylight in interiors

Kino-Flo

fluorescent lamps designed for use in film, they are long and flat, and an order for them would be designated in the number of "banks" at a given wattage

baby fresnel

50- to 200-watt lamps

(A note about lamp sizes: Lamps are available in 500 kilowatts to 10,000 kilowatts, and are therefore known as 1Ks, 2Ks, 6ks, 10k, etc.)

quad boxes

electrical boxes with have four outlets

snakes

power cables that look like mammoth, multicable extension cords

generator (genny)

a gasoline-fueled electrical generator for lighting in areas that do not have accessible electricity

car cigarette lighter

often used as a source of electricity when shooting in automobiles

GRIP EQUIPMENT

c-stand

A three-footed, extendable steel stand with a vice clamp at its top. It holds flags, silks, and kukaloris for lighting effects. An extra arm extension can be attached to secure equipment at any angle.

scrim

A light-diffusion material stretched over a metal frame, usually made of wire mesh, silk or other translucent material.

flag

A piece of fabric stretched over a metal frame usually suspended from a c-stand and used to cast shadows, direct light or to obscure light in order to prevent lens flare.

blacks

black flags

white card

a piece of white foamcore used like a flag to reflect light

silk

a flag with silk diffusion

gels

A light filter for changing the color temperature of a lighting instrument or source. Two specific gels: a CTO is "color temperature orange," which corrects for tungsten-balanced film. If you were shooting indoors and you wanted to use tungsten light sources, but there was a window that threw the color balance off, you'd cover that window with a CTO gel. CTB, "color temperature blue," corrects for outdoor-balanced film. If you wanted to shoot in a room that had huge windows and wanted to use sunlight (which is blue light) but wanted to light your subjects with tungsten lights, you'd have to correct the tungsten lights with a CTB gel.

MEET THE CREW

director of photography (DP)

Responsible for lighting, operating the camera, choosing film stocks, assembling the camera package, lighting equipment and all of the crew necessary to carry out his job. The DP works with the producer and director in budgeting and scheduling, and then with the director and production designer to create the project's visual look with lighting, colors, locations, sets and effects. The DP directs the gaffers on setting lights and leads the camera crew through positioning the camera, always checking composition and movements through the lens. After shooting, the DP works with the labs and reviews dailies and transfers.

camera operator (AC)

Supervises the operation of the camera, including any movements (dollies, pans or tilts), focus and composition. Also responsible for the maintenance, loading and smooth operation of the camera. The first assistant camera operator is generally the focus puller, who moves the focus rings on the lens (though they never look through the camera, and instead focus with measurements and grease-pencil markings on the lens) and makes sure the camera is mounted with the proper lens. The second assistant camera operator is primarily responsible for loading the film into the camera's magazines, operating the slate and filling out the camera reports that list the scenes and takes finished each day to be used as a reference for the lab.

grips

The DP and AC supervise grips that are attached to the camera crew, for example, the dolly grips that push the dolly around.

A LIGHTING PLOT FROM MOTT

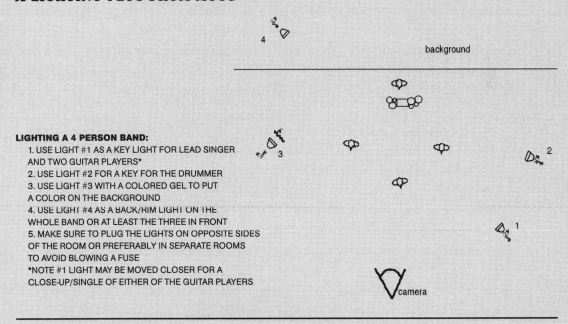

background

LIGHTING A 4 PERSON BAND:
1. USE LIGHT #1 AS A KEY LIGHT FOR LEAD SINGER
AND TWO GUITAR PLAYERS*
2. USE LIGHT #2 FOR A KEY FOR THE DRUMMER
3. USE LIGHT #3 WITH A COLORED GEL TO PUT
A COLOR ON THE BACKGROUND
4. USE LIGHT #4 AS A BACK/RIM LIGHT ON THE
WHOLE BAND OR AT LEAST THE THREE IN FRONT
5. MAKE SURE TO PLUG THE LIGHTS ON OPPOSITE SIDES
OF THE ROOM OR PREFERABLY IN SEPARATE ROOMS
TO AVOID BLOWING A FUSE
*NOTE #1 LIGHT MAY BE MOVED CLOSER FOR A
CLOSE-UP/SINGLE OF EITHER OF THE GUITAR PLAYERS

camera

YOUR MOOD DOMINATES THE SET

Here's one of my favorite film-production stories of all time. Peter Clarke, now a propmaster on features, started in the business by working on commercials in Boston. The story begins one day on a run-of-the-mill job with a youngish director. Shortly after call time, this director gets everyone to gather around in a circle for a little pep talk. Even at this early point in his career, Pete had mastered the cool disposition of a jaded film technician, and he was wary of any touchy-feely, pep-talk stuff: You're there to make money, not friends, and all that. The director opens the colloquy with the old wheeze, "I know we're not making *Apocalypse Now*, but let's try to make something good here, people. Let's not just go through the motions of doing our jobs. Let's make today special." Suddenly moved, Pete looks around and notices that everyone's listening seriously. Pete thinks to himself, "Maybe today is different. Maybe we can take more pride in our work." He notices that the woman sitting beside him is so moved by the young director's speech that she's even taking notes. She catches Pete's eye, and holds up her notepad to show him what she's written: "Who does this asshole think he is???"

The director's dilemma: You don't want to alienate your crew with bullshit, let's-go-team enthusiasm, but your mood, your disposition, and who you are sets the tone on your set. You need everyone on your side, working with you, and it's important to set that tone early in the day. If you're also the AD, which you will be on any low-budget job, you should attempt a variation on that quixotic commercial director's speech, but make it practical information. Take ten or fifteen minutes to go over your schedule with everyone on the crew. In the world of big budgets, the AD would keep everyone informed as the day progresses. Since you can't do that because of all your other duties, use a little crew powwow to get the shoot going on the right note.

As you would imagine, the morale issues multiply whenever a group of people have to work together. All the cliches about the director being captain of the ship and keeping up crew morale have some validity. The atmosphere on a set run by a rageaholic asshole is unquestionably different than the atmosphere on a nice-guy set, and as AD Mike Dignum told me, "You'll get ten times more out of a crew that's happy than a crew that's grumpy and complaining. It just takes one guy to get totally pissed off, to tell all his buddies on the crew what a lame show it is. Next thing you know, the guys are dragging their feet."

As a director, your mood affects the set and the whole shooting process. That's why, as with so many other endeavors, having a sense of humor helps enormously. Nancy Bennett uses double-speed playback so the band has to play at double speed while she shoots at double speed (which delivers slow motion when transferred at normal speed; picture the running dogs in Spike Jonze's "The Sweater Song" video for Weezer) to inject some energy into a flagging set. "Sometimes just to wake people up I like to use double-speed playback because there's something really beautiful about slow motion," she says. "Of course, it gets beaten to death but slow-motion-synch's pretty elegant and can be particularly effective with really horrible rock. After about eight hours of the band doing their twentieth play-through of a song, I like to wake everybody up by laying double-speed on them without telling them. They have to rise to the occasion and usually it's good comic relief anyway."

One very practical reason for maintaining your sense of humor on the set is so that you can cheer the band on. When they play on set, you should applaud them after every take. For a band, doing a video is like the worst gig they ever had. It's simultaneously like a twelve-hour soundcheck, an eight-hour photo shoot, and one of the most poorly attended shows they've ever played. One of the best ways to get the performance you want from the band is to be totally supportive. They're used to audience response, and if you're enthusiastic about them, the rest of the crew will be, too.

> **CALL TIME**
> the time the band and crew are necessary on the set, as found in the day's call sheet

Sometimes it gets a little too enthusiastic on the set. Darren Doane tells a great story about a shoot that got way out of hand. "We tried to do a video for a band called Voodoo Glow Skulls," his story begins. "They wanted to have a huge party out in Riverside and we'd shoot the band playing the party. The song was called 'Fat Randy' and it was about one of their friends, a guy in high school who went to parties and got in fights with people. They wanted to use the real guy, so they bus in people and throw this huge party. There must have been about a thousand kids at this place with pizza, beer, everything. By the time we get to shooting the conceptual stuff, Fat Randy is so drunk that he can't stand up or do anything. The idea was that he was gonna pull up in a van in front of the party, get out and everybody was gonna go 'Whoo!' and cheer for Fat Randy as he was walking through the house drinking beer. Though we have the cameras set up, ready to go, you can't control a thousand people. The van pulls up and the first take when he gets out everyone charges at him and you can't film because now they're in front of the camera. In the midst of all this, somehow Fat Randy picks a fight with somebody and suddenly there's about forty people beating the crap out of him. Beating him to a pulp. The party turns into a riot, things being broken and lights smashed. Next thing you know, helicopters are coming in, lights shining down, and the cops finally get there. They're arresting everybody and

I'm sitting there thinking, 'Wow, we're done.' The shoot just ended, it was over. We hadn't shot a thing and now the shoot was over. Our main guy was on the ground, bloody, beaten to a pulp, we spent the money and we had nothing shot. That's when you call the record label and you have to be human for that one brief moment when you say, 'It didn't happen. It got fucked up. These things happen and we need to shoot again tomorrow. We need to change the concept and we need another five thousand dollars.' Those are the hardest phone calls to make but when you make those phone calls you feel good that you did it. That you were professional."

SHOOTING FOR COVERAGE

A disaster on the shoot means that there's no way that you can execute your cherished concept. Your shot list gets thrown out the window, and suddenly you don't have your road map to success. This is the worst day of your life. Too bad. This happens all the time and you have to deal with it. You have equipment, a crew, a camera, film and a rock band. You can still make a video.

Jesse Peretz tells about traveling all the way to Berlin to shoot the Lemonheads at a big outdoor festival. "It was supposed to be a live performance video of 'Confetti,' so I just went with Elliott Rocket and his camera," Jesse recalls. "Huge stage, one camera. The production people from the festival wouldn't let us anywhere near the stage, so we could only shoot from below. They played six songs because it started raining. Evan didn't move at all. It was a long-lens shot, which ended up being about medium-wide because they were so high up and we were so far away. Evan was standing at the microphone not moving and the stage was cutting him off at the knee. We couldn't even get a full-length shot. It was not even like the worst video ever, there was nothing in the camera. They had the next day off, and were traveling with their friend Polly, who's a totally good actress. We had a friend who had an office in this amazing-looking paper warehouse, and basically we just shot the band in there. We dressed Polly up like an East German spy, and she ran around talking into her watch. We had a scooter and someone driving Evan. We created a little narrative that you can't follow, but it looks like a spy movie. It's not a great video, but for $5,000 in East Germany with no prep . . ."

Some folks are going to be better than others at the "save," making up the whole shoot on the spot when all else fails. In order to shoot when your plan goes out the window, you should understand the concept of "coverage."

When shooting a scene in a narrative film, a director positions the camera to film wide shots, medium shots and close-ups. Generally, the actors play the entire scene for each of those camera positions. Even if the director knows that one of the characters has a big dramatic line three-quarters of the way through the scene and has determined that they want a close-up of this character delivering that line, they still shoot this character saying all of his lines in all of the other camera positions. This ensures that the scene is "covered," or that you have the entire scene shot from all possible camera angles. This gives you a number of different options in editing. You'll hear filmmakers say, in reference to a film they're working on, "Well, we've got good coverage for that scene," or, "I've really covered that moment to death," which means that they've shot the scene from all the possible angles. They reached their goal on the shoot day; they shot more than they needed.

The concept of coverage illustrates the craft of the director at work. On the one hand, a good director has edited the movie in her mind before she shoots it, so she knows what shots she definitely needs and focuses on those shots and very little else. When people describe a director as being "fast," this is partially what they mean. An experienced director makes decisions about everything on the spot and can automatically prioritize what needs to be covered and what doesn't.

Shooting much more than needed shows a lack of precision, but there is a certain amount of coverage needed to provide flexibility while editing. In his book, *Making Movies*, director Sidney Lumet explains that in the classic Hollywood studio system, coverage was derived from a rigid formula that directors followed to meet studio executives' budgets. In that world, studio editors chose the shots for the final cut and directors were only responsible for capturing options from which an editor would select.

Being "well covered" also means having enough overlapping action for successful match cuts. Say you have a scene in which an actor runs toward the camera, stops, raises his arm holding a gun, aims, and fires. You envision going to a close-up only when the character aims and fires. It might seem expedient to shoot the actor raising his arms and firing only while you're framed for the close-up. However, for a seamless transition during the cut from medium shot to a close-up — for the audience to register the illusion that the cut is just a shift in perspective on the actor's continuous action of running, aiming and firing — the actor should complete that action as one continuous activity during both the medium shot and the close-up. There has to be some follow-through with the actor's activities, otherwise you run the risk of the cut between medium shot to close-up not matching. The actor might be in a slightly different position vis à vis the rest of the space when you shoot the close-up, which will look jarring when you insert that close-up next to the wider shot. The actor's actions could look unnatural, as though he stopped, then started again — or worse — that the camera stopped and then started again after he repositioned.

In a sense, coverage *is* the active work of a director. The grips and the camera crew get the camera in position. The grips and electrics do the rigging necessary to get the light for the shot. The talent stands in front of the camera. Now it's the director's job to cover the scene. As you're watching the band, wondering if they're comfortable and making sure they look good in the takes, you should also be constantly thinking, "What else could I shoot from this position? Here's a shot I could get without repositioning the camera. Do I have enough angles of them playing this part of the song?"

Thinking in coverage mode demands concentration on what's in front of you. Suddenly you realize that guitar player has this weird tic — he makes a really cool movement with his arm whenever he plays a certain part of the song. Make sure you get that moment on film. You realize that on every take when the singer finishes a chorus she looks to her left. Make sure that you get a take of her in which she looks toward the other direction so that it doesn't look like you're using the same shot over and over again.

> **MATCH CUTS:**
> editing that maintains the continuity of an action by matching the space, time and angle of one shot of the action with the space, time and angle of the shot following

COVER THE BAND PLAYING THE ENTIRE SONG AND THE SINGER SINGING

I remember the first time I visited the set of a real-budget video. I was astonished. For each take, they'd roll the entire song and shoot nonstop. Each performance take was at least three and a half minutes long, the length of the entire song. This seemed like such a luxury to me. Up until that time I had only run pieces of the song for a take. If I knew that I wanted to see the band performing their song during a chorus, I would only play back and shoot the chorus.

When you schedule the video, you try to get the performance out of the way to relieve some of the pressure: After half a day of shooting you at least have a performance video. You will certainly relieve the pressure by shooting a single take of the singer singing the entire song. If you're going to be indulgent and waste film, this is the most useful way to waste it. If you've planned for one close-up of the singer singing — and if you haven't, take one step backward and add it to your shot list — shoot him/her singing the whole song, making sure that you have the singer singing every line. Mike Dignum notes that getting the performance out of the way first usually clears the room of record-label observers as well. "I tell new guys if you have a record company peeking over your shoulder what they want to see is the guy standing with his guitar, singing. What I recommend is to shoot a full pass of the song, get it in the can, maybe do a couple of them. Make the record company feel, 'Okay, we've got it. He sang the whole song, it looked pretty great, he performed well.' Kick the day off that way and they're off your back. Then get into your conceptual stuff. A fine example would be 'Tonight,' the Smashing Pumpkins video. It was shot in two days, and that was a mammoth undertaking for two days. But we knew exactly what we had to shoot, we had every shot written down, broken down shot-for-shot in an order that made the most sense for me, the directors and the DP. The very first thing we shot was band performance. The band showed up with the record company, and then the label people left. We had a day and a half to be shooting all the conceptual stuff."

I didn't do this, I think, until my sixth video, which is ridiculous. I was wedded to a logic that proposes the singer getting from point A to point B, singing a certain part of the song at a certain location. Then something terrible would happen in editing. Someone would inevitably say, "Don't you have a better shot of her singing such-and-such a line. Maybe in that other location?" I would reply, "No, you don't understand, she's singing in the 'chorus world' here so I only shot her singing the chorus. She only sings the verses in the 'verse world.'"

At the end of the day, no one cares about your artistic agendas; everyone wants good shots of the singer. If you're married to a rigid structure — the singer only sings a certain part of the song in a certain location — then you have to make sure that you've got the best performance moments in the location you want. "In the beginning, performance was not my top priority and I didn't like doing performance at all," Tryan George says. "I had this story to tell, I've got this visual thing and I'm making this great thing, and the performance will just fall in there somewhere. That changed real quickly. I realized a strong performance is gonna get that emotional connection. If you make a performer look incredibly enticing, interesting, sexy and introspective or whatever, you're gonna get the most emotional impact out of the music video. So now I take the performance really seriously."

There are few directors who can ignore the dictate to cover the band's performance, even if it's not the most exciting creative work for the director. Spike Jonze is one of them, and he tries to create a meaning to the performance or as in his Wax video that featured only a slow-motion dash by a man on fire, he eliminates it completely. "I try to only shoot performance if I come up with a good reason to shoot it," he maintains. "If it works well for the entire video, rather than just arbitrarily cutting to the singer or the drummer or the guitarist. I don't really like that kind of thing. I'll try to come up with a performance that works into a bigger idea or a more interesting way to do performance. I've done videos where the whole thing is performance like that. I did the Weezer video ["Come Undone — Sweater Song"] where the whole thing was one take of the camera wandering around. I just took that idea and went all the way with it as opposed to doing it a little bit and cutting it in."

Using performance in a rock video may seem like old hat, but maybe that just makes it more like rock itself. Part of the enjoyment of listening to rock music comes from the familiarity of the form and hearing how the artist twists or conforms to the form. At this point, seeing bands perform in music videos may be the equivalent of a twelve-bar blues or a I-IV-V harmonic progression, and there is joy in finding new ways to use that form. "I think that people nowadays get caught up in doing these overwhelming concepts," says Norwood Cheek, "these conceptual videos that the band ends up getting lost in. I really enjoy shooting the band, letting the band choose where they want to perform, in their practice space or in their living room or hanging out in their favorite diner. I don't think that stuff ever gets old. It's like rock and roll. All the songs are essentially the same, but I just can't get enough of seeing somebody playing in front of the camera, if they're pumped up about it and if they're comfortable. It's great to be able to see them play their instruments. That's what people like. There's nothing wrong with going back to the basics."

> **PERFORMANCE BED:**
> laying down in editing one complete performance as a "bed" on which to rest narrative or other performance shots

No matter your feelings about using the band's performance, when the band revises the video, you can't claim that you need a certain shot on the basis of the video's logic alone, and you want to be able to present options. If the singer's vanity is the issue, you're only going to win your argument for your artistic choice by showing them that you did, in fact, shoot alternative takes, and that they don't look especially worse or better in those takes.

Also, one of those single takes of the singer singing can be a simple "performance bed" for you to cut around. Especially when you're doing a low-budget video with non-synch footage, it's good to immediately have something to synch-up so you won't have to look at a dark screen when you're shuttling past parts of the video you haven't cut yet.

If you're worried about ruining your concept, and it seems too random to use shots of the singer performing throughout the video in different locations, make the singer's "special" close-up in a non-specific place — an extreme close-up, or in an unrecognizable environment. This is only for the most straightforward, interlacing narrative formulas: If your two main categories of footage are narrative/conceptual and performance, it's useful to think of the singer's takes separately, as a third tier of footage. Obviously, this only applies to rock-band situations in which you can differentiate between singer with band and singer alone. Videos that feature a single performer are another story entirely. Every close-up of Babyface in a Babyface video is a special, and, since he enjoys a huge budget, every nice close-up came from a take in which he sang the entire song.

Just as you should feel great relief at lunchtime if you know you have all of your performance footage out of the way, you'll feel even more relief knowing that you got at least one single, continuous take of the singer singing the entire song. Period.

GET SHOTS OF THE DRUMMER

Producer Steve Albini claims that there are really only two camps when it comes to rock appreciation and rock record producing: those that favor guitars and those that favor drums. He prefers the latter, claiming that, even though he's a guitar player himself, he'll never embody the true spirit of rock in the way Led Zeppelin drummer John Bonham did. Certainly, Albini's production work with Nirvana, Bush, P.J. Harvey, and his own band, Shellac, celebrates drumming. Drummers make rock rock. Rock drumming makes non-rock rock. An MTV interviewer asked E.P.M.D. where they find drumbeats to sample for a hip-hop groove, and in unison, all four African American members of the group shouted, "Rock!" Yes, the guitar riff in AC/DC's "You Shook Me All Night Long" is infectious, but where would it be without the drums? Why did Aerosmith's "Walk This Way" work so well as a Run DMC crossover hit? That incredible drumbeat intro.

As an unabashed rockaholic, I accept my rock-drumming fetish. Watching a drummer is my favorite sound/image relationship. Watching a great rock drummer is like watching interpretive dance or a manic baton-waving conductor, and, like a conductor, a drummer's movements propel a song. Whenever I see a video or a live multi-camera shoot of a performing rock band, I always want to see the drummer. Even if the drummer is a real goofball, I become annoyed if I think he's underrepresented. When there is a dramatic cymbal crash or a dynamic drum fill that's not shown, I feel cheated and I disengage. This is why I make a rule of getting as many shots of the drummer as possible. The moment you have good shots of a drummer beating the set, the video rocks. On a truly low-budget job, you might not have enough film to burn on takes of each individual band member playing the entire song, but make sure you get drum coverage. Even though the record company and the band will plead for equal representation of each band member, you'll want shots of the drummer to raise the rock quotient of your video.

MAKE SURE YOU'VE GOT ALL MOVEMENTS AND ANGLES COVERED

Music-video acting may be mere movement, but all this movement demands the correct coverage. There's never adequate time to reposition the camera, so you're not always able to get different angles on the same actions. If you're prepared for this misfortune ahead of time, you realize that there are some directions you can give your subjects that will make life easier for you in the editing room. No matter the action in front of the lens, in my bizarre game of Simon Says I always hear myself saying, "Now, go back and do it the other way." If they pick up the bottle, make sure they put it down. If they walk down the street left to right, make sure you have them walk down the street right to left.

This isn't only about repetition. This is also a safety against screen direction issues you might have later while you are editing. Ideally these issues get worked out before you get to the set, but you want to make sure every set-up is usable. Remember the discussion of film syntax and visual grammar? You have to pay attention while you're shooting to make sure you have the elements you need to cut together a coherent visual sentence. "Make sure that the performer's eye line is always to the correct side of the camera, and make sure that the guy exits and leaves frame in the right direction," reminds Mike Dignum. "Make sure that if a band member's looking a someone [in close-up], he's looking the right way, and they're looking in the right direction back at him. Often people make a mistake and it looks quite funny when you see it on TV. Music videos very, very, very rarely have a script supervisor. So you're kind of filling in on that job, too. You're thrown into being in the script supervising position by being right next to the camera." Also, if you're integrating narrative or conceptual footage with performance footage, sometimes there is a really great performance moment in which your DP quickly panned the camera in one direction over the subject. You won't want to micro-manage the DP's hand-held camera moves, so if you catch your subjects moving in all possible directions, you'll have an easier time integrating spontaneous shots.

COVERAGE IS COLLECTING FOR THE EDITING ROOM

This coverage discussion may sound like a contradiction. It may be good for your development to work with constraints that force you to be economical with film stock, but by the time you get on the set, you want to shoot as much film as humanly possible. Think of the shoot as collecting for the editing room. Since you usually have only one shoot day, you've got to be shooting all the time — yet another example of how music video is sometimes more like photography than filmmaking. At a photo shoot, you find the location, style the band, then take as many shots as you can, searching for that perfect moment, the photograph that crystallizes the band's identity. Many music-video directors think about shooting film in the same way: Shoot continuously and editing becomes a process of finding those perfect moments that bring the band to life.

Now it's 4 A.M. and the last grip left hours ago. The PAs picked up the pizza boxes, took the band's beer cases to the Dumpster, and swept the location. You, your producer, and the DP sit on boxes, blowing into your hands on a cold set lit only by the DP's flashlight. You're all silent but pleased with a long day's work. Now you have to make the video.

chapter five

"Okay, I've set my in-point on the record deck. Now, I trim my in-point on the source deck back about three frames so I can get Peter to hit the snare. Preview. Okay, and . . . shit . . . this deck never gets it right. Peter isn't even playing that part of the song here. Okay, we're going to start all over again. I'll re-mark my ins and outs. Preview. Hey, why does it keep doing that!? That's not how I wanted it to . . . shit!"

It's apparent that you don't know what you're doing, and the editing system you're working on looks like something you rescued from your high school AV department. You thought your biggest challenge would be playing director on the set of your first video, but nothing could prepare you for the horror of editing a music video for the first time.

Who were you trying to kid? You're no editor. What's worse, the footage you're cutting, the only footage you will ever have, doesn't include some of the shots you dreamed up when you were writing your treatment and shot list.

editing >

Why didn't you get that shot of the guitar flipping through the air? Now there isn't enough material to cover the whole concept. How is it possible that you've worked all night and you've completed only the first ten seconds? You moan in agony as you watch that first ten seconds then the subsequent two minutes and forty-seven seconds of black, over and over again. How will you cut something that rocks? It's now a few days after the shoot and your friend the guitar player wants to see a rough cut already. You knew you should've gotten an editor to help you.

THE PLEASURE AND PAIN OF EDITING

Don't despair. Editing doesn't come easily, and unless you've had video-editing experience and know the equipment inside and out, editing a music video for the first time is going to be a long, slow process, which makes editing a lot like writing. (Remember writing your first treatment? The pacing back and forth? The endless trips to the boom box for one more listen?) When you're first cutting together shots — as when you first blast out a rough-draft treatment or story — your video looks terrible. It takes time to shape the sound and images into something recognizable, something that moves forward. When it begins to gel, however, nothing is more satisfying.

Old-school editors rhapsodize about the tactile pleasure of cutting on film. By holding the actual pieces of celluloid in their hands — instead of the alienating practice of pressing buttons on a video controller or key-stroking a computer — they can actually see and count the frames, which makes them feel at one with their work. I would argue that the sense of feeling at one with the project can be found in all editing, film or video. When you manipulate images, place characters and objects into brief windows of screen time, create editing illusions (these two people are in the same room, this object seems to be moving at a certain speed), you feel your project taking shape in your hands.

When I'm shuttling tapes back and forth, ejecting them and swapping them in and out of the playback decks, I feel plenty of tactile pleasure. These plastic casings hold my project, and nothing compares to the moment I hold a tape in my hand and say, "This is my rough cut." This feeling gets diluted somewhat when I edit on a computer, but if you don't edit your video at all, if you hand over your project to an editor, it literally feels *out of your hands*. I promise you will get a creative/productive rush while editing your own video.

Feeling that rush isn't the only reason you should edit your first video: editing teaches you to direct. In the editing room, you really understand the notion of coverage. You'll sit agonizing in front of the sad little editing system, wishing you had gotten another shot of the drummer playing a certain fill. "Why didn't we shoot that?" you'll wonder, then remember that getting thrown off your location ruined the plan. Then, even worse, you'll remember making a decision not to shoot the drummer because you wanted more of your narrative/conceptual footage. Most directors pride themselves on editing their first videos and consider the experience, no matter how painful, invaluable in learning how to plan a shoot. "Editing is the best way to learn what kind of coverage you need and what's really important," agrees Jesse Peretz. "You inevitably end up saying, 'I can't believe I always pan off the drummer when he goes into the drum roll because it seemed to make sense to go to the guitarist because the guitarist goes *rhoooommm.*' The next video, you remember to cut to the drum roll and like, oh my God, that rocks the song so much harder."

Sometimes editing represents the last hope for a badly bungled shoot. Editor Jonathan Horowitz speaks in a low whisper, taking long pauses between each word as he carefully considers the next. He adorns his skinny frame with bizarre clothes like a silver Caesar's Palace baseball cap and '70s-vintage boys' track shorts. Horowitz studied video art and cinema: When working with Horowitz in his tiny apartment on New York's Lower East Side, instead of the obligatory issues of *Spin,* I found old *ArtForum* magazines. He remembers a particularly impressive screw-up. "I once edited a video for a band called the Metal Church," he relates. "It was supposed to be a performance video. The record company had hired someone to do a three-camera shoot. They sent me the tapes and they were all black. The camera operator made a mistake and nothing was recorded. They needed a music video, so they just sent me every bit of video footage of the band that they had on VHS and 3/4" tapes. I managed to make something that more-or-less looked like a music video, faking synch. Because the image quality was so bad, we tried to make the footage look grainy by putting static into it, which didn't work very well. But we letterboxed it and had lyrics going across the screen. That was the worst footage that I ever had to work with."

Editing will teach you to have plenty of coverage in case something goes wrong with the footage. For example, when you realize that your only shot of the drummer hitting a cathartic cymbal crash is totally out of focus and unusable, you need to find something to put in its place. Instead of a performance shot to illustrate this moment, perhaps you find a shot of a slamming car door, or a foot pounding the pavement. If you planned ahead, you shot all kinds of percussive movements, if that's what the song demanded. A new understanding of how various images work with different sounds blossoms when you solve footage problems with editing — and even make the result suddenly seem musical.

Only by confronting the limitations you created for yourself will you understand the tactical errors you made on shoot day, a somewhat painful experience. Often what seemed so important to shoot while you were on location barely makes sense in the video, and you don't have enough of the best footage. "We should have gotten the performance shots earlier," you'll think to yourself. Major revelations — though we tried to warn you! — about how to direct a shoot day will come to you as you sort your footage for editing.

When you've watched your footage a million times, in reverse and slow motion, shuttled it back and forth and examined it frame-by-frame, you'll see how an activity "plays" on the screen. You'll get a sense of the rhythm and timing of movement and see what feels like a natural duration for an activity or the time it takes to get from point A to point B without seeming awkward. This newfound sense of rhythm will help you direct because, if you've been through the editing process once, you'll be forever conscious of how fast or slow your subjects move on the set. You'll modify the game of Simon Says to get the proper rhythm from your subjects.

The final argument for editing your own video: as a beginner, you're not subject to the routine creative decisions of the jaded editor. "Videos can definitely come together or not come together in the editing room," Spike Jonze declares. "The main thing is to find an editor with whom you share similar aesthetics and taste. If you don't, then you're always going to be going in different directions. The last thing you want is to have an editor whose opinions you don't trust making these decisions." Working with an editor, though, can also be a learning experience and can actually reveal aspects of your work that you hadn't seen.

"What I like to do is give an editor three or four days without me in the room at all to show me what he thinks is a really good cut," explains Kevin Kerslake. "Sometimes I will already have a preconception, and sometimes there's no other way to cut the film. At that point, at around four days, I'll basically step in and spend every waking hour in the editing room molding [the final cut]. I like to step in after the [editor's rough cut] assembly. [The rough cut] tends to exhaust the creative bone because at that point you're just trying to put shots together that work. The model for my relationship with an editor is something I took from Brian Eno, who once said about producing music, 'The best thing I can offer you (meaning the band) is how little I'm there.' What he offers to the music is a totally fresh perspective."

But now that you've dreamed your video into being and you've run the shoot and have the footage you need, you've done the hardest work. The technical aspects of editing aren't that hard to learn, so we say do it yourself. You'll have plenty of time later to learn from the masters.

Before you start giving the images life with editing, you complete a process that is pure music-video magic: putting your film image on videotape. As with other media, the evolution of music video coincides with the evolution of specific technology, in this case, film-to-tape transfer, or telecine. Originally, to get a film negative on tape, a device called a film chain projected the film image directly into a special video camera. Now, special flying-spot-scanner cameras capture the film image through special color receptors and lay it directly onto videotape without "flagging" or those trails you sometimes see when a video image records something bright. Digital controllers for these scanners can manipulate the film image in countless ways: On some machines the frame-per-second rate ranges from 2 to 90, which enables you to create extreme fast or slow motion. Color, contrast and brightness can also be finely controlled.

Creative use of this transfer process is what sets music videos apart from the naturalistic look of prime-time dramas or feature films. Have you ever seen a video and wondered, "How did they get it to look like that? Did they process the film strangely? Did they use a weird film stock?" Sometimes they did both of those things, but often telecine created the look of the video, manipulated by an engineer, or "colorist," who makes a living by creating new looks.

PROCESSING

Before you get to play in the telecine bay, you have to pick up your film. As with all stages of post-production, don't get caught up in a feeling of post-shoot euphoria that makes you feel like everything's done. Until you're sitting in the on-line editing suite, you have as much, if not more, work to do than when you started. Like all good low-budget video directors, I've had my moments clutching the exposed negative to my chest as I waited on a subway platform for the train uptown to the lab. The film negative is priceless until it's transferred onto video. Keep it by your side at all times and away from heat or light. It shouldn't be a problem, unless you're neurotic and keep calling the lab . . .

Remember the logistical nightmares Mott and I experienced on the Helium video? A true bonding experience, the shoot was incredibly wacky and too ambitious, but we got it done. In the car driving back from Boston to New York, however, we barely spoke to one another. We didn't say five sentences during the five-hour drive. What happened? Were we so emotionally drained from the harrowing shoot experience that words failed us? No, Mott had spoken to the lab that morning. They said we had a "high level of base fog" over the entire negative.

I remember precisely when Mott dropped this bomb. It was unfathomable. After all of the struggles finding the location, the crew, on-set electricity, now this? Freezing, I paced the length of the porch at the house in Cambridge where Mott was staying. I puffed rapidly dissipating little clouds into the winter air like exhaust from a wheezing old car. "What does that mean?" I panted, panicking. "Does this mean the footage is unusable?" All those folks who worked for free. All that heartache. Five thousand dollars of the record company's money.

"I don't know what it means!" Mott puffed back. For all his bravado on the shoot, I could tell that Mott didn't press the lab technicians when he talked to them. He didn't want to know, couldn't think the unthinkable. "I don't know if it's usable. They said it was all about thirty percent fogged. Could be the result of a light leak or the film being exposed to heat. They said that what's there will look pretty orange."

"What's there!?"

When he was a production assistant on *Saturday Night Live* in the mid-'80s, the producers gave Mott a case of unused Kodak 7298 film stock as a bonus. It stayed stashed in the bottom of a closet in Mott's East Village apartment for seven years — not the climate-controlled storage facility that Kodak prefers to see for its products. Occasionally, Mott would dip into this stash to supplement stock on a student film he was shooting. While we were prepping the Helium video, I found it and thought, "Yes! Free film stock. Perfect!" In a moment of cost-cutting craziness, Mott and I decided to shoot on this vintage stock. Though potentially not as dicey as recans, this film was old, while recans are usually gleaned from a shoot that took place a week before. I wouldn't advise taking a risk like that, no matter how little money you have. But what's truly pathetic is that this film stash of Mott's became like a drug for us. We kept saying, "Never again," but I think we used it for at least two other videos after the Helium experience.

The "high level of base fog" was like having light spill over the entire image. Ultimately, I wished Mott hadn't called the lab because the level of fogginess was out of our control. The lab can give you a pretty good sense of the quality of your footage based on a chart, or "timing numbers" that come with the negative. For a color stock, the numbers tell you the levels of magenta, cyan and yellow you have on the negative. If you have around thirty percent of each, that's good news. Needless to say, the numbers for the Helium negative were way off.

LABS

In New York, Los Angeles, and Chicago, the film labs process prints of the movies you see in multiplexes as well as your low-budget rock video. The big labs are scary for little projects. I always get paranoid that among big jobs for Paramount, Universal, or Miramax, my little rock video for Burning Bridges Productions will get lost — another strong argument for affiliating with a production company. If your project goes into the lab under the name of a production company that works frequently at that particular lab, it's easier to deal with the salespeople. For example, they know how much to bill for the job because the big company's account information is readily available. I also found that billing to a big account alleviated my lost negative paranoia.

If you're in a smaller city, you want to use big-city labs because of their quality control and turnaround. If you're in Boston, for example, you want to ship your film to New York, and DuArt has it's own delivery service. If you're in a more remote place, FedEx the film to the lab. Make sure you have some work orders from the lab so you can send those with the film. Stay on top of the lab: Call them to make sure they got your film and check on their delivery schedule. Exposed film is incredibly vulnerable — don't hang on to it. Guard it with your life, protect it from heat, and get it to the lab soon after the shoot.

For the most part, salespeople at the labs treat your project, no matter the size, with respect and will tolerate you as you learn the process — and some sterling individuals will even dispense priceless advice and counsel. Keeping their clients up-to-date on technological developments with stocks and processing, advising on procedure and making recommendation on timing and exposure is part of their job and a function they perform for postproduction supervisors even on big-budget features. Be aware that labs in the major motion-picture production centers of New York and Los Angeles have busy seasons. Two or three months

GETTING STARTED: KEVIN KERSLAKE

"One of the reasons I got into [music videos] was photography. When you print your own stuff, you're dealing with it. You get your hands dirty, your body nice and sick from the chemicals. With film, it's easy to get far away from that because you send the film to a lab, which is sort of like sending it to the bank. It's an institution. As a photographer, you need that regular rapport with the materials. There's so much stuff you can do to work [with music videos] on that level, like hand-processing your film in your own bathtub, sending film through chemicals it has no business being in, for example, cross-processing Ektachrome, which is a reversal film, by sending it through the same process you would send negative film through. And vice versa. Experimenting with printing techniques, like multiple-stage printing and whatnot. Scratching film, melting film, putting it in the oven. Keeping it close to the engine of your car for a few months. You've got to show film who's boss. "

<<<

>>>

prior to the Sundance Festival in January and the Cannes Festival in May they invariably get backed up as they deal with the flood of features large and small that vie for attention at these increasingly busy film markets. If you have a tight deadline during these windows, ask repeatedly about the lab's schedule and if they're experiencing delays.

If you're shooting black-and-white, or doing any creative processing, you won't necessarily want to use the big labs. They run baths for black-and-white film only once every other day in some cases, and the quality isn't up to the standard of a place that specializes in black-and-white. In the U.S., that means Alpha Cine in Seattle — everyone sends their black-and-white negative there. Even adding on shipping time, they usually have a faster turnaround than if you were in New York and brought your black-and-white neg across town. And Alpha Cine does good work.

When you're working with a big lab, always ask for a student discount. You're going to end up paying 12 to 14 cents per foot for processing, but you might get 20 percent off if you ask for that discount. If you shoot five to six 400' rolls of 16mm — about an hour of screen time at 24 frames per second — you'll spend around $300 for processing. To prepare your negative for telecine, however, labs add costs for cleaning, attaching leader, and splicing the rolls together in 1200' reels. This runs you an additional $30 a roll. For some reason, processing costs always seem surprisingly low to me. I always think that processing will add another thousand dollars to the budget, but I always end up spending $500 or $600. The simple, conservative, rounded-up rule of thumb for stock purchase/processing: around 200 bucks for each 400' of film. That's $200 to purchase, process and prep 400' of 16mm film for telecine — and that's conservative.

When you fill out your work order, remember to write "process normal," and "prep for telecine." If you're not processing "normally," meaning you want to do something unique to the chemical composition of the processing bath, or you want to have the negative "pushed" a stop, which means you want to increase the light exposure on the negative by increasing the processing time, you have to specifically indicate this on the job order. Hopefully you've had someone fill out camera reports for every roll of film, and you should include those with the work orders from the labs. Consider your decision to push the film carefully. Remember, if you're making up for the sins of a few underexposed shots on a roll with many other properly exposed ones, all shots on the roll will be effected by the pushing process. Also, the resulting image will be more grainy and contrasty. Most stock can only be pushed two stops before it looks terrible. If it's only a question of a few stops, consider repairing those few botched shots in telecine.

Processing can be put to creative uses. Many directors, including Kevin Kerslake and Dean Carr, experiment with chemical formulas to enhance the contrast or the color of their negative. Certain directors use obscure specialty labs that will try arcane formulations for them, and these directors keep their favorites a deep, dark secret. A few mad-scientist directors take the secret-formula routine to its logical conclusion and use their own bathtubs for processing. Kerslake has turned chemistry into a strikingly original body of work. "It's pretty reckless how I approach a lot of the experimentation [in processing], just because there's not enough time to test," he says. "I want to be surprised, too. Sometimes I don't even know what I'm going to get in the telecine. Ninety-nine percent of the time — having done all the second-guessing of how the film is going to react to a certain light or certain chemicals, or missing a process in the development, or doubling up on another one — you can gauge within a safe measure how the film is going to react.

Foto-Kem/Foto-Tronics
2800 W. Olive Avenue
Burbank, CA 91505
(818) 846-3102
35mm: CN, BWN, CP, BWP
16mm: CN, BWN, CP, BWP
S-16mm: CN

Four Media Laboratory
3611 N. San Fernando
Burbank, CA 91505
(818) 841-3812
35mm: CN, BWN, CP, BWP
16mm: CN, CP, BWP
S-16mm: CN

Super 8 Sound
2805 W. Magnolia Blvd.
Burbank, CA 91505
(818) 848-5522
S8mm: BW, C

Technicolor, Inc., L.A.
4050 Lankershim Blvd.
North Hollywood, CA 91608
(818) 769-8500
35mm: CN, BWN, CP, BWP
16mm: CP

Technicolor, Inc., N.Y.
321 W. 44th Street
New York, NY 10036
(212) 582-7310
35mm: CN, BWN, CP, BWP
16mm: CN, CP

Western Cine Film Lab
312 S. Pearl Street
Denver, CO 80209
(303) 744-1017
35mm: CN, BWN, CP, BWP
16mm: CN, BWN, CP, BWP
S-16mm: CN, BWN

<<<

LAB FORMS FROM DUART

You know you're going to get something. It's just play, trying to take a little detour, and there's no great philosophy behind it. I'm eager to see new things on film, and how film reacts. Sometimes I've called my producer saying, 'Do I have any time to . . .', and they reply, 'Nope, it's already gone through the bath.' And I know I'm fucked. I don't sleep well that night. I know that I've just foolishly gone down the wrong road. Then, 'Ahhh, that looks great.' I've been really lucky, really, really lucky with that. One of the reasons is that you just cover your ass, you shoot more than you need to because — especially with some of the processes I use — you are deliberately destroying twenty or thirty percent of what you shoot. What you're going to use are the points where the image recedes or appears out of the burnt-out film, before it fades back into whiteness. That's the moment that you're dealing with now.

You're not dealing with the performance, you're dealing with a filmic transition." Now you know that processing can be more than popping your film in the mailer and shipping it off. Lab work can be another tool, and an interesting one because it relies on chance and experimentation when so much of filmmaking needs planning and preparation.

TELECINE

The telecine transfer session for the foggy Helium video was only my third. It was scheduled for 9 A.M. on a wintry morning, certainly a first since we could usually only book sessions in the middle of the night. I remember once scheduling time at a postproduction house in New York that gave us an impossibly low rate of $175 per hour. The colorist was an older gentleman who might have been more comfortable with Tommy Dorsey, but the footage we were transferring was pretty straightforward. For some reason, probably poor planning on my part, we had to transfer the footage in two separate one-and-a-half-hour sessions. We did one of them on a Tuesday night, and the other was scheduled for later in the week, Thursday or Friday. When I called to confirm that second session, the salesperson explained to me that "The people from L.A. came and shut us down." Between my two sessions, this place had gone out of business. At least I got a bargain on the first session.

> **STOCK AND PROCESSING RULE OF THUMB:**
>
> You'll spend around $200 for each 400 ft. of film for stock and processing.

On that cold day, when the first image of Helium's Mary Timony came up on the screen, Mott and I gasped. She looked like one of those prehistoric mosquitoes preserved in amber. The entire image was orange. "Yeah, when the lab said you had a high level of base fog on this negative, they weren't kidding," chirped the nonplussed colorist. Base fog seemed to be the only thing on anyone's mind, and I flinched every time I heard the words.

Minutes after our initial despair, a remarkable thing happened. With a perfunctory twist of a wrist, literally a flip of a switch, the image looked normal. Well, almost normal. With its warm, golden haze, the footage looked something like a slightly faded Kodachrome snapshot remembered from childhood — which was great. These are the moments when you enlist in the rationalization squad, proclaiming, "Hey, we planned it that way." To this day, I worship the gods of telecine. Later in the session, as we were ruminating about the particular color of Mary's cheeks, I couldn't help reminding myself how wonderful it was to be able to use this footage at all. When production goofballs make the tired

"We'll fix it in post" comment, they're referring to telecine and moments like this.

Mott, though, perhaps because it offends his sense of craftsmanship, doesn't encourage directors to rely on telecine for the big fix. "To depend on telecine in any way, or to depend on video-generated slow motion or fast motion [as opposed to film that was exposed fast or slow], is a huge mistake. The slow motion looks crappy. And if the girl in the video is wearing a red shirt, and you want it to be brighter, you can make it brighter [in telecine], but it will also make her lips brighter, the lines in her eyes brighter, the red tints in her hair brighter, and the red in the car across the street brighter, everything will start to look fake. What you can do on the set, you should do on the set. I think that it's a big mistake to think everything is going to be fine in post."

Technical aspects aside, the nice thing about going to a film-to-tape transfer session is that it's the one part of the low-budget video process that makes you feel like a human being. And you don't have the option of cheaping out. You must go to a fancy postproduction facility, and most of the machines don't exist outside of New York, Chicago or L.A. Though you can't skimp on this part of the process, there are perks. You're no different than the client down the hall who's spending fifty thousand a week. Since it's a competitive market, these places want your business, and theoretically, even if you're doing a $5,000 video today, you might be back with a big-budget job later. Transfer facilities have client services, which means that while you sit comfortably on a big, inevitably leather couch behind the colorist who faces several large TV screens, you can order up cappuccinos and fizzy water. It's like room service: There are bowls of candy, and, right next to the couch, refrigerators sit stocked with sodas.

When you do a real-budget job, the film-to-tape session becomes less fun because of the record company personnel and band management in attendance, but the food gets better and better. When there's money at stake, the record label's video commissioner looks over your shoulder during the whole session, but they often bring a bottle of wine. Remember to book your session around dinnertime or lunchtime, because that means a free meal from the postproduction house's in-house caterer, and they can be quite good. I remember trying to appear nonchalant about eating during transfer sessions and secretly wondering if I could sneak doggy bags under my coat because I hadn't had a meal that good in days.

COLOR THEORY

To prepare yourself to speak the colorist's language, brush up on your knowledge of color photography and color theory. There are the additive primary colors: blue, green and red.

Think of these colors as "additive" because if separate light beams of each shone together — if blue, green and red are "added" together — the result is a single white light: blue + green + red = white. Combining just two of these primary colors at a time yields three new colors called subtractive primary colors: blue + green = cyan; blue + red = magenta; and red + green = yellow. It's easy to think of these as subtractive because one of these colors forms when one of the primary colors is subtracted from white light. For example, magenta is blue plus red, or white minus green.

Each of these subtractive primaries is also a complementary color to an additive primary. When the complementary color is added to its additive primary, the result is white. Since cyan = blue + green, or white − red, cyan is the complementary color to red. Cyan + red = white. It follows that since magenta = red + blue, or white − green, magenta + green = white. Magenta complements green. Yellow = red + green, or white − blue, so yellow + blue = white. Yellow complements blue.

This notion of complementary colors is important to understand for telecine. When your image looks too green, for example, tell the colorist that you want to "dial in" more magenta, and what was greenish in your image will go toward white. If everything looks too red, tell the colorist to dial in more cyan. In general, you should be comfortable with knowing what color added to what color equals what. Color receptors in the scanners (depending on the machine) can control levels of all six additive and subtractive primary colors. As a music-video director, your grasp of color theory should be better than a feature filmmaker. Timing an answer print for a movie isn't usually as involved or creative a process as tweaking colors for a music video in a telecine session.

For example, you can desaturate the colors so the footage becomes black-and-white, or dial in color to black-and-white stock. Think of all the videos you see that are monochromatic, sepia-toned or cobalt-toned black-and-white: Most were created in telecine. And color isn't the only element you can manipulate. You can defocus a shot, stretch it, flip it, shrink it, enlarge it, speed it up and slow it down. Certain frame rates give you classic music-video effects. If you shoot at six frames a second and then transfer at six frames a second, you get a

COLOR RELATIONSHIPS

Primary additive colors
blue+green+red = white

Subtractive primary colors
blue+green = cyan
blue+red = magenta
red+green = yellow

Complementary colors
cyan > red
yellow > blue
magenta > green

THE "LOOKS"

Grainy

Means what it says. The film negative is made up of "grain," little particles of silver oxide that comprise the film image. When an image is grainy, the larger grain structure creates a less sharp image. You can see the grains of silver in low-light situations, and with the fast stocks (higher ASAs) that are appropriate for low-light situations. To the visually literate, a grainy look suggests home movies, low-budget independents or documentary films, because the result indicates production circumstances in which you couldn't afford lights.

Clean, sharp, or slick

The opposite of grainy, a sharp, clear image denotes money and production value. Creating a sharp image indicates the equipment you used, the quality of the lenses you had, and the expense of your telecine suite. "Slick," however, doesn't always mean sharp focus. One of the classic telecine tricks used in many slick videos is transferring the film twice, particularly popular in R&B videos. First the film is transferred normally or with attention to bringing out detail. During the next pass, the image is defocused and the whites are "blown-out," which exaggerates the highlights on the image and everything else becomes out of focus. When you defocus an image in the telecine process, it doesn't look like the usual out-of-focus film: There is a uniformity to the out-of-focusness. Before the video is edited, these two

>>>

very popular if overused effect in which a blurry trail follows everything that moves in your frame. And it's low-budget video friendly: At six frames a second, you shoot one quarter of the footage you'd normally use, and the slow frame rate allows so much light into the camera that you never have to augment the natural light. Six-frame shooting for action sequences looks cheesy, but compelling in a retro-'80s way.

The image quality can also be manipulated. A colorist can bring out the grain structure of the film, amplifying the graininess or sharpening the image. The colorist can control the contrast, the difference between the darkest part of the image and the lightest. In a high-contrast image, the blacks can be "crushed" to the point that you see no detail in them, yielding an image that looks more like a weird lithograph than a motion picture. All the definition within the blacks found in a low-contrast image can be pulled out. More advanced techniques in telecine involve special filtration. For example, you can insert diffusion filters into the gate that holds the film in front of the scanner. In fact, you can insert all kinds of foreign objects — plastic sheets, paper, water bottles — into the gate.

Spike Jonze has good advice for the first-timer: "In telecine, it's good to bring in photo references. If you shot something and you know you want low-contrast, soft colors, try to get photos that look like that. If you want it to be contrasty black-and-white, try to bring a photo like that because it's hard to describe those things in words. I've worked with the same guy for a long time, so it's easy now. If you've never done it before, you don't know what 'warmer' or 'cooler' means, or 'flatter,' or 'blow the whites out,' 'crush the blacks,' or what all the terms are. You learn that the more you do it, but the more specific references you have, the closer it's going to get."

Everybody runs into a situation that has to be fixed

in the telecine session, but most directors will tell you that they go into the session with the best-looking footage they can possibly achieve and use the telecine only to create effects that add a big visual payoff. As Nancy Bennett says, "I don't want to rely on gags to know my stuff is going to look good." But Darren Doane thinks about telecine as soon as he walks onto the set. "Always. Every video," he declares. "When I start a video, I start thinking immediately how telecine is going to affect the project."

BOND WITH THE COLORIST

To be able to explore the range of options available, you have to bond with the colorist. Remember, colorists spend most of their week working with elegant but boring and demanding advertising clients who obsess over every aspect of the image. You're a refreshing change of pace, especially if it's just you and your DP in the transfer session. They don't have to deal with a crew of producers and clients, and they'll see the session with you as an opportunity to play, to try out new looks they haven't used before.

Engage the colorist in what you're doing. There's nothing worse than a session with a colorist who stays on the phone with his girlfriend the whole time. You can sense right away when you walk into the room if you're going to get along with the colorist or not. Make them laugh and tell them funny stories about your pathetically low-budget shoot. Flatter their intelligence by asking questions about film stocks and equipment. If they don't watch MTV and think your footage is a joke because you didn't light anything, or they're rigidly bound to broadcast engineering specifications, you can be in trouble. In a bad situation, there's inevitable and boring conflict over the amount of red in your image, for example. They'll point to their vector scope — a machine that monitors color in the frame — and

images are married and the effect is incredibly slick. The darker parts of the image retain sharp detail, but the highlights in the image seem to glow with an out-of-focus halo. It recalls the soft-focus, soft-core photography of David Hamilton.

Saturated colors

Saturated colors can mean many things, but the term generally refers to their intensity and richness. This is the opposite of saying the video has "desaturated," intentionally faded colors.

Crushed blacks

When the blacks are crushed, they lose detail. Dark areas in the image "crush" together to form large swaths of deep shadow.

The clean, well-exposed, in-focus look has made a resurgence recently after years of video obfuscation. A&R people have told us that out-of-focus is out; clean and simple looks good right now.

say, "Your red is way off the map here, buddy, it doesn't meet broadcast specifications." Too much of a certain color, especially red, can distort the image, and the more rigid telecine engineers act like television stations won't broadcast it because the folks at home might see their television sets blow up. Sometimes colorists just want to be difficult, see if you know anything, or are too lazy to work with you on your low-profile project.

"With everybody I work with, even on the crew, the primary step for me is to feel somebody out to see what they're capable of, in order to have a blind faith that they are going to rock my world," says Kerslake. "And I treat everybody as if they have the goods to offer. With colorists, it's a really funny thing because you're coming in with footage that is obviously sacred to you, and it's difficult to communicate your palate. Color affects everyone in different ways: It's just like finding a mate. The best way for me to find out if someone has a feel is to go in and let them do it, without me saying anything, and see where they end up. That's a really critical phase. I've only become comfortable with two people, out of thirty or so, because they have had the same critical nature as I have. You're basically asking somebody to paint for you, but you're standing right beside the canvas, saying, 'A little more green here, a little darker there,' and it takes a lot of finessing. It's a funny relationship."

As with directing a crew of experienced technicians on set, the most important things to remember when working with a colorist is to be straightforward, friendly and know what you want. If it's your first time, it's a good idea to bring videotapes of other music videos or commercials that you like so you can use them as a frame of reference for your footage. If you have questions, talk to the colorist on the phone with your DP before the shoot. Tell him or her the look you want to get, and ask for suggestions on how you should shoot to make it happen in telecine. This will be flattering and they might take more of an interest in your project. Telecine artists hate to think of their job as just saving bad footage, and they truly are best used to enhance a video, adding their own talents. "As soon as I get a color set," offers Julie Hermelin, "I always ask my colorist to show me something completely different. They're creative, too. This is what they do all day long, every day. They must know their equipment. They're like a DP; they're like an art director. They are a valuable part of the process, the colorist."

In the best possible scenario, the post house will let you spend fifteen minutes watching what their machines can do before you actually work on them. This is difficult, and sometimes you have to convince the sales rep at the company that you are going to be a big client. Luckily, sales reps, colorists and online editors pride themselves in providing good service. Charm these folks with your enthusiasm. No matter what, it's a good idea to sit in on a telecine session before you do one yourself, so ask other production people if you can sit in on an upcoming session of theirs.

Whether or not you see telecine magic at work before your project, it's important to learn the visual vocabulary of the system right away. Though the colorist will probably suggest it anyway, ask them to bring up an image on which you can start to work. This should be a representative shot, something that you had time to light. If you're making a performance video, this shot should be a master shot in which you see all members of the band. If you envision many different looks, for instance, different looks for the performance versus the conceptual footage, establish those looks quickly, because time is your biggest concern. With $400 per hour telecine fees eating into your $5,000 budget, you don't want to be wasting time. Get the fiddling around out of the way before you start rolling tape or laying down your material.

When you begin to lay the material onto tape, pretend you're directing the video all over again. Watch the footage carefully. Even though he/she is a million more times experienced than you are, make sure that the colorist is aware of slight fluctuations in the image. You don't want the bass player to look pink in one shot, then orange in the next. Also, think about a new level of coverage. If a shot you're watching on the screen looks terrible — the action is unclear, the composition is lousy, the angle isn't dynamic, something is in the frame that shouldn't be, the subjects are moving too slow or too fast — stop everything and try to fix it. If you didn't get the proper coverage of an action during the shoot, you can make up for it in telecine. For example, run the shot in reverse or zoom in so it looks like it was shot from another angle. As much as you want to sit back and enjoy watching the images you created, you have to pay close attention.

TELECINE TRICKS

Here's some telecine advice, courtesy of Nancy Bennett:

"There are certain effects that telecine can put in the film. One of them is D FX, which is amazing. It gives you that defocused edge that adds luminance and softness of skin. It's a beautiful look and very popular. Some very typical music-video guys stick lens tissue or cellophane or wax paper in the Rank [telecine]. But I think if you don't have a lot of money to spend in telecine you don't want to screw around with that stuff too much. I think you want to go in there with good, clean film that's really well exposed and focused."

<<<

More often than not, you don't enjoy watching the images as they fly by. Shots you thought would be genius look totally ridiculous, while other shots simply don't work: "What do you mean you forgot to turn the camera on?" Do not become morose in telecine. To avoid the inevitable telecine depression, bring a tape of the song with you to the session, even if you are transferring MOS (without synch). There's nothing worse than giving the colorist the opportunity to listen to their own music while they're transferring your job. When they ask, "You don't mind if we listen to . . . ?" it's simply bad karma to say "Yes, I do" but I remember enduring classic-rock radio when we were transferring the foggy Helium video. It made me even more depressed. When you have a smart slate and synchronized playback, the machines automatically synch each shot to the DAT tape. Watching synchronized footage is more fun, because you get to see which performance takes are usable, but it adds hours to your session. When the colorist sees the slate numbers on screen, she punches those numbers into a computer that controls the video and audio machines. Both the film and the audio are rewound to a precise moment when they are in synch. Even though this is a fully automated process, all of this rewinding takes time. You'll spend many more hours syching up the footage yourself, but it's cheaper.

THERE'S A REASON THEY CALL IT VIDEO

Because they're almost all shot on film, the "video" in music video gets added in the post-production process. Many of the first music videos were actually shot on video, but one constant remains: video editing. All those quick "flutter cuts," shots of only one, two, three frames, would be too labor-intensive for celluloid. Video editing allowed a particular editing style to evolve, a style that became inextricably bound to the audience's impression of music video. The audience demonstrates an ever-increasing agility with visual material, an agility that moves in lock-step with technology's ever-increasing ability to cram more images into every moment of screen time.

Once there were lefty, progressive connotations to the word "video." Local cable-access channels were going to take television production away from the big corporate networks and bring it onto the street with the people. We were going to be a real television democracy, surrounded by grassroots guerrilla documentary videos. In the mid- to late-'70s, video held the space in our culture now occupied by the Internet. In this spirit, my parents enrolled me in a video workshop with a hippie woman who lived in a downtown Manhattan loft filled with decoupage. Come to think about it, is there anything more '70s than a video workshop? I was in third grade. Along with the other third-graders, I would come up with goofy little scenarios, and she would videotape them. I'd like to believe that we learned something about the equipment, but I can't really remember it. I can see the clunky reel-to-reel video machine with orange-brown panels. During a hide-and-seek scenario, I ran into a closet and found a naked man sitting cross-legged. This I remember.

When I got to high school, I took another video class and worked again with reel-to-reel videotape. The first piece I ever cut on video, my own little music video for my favorite rock band, Mission of Burma's song "Learn How," was edited on reel-to-reel decks. I shot lots of wheelchair tracking shots of classroom seats ominously moving by the camera. With the experience I have now, nothing seems more primitive than the physical process of editing on those reel-to-reel decks. To make a proper edit — and there was really no such thing because each cut produced a glitch — both reels had to be held in place while the machine tugged at them. At the right moment, after all sorts of grinding noises, the reels had to be let go.

ANALOG EDITING

Our hazy nostalgia for reel-to-reel video must mirror how folks who are accustomed to editing digitally (by computer) feel about "analog" editing. Rapidly becoming outmoded by computer editing, analog editing actually requires using videotape. With 3/4" U-matic video-cassette tapes as submasters (copies of the Beta or D2 tapes you transferred your negative to in telecine), you record your shots from the playback deck onto a tape in the record deck.

These 3/4" tapes are called "window dubs" because you lay down "vis code," or visible time code on them. Time code is information encoded on a videotape that functions like a running counter number. It clocks the hours, minutes, seconds and frames of your video. Time code becomes crucial in your on-line edit when computer controllers put together a final version of your video based on your off-line rough cut. Computers and video controllers can read time code and cue up video machines to a particular frame. On your master tapes, the time code is only read by machines — you can't see it. Your off-line edit tapes, or window dubs, don't have time code encoded on them, but the window displays time-code numbers that correspond to the masters.

You can strike these window dubs from the masters either in the telecine session while the masters are being created or, and this is the low-budget option since post houses charge upwards of $25 for a 3/4" dub, you can have them made at a special dubbing facility. In New York I always had my dubs made at a place called PDQ, where a friend of mine had an account. The place dripped with New York atmosphere, run by old garment district–style Jewish men and staffed by young African American homeboys. Having the dubs made there meant that I had to make another trip, and that I couldn't start editing right after the telecine, but I was saving about ten bucks a tape for dubbing. In either case, when you're doing a tape-to-tape edit, make sure that your window dubs are only 30 minutes long. Longer tapes mean you'll spend more time shuttling back-and-forth finding shots.

The relatively terrible aspect of tape-to-tape editing: You spend a lot of time fast-forwarding and rewinding. You'll do this with an editing controller, which synchs up your two video decks so that the edit occurs at the proper points. The simplest, and most ubiquitous, are the Sony RM440s and RM450s. These controllers were designed so that broadcast news crews in the field could quickly cut together stories for news broadcasts. They're straight-forward: You set in-points for the record deck and for the playback deck, preview the cut, and after trimming a few frames here and there, you perform the edit. Anyone with a basic understanding of editing would immediately understand how to use these controllers without recourse to a manual.

But you need to grasp the concept of insert and assembly editing. The RM440, or any equivalent controller, will allow you to cut in either assemble or insert mode. In assemble-edit mode, you cut your piece together by adding each shot onto the end of the previous one sequentially, like a row of bricks being laid down. Insert editing mode allows you to insert one shot into the middle of another. Whatever you do, don't make the mistake of trying to cut your video in assemble mode. A music video is an exercise in insert editing. After all, you are inserting shots right on top of one long shot that has no image but contains all of the sound for your piece: your audio master.

When you're making a real-budget video, a record company generally supplies an "audio package" to you before you shoot. It contains a DAT and/or a 1/2" audiotape reel of the song, as well as a master tape that's either Beta or D2 (whatever format they choose) along with a 3/4" window dub of that master. This ensures that the audio on the video you deliver them is a non-tampered-with version of the song. When you're making a low-budget video, you inevitably have to make your own master tape and a dub. Do this before you shoot. Even if you're just recording from a CD, have it done right. Have the place that's doing the dub make the tape black, with nothing but a window burn-in of the time code. The master tape itself should have vis code, so that the on-line editor can clearly see the first frame of the song. You're only going to cover this tape with images later. Have them generate the time code so that the first moment of the song starts at hour one on the nose, or 01:00:00:00. This lets the on-line computers know exactly where your video begins. Often, when an engineer sees that he has to dub audio from a sad little punk-rock CD on an indie label, he won't bother to do the job precisely, and the song will start "around" the one-hour mark. Make sure that they take this job seriously because it will cause headaches later if it's not done right.

So, with your 3/4" videotape dub of the audio master and your other 3/4" dubs of the master footage, you have at least three or four tapes to keep inserting and ejecting from the machines, which means you have a lot of fast forwarding and rewinding to do when you're editing tape-to-tape. Write thorough logs when you edit tape-to-tape with the complete time-code number and everything that's going on in the shot. As we'll discuss later, even slight camera moves are worth noting. Know your master footage inside and out, so that you aren't wasting time shuttling through entire half-hour tapes only to discover the shot you wanted on another tape.

DIGITAL EDITING

Most videotape, like most audiotape, is analog. This means that videotape records a waveform signal that gets electronically imprinted on the tape, maintaining the shape of the original waveform signal, the electronic reverberations of your sound and image. The ribbon of tape rolls by a magnetic record head, and, as time passes in front of the camera or microphone, the equivalent amount of time passes on the rolling tape. To understand this concept, conjure up the mental image of a lie detector test's scrolling paper that records all the fluctuations of the subject's responses as they're asked questions. Film is an analog format: The recording medium, the film stock, makes a representation of the light and shadow that the lens imprinted on it.

In a digital format, the signal gets broken down into a binary system — 1s and 0s — and imprinted on the tape with electronic pulses. Digital audio tape (DAT), and digital videotape formats (DigiBeta, and D2) rely on a time-space continuum, as analog does, but the digital signal can be stored in much less space. And it's not making a representation of the image or waveform, it's creating a series of 1s and 0s. The greatest advantage to any digital format is that the information on digital tapes and disks retains its integrity as it is copied. If you dub an analog videotape to another analog videotape, you lose a "generation," or, as video eningeers and TV producers say, "go down a G," with slightly faded colors and less-clear sound. This doesn't happen with digital formats. If you dub one digital tape to another, then that tape to another, and you do that a thousand times, the last tape has the same quality as the first tape.

The first wave of digital, or "nonlinear" editing systems — Montage, Ediflex, Editroid, Touch Vision, and the CMX 6000 — came on the scene in the mid- to late-'80s. Now, everyone working professionally in television and most film folks use digital systems. For the last decade, people have referred to digital editing as "nonlinear," but, as the guidebook to the most popular off-line digital editing system, the Avid, points out, "the process itself is nothing new to film. Film editors have always had the ability to launch into a project at any point, move whole sections and insert shots at will." Strictly speaking, nonlinear editing means that you don't have to cut your show in order.

When you cut digitally, you're never really "recording" anything as all of your cuts are virtual — they happen only in the memory of the computer, where they can be saved, deleted, and recalled at will. After you insert that shot, you can easily access the shot that you just recorded over. Well, isn't that just like the "preview" button on a tape-to-tape controller? There's no comparison. Editing digitally is like working with an endless chain of preview edits where nothing is permanent. You can remove or add shots without making holes or messing up your edit. On a digital editing system, one can undo commands with the stroke of a key, just as one would select the "undo typing" command to correct a mistake while using a word processing program.

What gets referred to as the Avid is really a series of Macintosh-compatible software systems. The primary tool of the Avid system is a software program called the Media Composer. No other digital-editing system has been as successful, but there are other Mac-compatible systems like MC Express and the Media 100 that are a little less expensive, and there are now all kinds of new systems like Draco and Trinity that seek to challenge the established systems. The PC-compatible versions, like D-Vision and Lightworks (the latter being the most popular digital-editing system for feature films), all share the benefits of working with randomly accessible footage.

What makes Avid and the other digital editing systems truly nonlinear is that your material can be randomly accessed — there's no need to fast-forward or rewind. Once your source material is stored on the Avid disks, it can be retrieved like tracks on a CD or frames on a laser disk. This makes digital editing much faster than analog editing. But that time saved in the actual editing can be used up by the preparation for digitally cutting a video.

In order to edit digitally, you must transfer your analog tape to a digital format and digitally store the video signal on a computer hard drive before you can use the computer to edit. This conversion of your videotapes into a digital format called, not surprisingly, "digitizing," takes time, but it changes your editing process itself. To digitize, you play your footage from the telecine session back on a videotape deck that feeds into the computer. However, you should babysit the computer. This radically changes your logging process. The software of an Avid, for example, is designed to force you to log and organize your footage as you digitize.

THE AVID SYSTEM OF YOUR DREAMS

Since all of your material is digitized, or converted from video information into digital information, it can now be randomly accessed. This means no more fast-forwarding or rewinding, but it also means that you have to have an entry or a "clip name" for every moment you want to use in order to randomly access a specific moment. In effect, you edit before you start editing. Since you have to type a name for each moment, you only pull "selects," or the best moments that you think you are going to use. You create "bins," which are the equivalent of folders in Macintosh programs, in which you can put together different types of footage.

The Avid seems designed for music-video editing. There's a function that gangs together shots if they're all time-coded. Say, for instance, you have close-ups of each band member playing the entire song from start to finish. You can gang these shots together so that they all run simultaneously. You look at each shot simply by dragging down a menu at the top of your screen. In this way, your editing can be like directing a multicamera shoot. Line up all these different angles and you can see what's happening in each one whenever you feel like it. This kind of luxury you can't even imagine while doing a tape-to-tape edit.

The Avid is also fairly easy to learn. With near-universal access to computers, the act of depressing and twisting a shuttle knob on a tape-to-tape video controller seems more foreign than pointing and clicking a mouse. The Avid comes with extensive manuals and has an easily understood built-in tutorial. It takes practice, but, like all Macintosh products, it's user-friendly. Learning by watching others use the Avid can be confusing, though. Once you're comfortable with the system, you develop idiosyncratic ways of working, since there are so many different ways to execute the same function. If you're trying to learn the system, dive in and go through the tutorial yourself. It's the only way to learn.

Nonlinear editing systems used as on-line systems can greatly benefit a low-budget production. Ironically, I first used the Avid on my lowest-budget project ever, the Girls

Against Boys video. I worked with an excellent editor named Candace Corelli, a devotee of New York's early-'90s, neo-punk/glam scene: D-fuckin'-generation, baby. Her whole demeanor — not to mention her incredibly excellent hot-pants-and-platform-boot outfits — was different from most editors I knew. Her concerns as a music-video editor were different as well: "That guy looks pretty sexy in that shot . . . Oooo, this rocks . . . Dude, you gotta use this shot 'cuz right here he looks pretty fuckable . . ." This made using new, scary, advanced technology so much more palatable.

Together we brewed up a plan where I would shoot the video on Hi8, input it directly into the Avid, do one cut that was both off-line and on-line, and output that cut from the computer onto a master tape to deliver to the record company. The scheme worked because the output didn't look as videoy as it did when it went into the computer. We used a digital-editing function to our advantage.

"Avid video resolution," or AVR, is a term for something that all digital editing systems have: varying degrees of digital compression. It's equivalent to the relative graininess of a film image. When you digitize your image at a low-resolution, or say, AVR 5, your image is going to look a little chunky because the blobs of digital material that make up your image are going to be bigger then they are at a higher resolution, or AVR 27, the resolution level acceptable for broadcast. Low-resolution material takes up less storage, or memory, on your computer than high-resolution material — it takes more 1s and 0s to describe all the detail in a high-resolution image. When you have an hour and a half of uncut music-video footage, you generally digitize this footage at AVR 3, or even 1, to save disk space. You work with that footage, generating an edit decision list as you do your off-line edit.

With high-resolution machines more readily available today, you can online on the Avid itself. After you've done your off-line, you redigitize your footage at a higher resolution. This process is called "batch digitizing." Working off your EDL (edit decision list), the computer grabs the shots you selected in the edit from your source tapes and redigitizes them at a higher resolution. This process is similar to an analog on-line, although in an analog on-line the footage goes directly onto a master tape. On an Avid, the shots get combined in the computer, then are output onto a master videotape. Now that AVIDs can output at AVR 77 — a resolution at which you'd never be able to tell the result was digital — on-line suites are becoming outmoded.

This marks a significant advance for low-budget videomakers. It's much easier to get a low rate on an Avid system for a two-hour on-line session than for an on-line suite that costs upwards of $300 an hour. You have to somehow generate an Avid-compatible EDL, but you have to write an EDL anyway. Darren Doane does exactly this. He cuts his videos on a dinky VHS-to-VHS pro-sumer editing system, then writes his EDL on Avid software he's got on his desktop computer. He onlines with his master tapes on an Avid, which generally costs him a couple of hundred bucks.

With the Girls Against Boys video, Candace and I input the footage at AVR 5 and output the footage at AVR 5. The chunkiness of this image worked in our favor, dulling the hard, video edge of the original footage. This technique used sophisticated, expensive equipment to achieve a low-budget result. The video doesn't look great, but at first glance it looks more like grungy 16mm footage than Hi8 video. After the record company sent them the videotape, MTV had to dub it again so that the signal conformed to broadcast standards. Normally this would be enough of an excuse for them not to play the video. Fortunately, Girls Against Boys were kind of hot at the time.

THE LOW-BUDGET/ROMANTIC ARGUMENT FOR TAPE-TO-TAPE EDITING

Still, many editors maintain that editing digitally comes easily only once you've edited tape-to-tape. Countless videos have been cut on tape-to-tape systems in colleges, high schools, community media centers and production companies. At one of the companies that represented me, I cut my videos on the system used to put together director's reels. This company struggled desperately to get me real-budget jobs, and I was mostly excited that I could use their off-line system after-hours for free.

At the risk of sounding romantic, I think you should use tape-to-tape editing when editing your first video — not to endure pointless frustration but simply for the learning experience. Since digital equipment has become the professional standard, tape-to-tape equipment comes cheap and is easy to get as production companies and schools unload their old editing systems. For what you'd spend to on-line and off-line a few low-budget videos, you could buy an RM440 set-up. For a little more, you could buy a couple of U-matic decks. Think of tape-to-tape as a rite of passage, and as you struggle with and curse those machines, think about how much easier it will be when you make the switch to digital. As much as I want to make some pro-analog, Luddite argument, the main advantage of tape-to-tape editing is economic. And with the advancement of digital editing technology, you'll likely be editing projects on your computer desktop sometime real soon, editing videos and generating an EDL with Mac-based programs such as Adobe Photoshop or Premiere.

Jonathan Horowitz began editing on tape but moved easily into the digital world.

OFF-LINE AND ON-LINE EDITING

When non-production people think of editing, they envision off-line editors, the folks who make all the editing decisions, piecing together the video from the masses of original footage. The on-line edit creates the final assembly of your video onto a broadcast-quality tape. The on-line editor uses a computer to gather up all the clips from the various master tapes (instead of the sub-masters used in the off-line) guided by an edit decision list based on the off-line edit. On-line editors work much more like colorists: highly skilled engineers who know how to operate fancy computerized equipment. The work of an off-line editor is editing.

<<<

"I cannot think of any advantages, except that it's cheaper to edit tape-to-tape over digital," he says. "When I was editing on tape, people would be really surprised that I worked on tape, especially if there were a lot of cuts. I remember one of the first videos I ever did had blocks of alternating two-frame edits and I had done all of it on tape. At the time, some people didn't even think it was possible. It really is. It's just that when something can be done easier in other ways, people forget that it can be done the old way. Everything is easier on a computer, but it's not that difficult on tape, either. Videos I've edited on tape are no worse for it, and a computer is not going to make a bad video good."

EDITING THEORIES

As an off-line editor, keep a few theories in mind. The classical Hollywood model assumes invisible edits, seamless transitions that change perspectives within a scene and build scenes into stories. Match cuts, for example, aren't meant to be read as anything more than a shift of position on a continuous action. By cutting on action (the moment a character raises a glass, for example, the cut from a wide shot of the diner to a close-up as he drains the glass), the edit becomes a seamless transition. The action makes the audience register that the transition into the close-up occurs sequentially, and they're never conscious of the camera turning off, repositioning and turning on again. Unsuccessful match cuts make us aware of the cut. The European art films of the '50s and '60s that overthrew Hollywood narrative conventions aimed to make cinematic devices visible. Though it's hard to imagine after three decades of assault on conventional film narrative, Jean-Luc Godard's films still look radical in part because of their liberal use of jump cuts: from the same camera position and focal length, a character will appear in one position — cut — then jolt into another position or into another part of the frame.

From the earliest days of filmmaking, there was an alternative to the invisible editing of Hollywood (though cinematic revolutionaries Eisenstein, Pudovkin and Kuleshov credit a contraband copy of D.W. Griffith's *Intolerance* that made its way to Kuleshov's workshop for inspiration). Russian intellectual/filmmaker Sergei Eisenstein (1898–1948) developed the notion of dialectical montage, in which the juxtaposition of shots illustrated Marxist theories of class struggle and conflict. Editing had to call attention to itself because, for Eisenstein, most cinematic meaning came through editing. A shot (thesis), cut with a shot of different visual content (antithesis), will form a synthesis which in turn will create a new thesis. Eisenstein's contemporary and fellow Soviet filmmaker, Lev Kuleshov, devised experiments in which he shot an actor with a blank expression. He cut this expressionless actor with a shot of a baby, for example, and discovered that audiences read love in the blank features. When cut with a bowl of soup, they read hunger. This is known as the Kuleshov effect.

A RELAXED REVOLUTIONARY. SERGEI EISENSTEIN

It's remarkable how directly Eisenstein's and Kuleshov's theories apply to music video. (Some of his other theories apply as well, including "typage," in which actors in his films portrayed "types" more than well-rounded characters, so that the audience more readily understood them. You can see this in the gloomy old men in music videos that represent death, for example.) Though many music-video editors aren't necessarily thinking about Eisenstein, music videos are often cut to enhance a visual clash. Generally, music videos thumb their nose at classical Hollywood editing. Even in cinematic clips, in which the cuts are logical, jump cuts are acceptable in the performance sequences. A shot sequence that goes from wide shot to medium shot to close- up is fluid: there's a progression toward the subject. But music videos freely intercut between wide shots and close ups. When record company people get involved, and bands themselves are involved, they're less concerned with visual logic than they are with pasting together a series of shots that make the band look good — a practical reason for iconoclastic music-video editing. Creatively, the editing in music video, as with other aspects of music-video production such as the photography and art department, calls attention to itself. Music video is, on some level, the bastard, capitalist grandchild of Eisenstein: cuts jar, not for any theoretical purpose, but to startle the eye of a visually jaded 14-year-old. Music video mandates a maximalist approach to editing. Given the reliance on editing for shock and the technological fascination with upcutting, it's no coincidence that video directors who seem truly innovative now experiment with making videos that are editorially spare or, as in the case of two renowned Spike Jonze videos, Wax's "Southern California" and Weezer's "Sweater Song," have no cuts at all.

Horowitz's only theoretical system is to demand some sense, some meaning to the order of the shots. "What constitutes sense for me might actually seem nonsensical to others," he allows. "If you're making a music video and you really care about it as more than just a job, there are many possibilities that the medium has for creating meaning. You have maybe 200 images over the course of three minutes. You have the lyrics, the different sounds and the combination of images. There's a tremendous amount of possibility [to create meaning]."

In the same way that match cuts whiz past without us thinking about them, we read meaning through editing without even thinking about it. Classic videos are one big exercise in the Kuleshov effect. In the traditional performance/concept interlacing-narrative model, when a rocker looks off camera while singing intensely and we cut to a shot of a young woman hitchhiking down a lonely road, we not only know that the singer is singing about the woman, we understand that the singer is thinking about her at that moment. When the camera rolls, the singer thinks about whether or not his hair looks cool, or whether the cute make-up girl likes him, but, through editing, we understand that he's living in the moment of the song.

Placed alongside certain musical or lyric moments, shots can take on new meaning. If the singer sings a refrain about hating someone, and at the moment he sings, "Ooooo and I hate you soooo much baby . . .," we cut to a shot of the bass player, we'll think that the singer hates the bass player. Editing gives you an enormous amount of power to create new, unintentional meanings with song lyrics.

Through editing, random footage can gain a structure. Perhaps you discover in your conceptual footage a strong image that the editor deems worthy as a recurring motif; a video that had no direction suddenly seems to make sense. Also, in editing you can create deeper sound/image relationships. This is really where a good music-video off-line editor's talent lies. Finding shots that accentuate musical moments is a unique and highly subjective ability.

As with all sound/image relationships, no one can explain why a close-up of a lead singer bobbing his head a certain way perfectly matches a guitar part at another place in the song. It's about movement. The subtle hand gesture of a model somehow accompanies a vocal line; a slowly rotating chrome hubcap perfectly illustrates a cyclical keyboard line; the slamming of a door emphasizes a snare hit; the breaking of a glass, a cymbal crash. Editors make these sound/image relationships come to life by placing the shots at just the right moments.

Whenever I think a cut makes sense, I give it what I privately refer to as a conductor's baton test. Either by squinting my eyes or by standing back from the monitor, I watch the video, purely for the sound/image relationship of the edit. I squint at the screen so that I'm not looking at the action in the shots to determine if, in the abstract, the movement within shots and the timing of the cuts match the music. If the video works on this abstract level, then I know that the cut is done.

Whenever I worked with Horowitz and I asked him why he put a particular shot where he did, he could always come back with a few reasons. If it was a performance shot, it could be as simple as that was the best looking moment of that performance we had. Then the reasons got more obscure. "Well, right there, they're singing about falling down, so I wanted to use that shot where that guy in the back is bending down, because it kind of matches the lyric," or, "Well, in both of those shots the camera pans left-to-right, so it flows better."

Good editors, like Jonathan, also find all kinds of "graphic matches" in the footage, meaning that one shot flows into the other because they're graphically similar. For example, on one side of the frame there's a circular object, say a satellite dish. This cuts nicely with a close-up of a spinning hubcap in another shot if that hubcap is in a similar space in the frame. Circular object meets circular object, and suddenly the cut becomes motivated.

All meaning and theory aside, that's the goal: motivated cuts. If you're trying to avoid randomness in your concept, you certainly want to avoid randomness in your cutting. If, when you were dreaming the video, you listened to the song and asked yourself, "What am I looking at now? What am I looking at now?", then you should be taking a similar approach when you watch your cut as it comes together. "Why is this shot here? Why are we looking at this?"

Cutting the video is like writing the video all over again: You brainstorm ideas, problem-solve, polish, and refine. You rethink your story and rework the ways you show the band. A cut that works really well with the music rocks. It moves. You tap your foot to it. You see what you want to see when you want to see it. This is the job of the editor.

THE PROCESS

Even if you're not preoccupied with theories, the off-line editing process remains the same. You log your footage and you sort it out into categories that let you easily select shots later. As when you cut tape-to-tape, you also create a "bin" on the Avid, that is, make reels of like footage: all the performance shots on one reel, for example, all the conceptual footage on another. Again, don't log your tapes just for actions or locations. The more thoroughly you flesh out your logs, the easier it will be to problem-solve later. All of those cool little whip pans and camera wiggles, weird rack focuses, unintentional flash frames, high-speed moments when the battery died — if it looks cool, it should appear on the log. When I edited tape-to-tape, I would almost always have a separate reel of "cool shit," a reel on which I dumped all the cool moments I wanted to have close at hand to try in various places. Approach the process with detailed, methodical planning because, as we've seen with other aspects of production, planning equals savings — of time in this case. Also, many directors point out that, with a small budget, you can't afford a second chance in the editing room. Videomakers working for major labels and big bands often endure ten or more re-edits while incorporating changes from band members, managers, label video commissioners, A&R people and the singer's girlfriend.

When you cut non-synch footage tape-to-tape, synch the footage before you do anything else, including logging. For the first few videos I ever cut, I didn't systematically synch the performance and that probably doubled my editing time. Though slightly easier on an Avid system, synching shots by eye is an arduous process. A director's musical knowledge really helps here. If you can watch a guitarist and recognize the chord he's playing — literally recognize the hand position of an E chord so that you can match it to a moment in the song — you have an advantage over many editors. "There is something really musical about editing, and an editor really needs to have that in his bones," maintains Kevin Kerslake. "You rely on that. The rhythm of the piece [becomes important]. I used to cut everything I did, and you get into what we call 'frame fucking,' where sliding a shot a frame or two really has a dramatic impact — just for you. Somebody else might not even see it."

But Horowitz cautions not to obsess about having the exact hand movement match the exact sound. "I'm not a musician and it's not always entirely apparent to me what hand movements on a guitar correspond to what sounds," he says. "Ninety-nine percent of the people watching music videos aren't musicians either. Changes that band members often request are where the synch is wrong. Most people who watch a music video never notice these things."

You'll want to get it as close as possible, though, and remember you will have to answer to the band, who will almost certainly notice. To synch up a shot by eye, you have to find a moment in the take at which you recognize the precise song part being played. That's easiest with the vocals because you can precisely match the lyrics to the singer's mouth. If you synch to the vocals, find a moment at which the singer sings a consonant, when he's closing his mouth to make a hard sound. When you've found a moment on the audio that you think matches the precise moment on video, set in-points on your play and record decks. Preview the shot. If it looks in synch, the tapes are exactly where they need to be, so roll back to the beginning of the shot, and roll the audio back exactly the same amount using the sad little control-track-driven numbers that you have on an RM440. If you use these controllers, remember the three-frame slippage. Inevitably you will have to try it more than once, which is frustrating. On the Avid, the process is the same. You'll have your audio track in an audio bin, and once you've found a synch point, all you have to do is scroll back the audio with a clicking and dragging of a mouse.

It helps to anticipate the synching process while you shoot. On a synch shoot, the camera has to find the smart slate at the beginning of a performance shot. This means that the DP must adjust back into position after shooting the slate, which takes a moment. The same thing can be done on a non-synch shoot. If the singer sings a particular line to which it would be easy to synch, or if the drummer plays an easily synchable drum fill, train the lens on that musical moment at the beginning of the take. Work these inserts out with your DP ahead of time and it'll make your life easier in the edit suite. Some folks try to shoot an entire song in one take when they don't have a smart slate. That avoids any ambiguity about which part of the song the band plays during the take. "I think you have to consider what you can expect of the editor," suggests Horowitz. "If you give someone a lot of footage with wild camera movement and there's no way to synch it up, the editor's job is going to be more difficult. If you're going to shoot performance footage and there's wild camera movement and no synch, I think it's important to indicate somehow where the take is starting in relation to the song, or just shoot the entire song."

A word about synch. The human mind desperately wants to synch image to sound.

After years of growing up watching people speak, the human eye is quite accustomed to that sound/image relationship. Bands are real sticklers when it comes to shots in which they may or may not be playing a certain part of a song, but when most folks see an image of someone playing the guitar, and they hear a guitar on a soundtrack, they assume they're being shown that the guitar player is playing that particular guitar part. If you use a shot of the guitarist playing a different part than what is seen, their brains make up for the discrepancy between sound and image.

All editors work differently, but most like to first lay down image over the entire audio track. "For me it's like oil painting," claims the methodical Adam Bernstein. "First you do a sketch on the canvas, then you do a wash layer, then you do another layer, but you're constantly working the whole image in stages. You don't get hung up on cutting your first verse, then fine-cutting your first verse, and then moving on. What I would do is lay down a performance, a synch performance level. I build the performance footage for one or two days so I know I have the best performance video I can possibly have, almost a performance video that could play on its own. If I start covering shit up, I know that I have the best moments. The worst thing you can do is to not look carefully at your performance from the very beginning 'cause then you lock yourself into decisions, and you're never going to go back and change it. Things have a way of really getting set in stone. I basically follow my massive chart, so I know that the girl in the bikini will smash the burning Buick in the second verse, and I have twelve seconds to get that done and preserve these good performance moments. It's like a jigsaw puzzle."

"I usually start with laying down the performance footage, even if there's a lot of narrative footage," agrees editor Horowitz. "Then I work the narrative footage into a bed of performance footage. The advantage to doing that is that there's more leeway as to where you can put narrative footage. If there's a really good synch performance shot, it might only be able to go in one or two places. So, if you start by editing the performance footage, it enables you to include more of the best performance moments." After one session of editing, I don't want to see any black holes in my program, and I'll throw down shots, even arbitrarily. This makes me feel as if I've reached my first editing goal. After that, I try to build sequences, narrative or performance, and work through the whole video chronologically.

Endings and beginnings need special attention — there's nothing worse than a video that fails to get attention or loses steam at the end — so I'll work on them first.

"It's kind of hard to say when you know a cut is good or done," says Horowitz, shrugging. "It's more something that you feel. I have to just look at it and feel that every shot is properly placed and every cut is properly placed. If there's some meaning that's trying to be communicated that it's successfully communicated. Things have to be evenly spaced. If it's a performance video, you don't want three shots of the guitar player next to each other. You don't want him to disappear until the end. You want it to be balanced, musicians or the shot elements, in a comfortable way."

What with arcane theories and unfamiliar equipment, deadline pressure and perhaps the limitations you discovered in your footage, editing becomes an exercise in the possible. But editing is truly the act of making the video sing, when all of the images you collected get the chance to vie for a place in the video you dreamed. Now that you hold the fruits of your hopes and many long nights, how do you share it with the world?

chapter six

What do you call an indie-rock music-video director without a wife or a girlfriend? Homeless.

This crack by some friends in film production sent shivers down my spine because I was the punch line. At that point, after many unpaid video jobs, an endless stream of borrowed equipment and broken promises, I still hadn't grabbed that elusive assignment for a cardigan-sweater-wearin', post-Nirvana, pseudo-indie, corporate alt-rock band that would have paid well and made me a Buzz Bin director. Was that what I wanted? God, where did my post-punk value system go? What about my aesthetic sense? When did I start evaluating my self-worth based on whether or not I was awarded a $15,000 video for a band I vaguely knew?

You want a career in music video? Really?

Music videos are fun to make, but managing a music-video directing career leads to pure misery and confusion, like most pursuits that are high-profile and creative. **working >**

If your first low-budget video efforts receive peer approval and even make it onto MTV, you begin to crave a directing career. You become obsessed with developing a reel and finding a representative to send it out. Then you get to write treatments, and you will go through the treatment-writing process dozens of times. I've written sixty treatments for huge bands such as Soul Asylum, the Offspring and Dinosaur, Jr., jobs for which I don't know if I was ever really considered. Video commissioners ask for endless revisions that keep your hopes alive. "Maybe I'll get this job," you think. "They want hot, young, new directors, right?" You fantasize about director's fees as you would daydream about winning the lottery. If you have directed one or two $5,000 videos then start writing treatments for jobs with budgets of $50,000, your potential earnings increase from $500 to $5,000, a significant raise for a wannabe director.

When you don't get the job, you feel rejected and dejected, even though the job was never destined to be yours in the first place. You start believing that the video industry exists only to exclude you, and you reflexively probe friends for information about about jobs and who's working on what. You watch MTV and wonder, "Why didn't I get this job instead of that person? I could have made a better video for $5,000 than the one that this schmuck made for $150,000." Feeling scorned, you retreat into passive-aggressive behavior, ignoring old musician friends who work with other directors. Julie Hermelin maintains that "It's all a matter of who's hot at the moment. You can have a solid reel and a good reputation, but that doesn't mean you're going to get the job even if your videos are on MTV. There's a handful of directors who get all the jobs, and then the rest of the directors work on and off. If you have a hot moment, you might do three videos in a month. And then five months might go by without work. You're gonna write, but you're gonna lose out by a hair to someone else."

EVERY DIRECTOR OBSESSES ABOUT CAREER

The panic and paranoia never go away, no matter how successful you become. All the directors you met in this book still obsess about their careers. Once you venture into the world, trying to get music-video directing jobs from bands you don't know personally, the process seems arbitrary. Even when you've got a plum job within your grasp, it often gets snatched away. Julie had just such an experience with one of the most renowned videos of all time. "I got flown to Atlanta to meet TLC, driven first class, taken out for dinner, met the girls," she recounts. "They're all set to do the 'Waterfalls' video, a three-quarter-of-a-million-dollar job. And then Left Eye goes on trial for burning down her boyfriend's house, so she couldn't leave the state, and the concept could not be shot in Atlanta. She was under house arrest for six or eight months. Then three months after that we were gonna do it again. I was totally connected with the girls. We were there for a week in preproduction, and then they decided not to do it again. In those eight months another director got involved. F. Gary Gray was getting hot; he did it, and I didn't. He made a lot of money on that video and I didn't make any. It was mine. We budgeted it. I was flown out to Atlanta. We had a shooting date and we were putting things on hold. Of course, 'Waterfalls' won best video of the year and now F. Gary Gray does a movie, blah, blah, blah [*Set It Off*, 1996]. I went to the awards and said, 'Gary, it was my job.' It was so hard. I mean, it was my video."

Directors also look over their shoulders at time and the younger crowd that's gaining on them because music video is a young person's game and your career lasts but a blink. Rachel Weissman notes that music video attracts a younger crew than commercial production, for example, and her partner John Owen points out "It's all an age thing, I think. If you're twenty-six, you think you're a genius. If you're thirty-six, you can still enjoy being told you're a genius. But how many fifty-year-old music-video directors are there that really believe they're fuckin' geniuses?"

GETTING MUSIC VIDEO JOBS

How do you even get to the point where you are up for a job? The great thing about being a video director (and many other jobs in the creative services) is that you don't need a résumé. You get jobs by presenting your portfolio, or, in the case of a music-video director, your reel, a videocassette compilation of your best work. You hear folks talk about directors "building a reel" as if they were redecorating the Sistine Chapel, but the reel must simply demonstrate your best, most recent work. I remember meeting the late Steve Brown — a low-budget music-video guru, and a mentor to more than a few of the folks in this book — and asking his advice for a new director. I handed him a sad VHS tape pasted with a label on which I had written in red marker my name and the word *reel* in quotation marks. He objected to this label immediately: "What's with the fucking quotes?" I explained to him that since I had only done two videos, I felt squeamish about putting the word *reel* on without quote marks. Nearly bellowing, he declaimed, "Don't ever send people the message that you are embarrassed about your work. Even if you've only done one video, your reel is your fucking reel."

Your work is your calling card and the key to getting any other work, so play your reel for everyone who will watch. As Darren Doane says, "You should never use the excuse that you gotta know someone in the industry. Everyone *does* know somebody in the industry. Anyone can say, 'I've got a friend who has a friend who knows someone.' Well then, get a hold of that person." If the band for whom you've done a video is happy with it and part of a local music scene, send your video to everyone else in the scene. If the band's indie-rock record label is happy with the video, send it to all of the other indie labels. The few truly independent labels don't have video commissioners, which means that you can talk to a decision-maker at these labels and they might actually look at your work. Video commissioners at major labels mainly deal with reps.

Gaining a rep marks the transition from making music videos part-time to making music videos "professionally," and the process of looking for a rep prepares you for the heinous challenge of landing music video jobs. Unless your first, self-produced video was a Buzz Bin pick, or you're the little brother of an executive producer, it's hard to get reps to look at your work.

WHAT REPS DO

Reps come out of the music business or the music-video culture, sometimes from video-producing backgrounds. Sometimes they are rock party girls. I've heard of one rep who was an ex–perfume salesperson. Whenever this pedigree was pointed out, it always prompted a chorus of, "Well, if she can sell Chanel, she can certainly sell directors." Reps sell. They send out director reels, targeting video commissioners and finding the commissioners as they look for directors. Like agents, reps shepherd new directors though record-company corridors to meet video commissioners. They research label activity to find out what band's doing a video, when, and if there is a chance one of their directors can write for the project. Your rep basically just knows a lot of folks in the music business.

Reps gossip and schmooze with video commissioners all day then go out and party with more video commissioners and band managers at night, all the while promoting their directors. "Hey, have you seen David's latest video? You have? You like it? Great! Who's coming up on the release schedule? Oh, he'd love to write a treatment for (fill in name of band I've never heard of), they're his favorite band." Sounds like a big party, right? Well, repping video directors can be a thankless job. Video commissioners, who get flooded with forty rep phone calls a day, rarely call back, while directors call constantly to complain about their careers. "When am I going to get to do the new Weezer video?" rings in a rep's phone earpiece all day long.

After getting the job, reps monitor the interests of the director throughout the shoot. If the rep's also an executive producer at a production company, s/he often drafts the budget for the bid, hires the line producer and makes suggestions about crew members. An executive producer/rep works with the video commissioner as an ad agency account executive works with a client: The rep knows enough about his clients' strategy to choose the right director for a particular band and budget. If the job doesn't go well — if the record company isn't happy with the video — the reps negotiate with the record company. Reps develop director careers, molding their young talents, helping them make choices about the jobs they take, and, if they can, prodding their production company to kick in money to augment a low budget.

Jerry Solomon at Epoch Films is a classic example of an executive producer/rep, and he's worked with some of the best directors in the business. "Before I started repping," he recalls, "I was working as a production coordinator with older directors like Paula [Greif] and Adam [Bernstein] who were working during the Renaissance, I guess the pre-Renaissance of music video. In those days, if the band needed to make a video, they would call up, the directors would write a treatment, and it was over. There was no money, but it was a chance for these guys to direct, and it wasn't like you had to make a million phone calls. It was like, listen to the track, write a treatment, band likes your treatment, budget the job, award, shoot. It was that simple. It's evolved into something much more corporate. With commercials, there's sort of a method to the madness. The video thing, I don't think there is a method to the madness. I think that the commissioners at labels have to adhere to the rules of these rock-and-roll guys, their managers, the marketing guy and the publicity person. Now everybody has their finger in the video. My job is to put my directors in the best position to succeed."

What does it sound like when reps guard their directors' careers from the detours and diversions created by the wrong job at the wrong time? Solomon offers a little dialogue that illustrates the dance between reps and commissioners and the personalities involved. "This guy who's a friend of mine," he recounts, "who used to be a rep, called me up and said, 'I got this video for Jeff Price, $80,000.' Jeff Price is a ten-million-dollar-a-year commercial director. I say, 'I can barely get the guy to do a shoot day on a commercial for less than $150,000. He's not going to make way for this.' He says, 'The band really loves his reel, man.' I'm like, 'I don't care if the band loves his reel, he can't do it. I'm not going to take a bath for A&M Records or this band so that they can get a great video from Jeff Price. Don't even bother calling me unless you got $200,000 or more for Jeff Price.' The guy's like, 'Fine. Fuck it.' Somehow *I* screwed *him* by not delivering a director to him! The label people that are cool, and there are some out there, will call you and say, 'Look. I would love it if Jeff Price did a video. I got $100,000. Can you do me a solid, dude? Can you at least let him hear the track? Maybe he'll love it and we can find a way we can get you a buck-twenty-five,' or, 'Budget it for as low as you think you can go, and maybe I can get it through.' That's smart. These other schmucks that call you up and just say, "Dude, I'm giving you an opportunity.' You ain't giving me an opportunity."

WHAT VIDEO COMMISSIONERS DO

My long-time rep was the well-connected Catherine Smith, who produced for music-video founding father Julian Temple, among others. She reminded me often of these connections and told me about the L.A. video commissioners to whom she could introduce me: "You don't even appreciate that I can get you a meeting with Randy Skinner at Warner Bros." I distinctly remember having one of these conversations with Catherine in her office while watching the MTV Video Awards out of the corner of my eye. As an inexperienced, ornery, ungrateful music-video director I said, "I don't care about any Randy Skinner. I don't care about anyone who works at a record label. I don't believe that anybody at a label can help me get a job." Meanwhile, on the screen, R.E.M.'s Michael Stipe shuffled up to the podium to receive the award for best video. The first thing he said was, "I'd really like to give a special thanks to Randy Skinner for her guidance and for setting us up with the right director."

Years later, I finally met Ms. Skinner on my own. I was walking out of a restaurant with a friend of mine who spotted an acquaintance Randy was lunching with. We walked over to their table, my friend started chatting with his buddy, and, after hovering awkwardly around the table, I introduced myself to Randy. She politely responded, "I like your videos," and immediately I became much more at ease. I moved closer, rested my arm behind her back on the banquette, and with broad gestures no doubt said something grand and ridiculous. "Are you glad you met Randy?" my friend asked after we left. "I'm sure you made quite an impression," he sighed as he glanced toward my completely unzipped fly.

If the label commissioners aren't taking your rep's calls, then how do they spend their time? Randy Sosin, a video commissioner at A&M Records, describes his function as a facilitator. "At the end of the day," he asserts, "I'm as concerned with the artist enjoying the process and feeling good about their music video as I am about making a good music video. I sit in between the artist and the director, and I want both sides to be happy. My happiness comes from them being happy. I'm not trying to drive it one way or another. I would rather have a good music video that the artist really loves than a great music video that the artist really hates." For Sosin, that position in between the artist and director extends onto the set. "Bands say 'What are all these people doing here? We spent this much on our record, how can it take this much just to make one video?' During the shoot, I try to make the artist aware of what is going on. Even though they've read a treatment and the director will show them storyboards, they don't necessarily understand it. Some directors are better than others at communicating with the artist, so it's up to me to kind of explain to the artist what they're doing and why they're doing it. For me, as long as my artist is on set, I'm on set. I don't know if everyone does that, but I feel like if they're there working, then it's my job, as their video person at their label, to do that. If they have to be there until six in the morning, then I should be there until six in the morning."

Some video commissioners, especially those such as Skinner, who oversaw Madonna videos in the '80s, are people you have to know if you want to be in the business. I think, however, as a novice director, I was right to question the degree to which video commissioners can help you. Jerry Solomon agrees. "Commissioners have zero power," he asserts. "I think that commissioners, in this day and age, have very little power getting a job for a director. The only thing that a commissioner can do is present, filter the reels that get shown to the bands, and make sure that the directors they bid are good ones. After that, in terms of the money, and in terms of the concept, and in terms of the actual creativity, I think they've become — and I don't think that they were always this way — glorified paper-pushers. Video commissioner: dead-end job. You've got nowhere to go at the end of the job. Very few of them have been able to find something outside of it. The weird role of video commissioner is that you ain't in the record business, and you ain't in the film-production business. So what do you do? They're not really like marketing people. They're not A&R people. They're not publicity people. What is it exactly that they do? They do one specific element. Can they really budget a job? No. Can they really line-produce a job? No. Can they direct any of this stuff? Well, we've seen a lot of them try, but they can't. They hang on to that job and that power for dear life because they're not in either world."

Susan Solomon, a former commissioner at A&M and now a producer, says that the video commissioner's power differs from person to person and label to label. She sees the job as being a communicator between lots of competing interests. "On the set, you're basically trying to keep everyone happy," she says. "You're trying to keep your director happy, if you've got a pain-in-the-ass band, you try to keep them psyched, you try to keep them focused. Certainly performance is a major interest of the record company, making sure that works. It's all about the band first. What do they look like? Do they come across as cool, or whatever they're supposed to be? Some directors don't communicate with you. I've been on a set where a director literally wrapped himself with a sheet so that he was in front of the monitor and I was behind it. I was like, 'Okay, this is not going to fly.'"

Young directors despair over the businesslike structure and systems of the music-video business. Reps and video commissioners get paid to talk to one another. They're paid to oversee the treatment-writing ritual that raises a director's hopes only to have them shot down again. But Sosin points to the opportunities that labels provide to young directors to experiment and grow in their craft, at someone else's expense. He sees the best work resulting from a collaboration between the artists and the directors — a collaboration he encourages and nurtures. "Even though we spend as much money as they do on independent feature films, it's much more of — for lack of a better term — an organic process with videos. A lot of times directors shoot stuff for the edit and then figure out how it's going to go together later. At the end of the day, the video director is being given a license, with very little credibility, to make a film. I think that's a really cool thing, that they're being given the opportunity to use music video as a medium to, if they want to become rich, make commercials, if they want to become filmmakers, to get into feature films. I think music video has become that medium. A huge number of directors have moved on from music videos to feature films, and not just David Fincher and Michael Bay." Directors are grateful for the opportunity, though also frustrated with inconsistent treatment at the hands of labels. Commissioners are, of course, as susceptible as the rest of the music business to the come-hither appeal of the new.

The suggestion that video commissioners solicit treatments to justify their jobs holds true for reps, too. Reps want to have a steady stream of songs coming in for their directors to write treatments, to assure the directors that they're doing their jobs. So they will convince reluctant video commissioners to send directors new tracks with only the remotest possibility that the director could get the job. In this way, treatment writing becomes politicized. Reps and commissioners will barter with one another using director treatments. Your rep will come to you and say: "Listen, I've talked to video commissioner X and he wants you to write for huge, rock-star band Y for a $170,000 budget. Isn't that great?" You think, "God, my rep is the best," and little will you know that later in the week X will call back your rep and say, "Look, I let that little schmuck write for Y. I threw the kid a bone. Now will you please convince Z (one of your rep's other directors) to consider shooting this other job I have, even though it's super low-budget? You owe me a solid on this one."

"I will say this," admits Sosin, "the process from which we go about making music videos is broken. I don't know what we can do to make it better, but the treatment's a really bad way to do it. It puts everyone at risk because it's completely subjective. It's hard for a marketing person to read the treatment and visualize it because it's not their job. They're much more linear. And bands don't necessarily read treatments and understand them. Some of my favorite treatments have not been made into videos, and I've subsequently seen other artists make them into videos. It's a frustrating thing from my perspective."

"I mean, the thing that's hard about music videos is that the input that you get from other people is so contradictory," says Tryan George. "You know, you'll have a video commissioner saying one thing. You'll have the singer saying something else. And then you may have a manager and another band member all differing. That's the point when you realize it's up to you as a director to just satisfy your idea because in the end you can't satisfy everyone. So you have to be selfish and let them know that it's gonna make a better piece if you just stick to one consistent vision." That vision comes under scrutiny again in the editing room when bands and labels will often ask for revisions to rough cuts, revisions that frustrate directors and bankrupt their production companies.

Directors, reps and video commissioners have a difficult relationship, as any relationship that's built on need and mistrust. Some directors ask, "Who are these people?"

"I've only worked with two video commissioners that I have any respect for, seriously," says Rachel Weissman. "I haven't worked with every commissioner but there's only been two occasions that I've felt that the client — when they are my client — is together, smart and knows their job. I think there are too many people who work in the music-video business because they were receptionists and then they were given an assistant job and then, boom, they're a commissioner. I don't think you need much on your résumé to be a music-video commissioner. I can't think of why else there'd be so many uninformed, crazy people as commissioners." Jerry Solomon sees the commissioners as corporate obstacles who prey on directors and production companies. "I have a lot of venom, actually, toward the industry," he says heatedly. "I really do. It's a nasty business. These commissioners are total corporate players and the music business is a corporate environment, and just because they wear jeans and T-shirts to work doesn't mean that they're not part of a corporate bureaucracy. It doesn't mean that they don't have their own careers and own agendas and they'll screw you if they have to do that to succeed. That's the truth. How many videos did you do for a Lee Rolontz [a Sony video commissioner] or somebody like that, for twenty thousand dollars, but never once did they give you a shot [at a bigger budget]. Or would pretend to throw you a bone and let you write something for a good band for a hundred [thousand-dollar budget], but you knew damn well you had no chance in hell of getting it no matter how good your treatment was. And you weren't even sure if your treatment was ever even read by the band or the manager."

"I know some labels, they'll send out a track to the director, and the director is all psyched before the band has even seen their reel," says Susan Solomon, sighing. "I don't play that game. Why waste everyone's time. Why waste my time, too, quite frankly. I try to get everyone on board, and then you pick three directors, tops. Best-case scenario is that you single bid, but that's rare. You find the three that you really like and you send the tape out to the directors and you give them your spiel. What the band is about, what we're trying to do, what they feel comfortable doing, maybe what the song's about, you hook them up with the artist, the lead singer usually, and then they can talk. Again, a lot depends on how well you know the artist. If it's a brand-new artist, you don't really know. I worked on Sheryl Crow's first video. You didn't know what she was going to be like in front of the camera. She wasn't sure about what situation she'd be comfortable with, and, honestly, the first video we did, her performance sucked. We didn't shoot her right, so you learn.

"I've heard all the stories," she continues. "commissioners can be awful. 'They know nothing. They are in positions of power, so they use that authority. They're on a set, and they throw their power around, even when they don't know what they're talking about.' I totally understand directors who have a problem dealing with that bullshit. On the other hand, it's the same shit [commissioners] get with bands. The minute they come into your office, they look at you and go, 'You're a label geek, I give you no respect.' You try to say, 'You know, I'm not that bad.' And there are directors who give you the same thing. There are directors who think, 'All commissioners know nothing,' without realizing that there are different ones in the world. The bottom line is, when you're in a business of art and commerce — commercials, music videos, feature film — someone's paying for it. You have to keep someone informed about what's going on. It's the nature of the beast."

The label's A&R staff takes a more active role in videos for high-profile artists, or if the individual A&R person has a close relationship with the band. Mark Kates, A&R at Geffen Records, says he tries to stay out of the process. "You want to be involved [with the video production process] because it's cool. It's interesting and it has to do with what you do. But I think the only reason to be involved is to help the artists get what they want, to increase their comfort level. Theoretically, that's what the video commissioner is there for. We have a great video commissioner here, and, generally, I don't feel like the situation demands my involvement. With some music videos, I've been involved every step of the way: multiple phone conversations, going over the treatment, going to the shoot, going to the edit. I guess there were some that were important to the company so I had that level of involvement. And then there are some that I see the treatment, and then see the video, and there's not much in between. I guess that's from trusting people that you work with to do their job."

Spike Jonze recommends relying on the band for support with their record label, another important reason to bond with the artist before beginning the videomaking process. He cites the one-image, non-performance Wax video as an example. "With the Wax video," he says, "[Caroline Records] was really freaked-out by it: 'This is our video?' The record company was like, 'Maybe we could cut in band performance.' And the band said, 'No, this is it.' The reason it went to MTV that way is that the band said, 'Send this in. Bring this to MTV. This is our video.' I did,

"First of all, you've got a reel. You've got a personality. So, if you get a meeting [with a video commissioner], you've got to sell your-self as much as you're selling the reel because personality's involved. I might see a director who would be really great for a band, but personality-wise, they'd never get on. Or you meet a director who doesn't have much personality, and you think he'd be hard to communicate with. With a young director, they got to be out there. You've got to hustle, you've got to be out there, and you've got to create your own chances and opportunities."

too, but, coming from a video director it's not a powerful as coming from a band. The record label is going to be scared, as any company is, of doing anything that's different. They think about marketing or what's worked in the past or what sells, as opposed to what would be great."

Don't think of video commissioners as the keys to the doorway of success. It's most useful to think of them as another kind of producer. They guide a band through the video-making process, as your rep guides you, rather than being the one solely responsible for hiring you. Once you think about them in this way, you'll stop thinking about them as evil corporate figures who keep you out of the loop.

MANAGE YOUR OWN CAREER

Employ a *You Stand There* strategy for music-video director career management. Everyone we know in the business agrees that a director is solely responsible for managing and developing his or her own career. Directors find their own reps, and when directors find themselves in high demand, reps often amount to nothing more than folks who field phone calls. Also, only the director can determine the kind of work that they want to do. "If there's a director out there who has done a couple of these low-budget clips and thinks to themselves, 'I just need a production company to help me out,' I think that they have to be very careful," cautions Jerry Solomon. "There are a lot of bad companies and bad reps. Anybody who promises you that they're going to get you this and they're going to turn you into that, stay away from them, because there are no guarantees. The best reps are the ones who are honest with you. It's the responsibility of the director to tell the rep, 'This is what I want to do.' I know certain directors who did, let's say, rap videos because that's what the reps could get them. That's where they built their reputation. All of a sudden, its fifteen rap videos later and they're thinking, 'I don't want to do another gangster thing, I don't want to shoot in Harlem, I don't want to shoot in East New York. I want to do alternative stuff. I really want to be working with U2 or Pavement.' It's important from the beginning, whether it's yourself repping, or a rep that you hook up with, to say, 'This is where I want go.' Although you've been doing $150,000 rap videos, call up Matador, ask if they can hook you up. Call up Sub Pop, call Merge, and ask Superchunk to do a video for them for like $5,000, just to have an alternative video on the reel. You've got to know what your sensibilities are, what kind of music you like, what kind of filmmaking you want to do."

"There's the whole issue of agents and representation and all that crap," says Bernstein. "Does being with a big, fancy company help you out? Maybe to an extent. Some people have kick-started their careers by being in the right place at the right time. You have to be persistent without being a pain in the ass; be in their face without alienating them. My strategy with those people is that whenever I would do something new and cool, I would send it out with a candy bar or some kind of weird novelty gift. Obviously, the important thing is the work, but the next most important thing is to do something fun that's going to stick out from the big pile of tapes they have on their desk.

"The most useful thing you can do to jump-start your career as a music-video director is to have been in a band or know a lot of musicians," Bernstein continues. "Also, you reach a certain critical mass when you've done enough videos that have gotten enough play that you become like a hairdresser. It took me two years to become a full-time music-video director, until I got into what I call a hairdresser mode. I did a video for E.P.M.D. so Hank Shocklee from Public Enemy calls Lear Cohen and says, 'Who did that video for E.P.M.D., it was cool. Oh, it's Adam Bernstein. He should do ours.' It's like the hairdresser thing. Frank Black calls me up because he's friends with John Flansberg, and he likes the videos I did for John Flansberg: 'Who did your hair, your hair looks great.' You get into the system like that."

No matter how powerful your rep, you must do some of the repping duties yourself. Make your own contacts with bands, shoot low-budget videos for reel-building and on-set experience and constantly provide your rep with extensively researched lists of performers whose jobs you want to book. "It's your responsibility to stay on the rep," advises Jerry Solomon. "You should be buying magazines like *Ice,* or something that's going to tell you what's coming up in the next three or four months. 'U2's putting out a new album. They're in the studio. Call the manager and get my reel seen.' It's your responsibility to say, 'I have a connection here,' if you know the manager or the band. You should help the rep with those contacts. You should not sit by the phone and wait for the rep to call. A rep is going to work as hard as their directors are going to work for them."

It's too easy to blame reps and commissioners for career stasis. Commissioners have to please the marketing departments of their record labels, the artist and the artist's management. The buck stops with the band: If they have a relationship with a director, or if they have been dying to work with a particular director, then they usually have the last say in the matter. Though your rep should always work toward getting you work by any means necessary, in the end, that isn't their only function. Like commissioners, reps are best-used as mediators and facilitators. They play good cop when you negotiate with a record company and keep the record company at arm's length so that you can do your job. When you see the importance of this function, you stop seeing them as only the avenue to a job, and you won't blame them for your troubles.

WHERE TO FIND ICE
P.O. Box 3043
Santa Monica, CA 90408.
Their current annual
subscription rate is $30.

"No rep will get you work," Doane asserts. "The reel and your videos get you work and that's it. You need to hang out with bands and show them your work. It'll definitely come back to you. When punk broke, I knew all those guys and they called me. I've done eleven videos for Epitaph alone. That gave me a career. You feel respected, not like you're beating down a door. Someone likes your work. Those are the kind of connections you want to have: with a label and with band people. You gotta find your own way to do it."

Some directors, big budget and low budget, start their own production companies and rep themselves. The obvious advantage to this approach is that your company makes the production fee. But bear in mind that those production fees must cover office personnel, rent, phone, utilities, messengers, postage and a hundred other things that make up office overhead, and there are inevitable cost overruns that come out of your pocket. It's not that easy to make real money making videos, even at what are seemingly high budgets. Also bear in mind that established production companies get preferred rates on equipment and services because vendors see them as large clients. A production company that has three shoots happening every single week represents large potential equipment rentals, for example. You won't be offering that kind of volume at first.

Mott and I called our company Burning Bridges Productions. I actually drew a pathetic company logo that featured the Brooklyn Bridge in flames with a group of weeping crew members on one side holding broken cameras and invoices that said "Unpaid." A thought bubble over the head of one crew member read, "I'll never work for free again." I stood on the other side of the bridge with one hand holding a shopping bag labeled "Matador Videos" and the other hand thrusting out the finger at the sad sacks across the bridge. Vendors didn't see the irony in the company's name, but we would often snicker to ourselves when one of them asked which company would be responsible for paying.

Having your own company can be a struggle, but it works particularly well for folks who only want to do low-budget videos. Some successful directors retain their own production companies in order to produce low-budget jobs that their bigger, fancier companies would reject. Sometimes you need a simple production entity to help with these jobs, one where you're the producer and rep, and you can edit on your own tape-to-tape editing system.

HOW DO VIDEOS END UP ON MTV?

When record-label video commissioners aren't dealing with you and your rep, they're schmoozing with MTV. You'll never see this part of their job, which just might be the most important. Just as a record label's radio promotions person works to convince radio programmers to play their label's songs, a video commissioner courts programmers at MTV. Commissioners ensure that the video is "serviced" correctly, that it arrives at MTV in time for the Monday acquisitions meetings, and with the required paperwork (lyric sheet, credits, etc.) attached. To generate some hype around a video, commissioners will let the video circulate among other music-video people and supporters of the artist in question at MTV. There have been stories, no doubt apocryphal, about commissioners leaving envelopes filled with cash under benches in Central Park.

The deep, dark secret is that the programmers who

decide what videos make it onto MTV truly love the videos they program. I was shocked once while talking about music with Sherri Howell, an MTV programmer who I saw frequently out and around in the New York night scene. Since we were in a too-cool-for-school, rock-enriched scene, I was jibing her about the band Live, which seemed to be on MTV constantly. When I shot her a comment, something along the lines of "Doesn't it depress you to show those videos all the time?" Sherri's response was direct and adamant: "I *like* Live."

Amy Finnerty has been a programmer at MTV for more than ten years. She describes a two-part weekly acquisitions process that features passionate debate among the members of the talent and programming department in which all present fight for their current favorites to see air time. "We have our acquisitions meeting on Mondays at 1:30 P.M.," she says. "In that meeting, we look at anywhere from 35 to 60 videos and decide whether or not we want to play them. We'll accept a video for general rotation if we're not sure exactly what we're going to do with it. If it's something we've been waiting for and we know what we're going to do with it, we'll put it in regular rotation, or we'll accept it for *120 Minutes*, or *Yo*, or *Amp*, some of the specialty programming. We don't do anything else in that room but talk about whether we want to play a video. On Tuesday mornings, we have our music meetings. That's a smaller group, about eight or nine of us. Those last anywhere from an hour to four hours depending on what kind of music we have in. We basically go through our rotations [the videos currently being shown] and duke it out. Generally, we start the meetings by talking about whether or not we have any world premieres for that week, because those are usually bands that are going to be getting a pretty heavy rotation. Making it work means being able to express your personal passion and get that on the air, as well as make the rest of the group know that you are well aware of our programming needs. We always balance having enough hits on the air to get the ratings that we need with creating enough room in our day-to-day programming so that we can develop new artists. That's generally where the big fights come in. But it's important that we reserve the right for everybody in that room to be able to express their opinions to the point of being able to put a video on the air. There are people in the room who are just as passionate about something that I can't stand as I am about the bands I happen to be into at the moment. You have to respect that, because they come in with real, genuine emotions. Because our audience is really wide, we kind of have to please all of them. "

Keeping track of the changes in MTV's programming strategy will prove fruitless for targeting your style or choosing a band with which to work: It changes too quickly and relies too heavily on personal passions and network ratings concerns for you to plan making videos that will resemble today's preferred look. And MTV's already restricted playlist promises to get shorter. "MTV has altered its policy, and they're probably going to alter it again before your book comes out," Kates advises. "Now they're saying that MTV's going to play fewer videos more often. From a record-company point of view, that means we're probably going to make fewer videos and spend more money on them."

No matter how jaded the music-video director, they all fantasize that the low-budget video they've done for an obscure band will become a huge hit on MTV and the phone will start ringing off the hook. Bands share this fantasy. Though few in the music-video machine will admit it, rarely has a band's career been launched by video. This reality is denied because the music-video business has become entrenched in the music business in general (what marketer wants to pass up the tens of millions of households that can tune in to MTV, VH-1, BET, Country Music Television, The Box, and others?). Though Kates sees the impact in SoundScan sales figures when a band's video goes into and out of MTV rotation, many in the industry regard videos as a general awareness device, much like press coverage. You can't track the direct influence of press on sales, but it undoubtedly helps. Aside from clear examples such as Blind Melon's "No Rain" and White Zombie's *Beavis and Butt-head*–inspired career boost, there is no way to chart the direct influence of music videos on a band's success. Bands break on radio, and that coincides with MTV presenting the video.

"We've talked about picking singles based on whether or not they'd make a good video," says Kates. "I've always shied away from that because you have less and less idea of whether your video will actually see the light of day on MTV. But you still have a fairly good idea of where you might end up on radio with a song, and, ultimately, if it goes on radio, it'll go on MTV. And if the song's a hit on radio, MTV will play it no matter what the video looks like. I can't imagine now some video taking over the world the way "Teen Spirit" did, and even that song, I can tell you firsthand, was burning the phones down at radio stations all over the country before MTV really started playing it."

Finnerty believes that the ties to radio play also depend on the genre. "Our relationship with radio depends on the type of artist," she asserts. "Pop acts develop differently. They come up and either hit fast or they don't hit at all. Rock stuff, underground, hip-hop stuff, and techno stuff takes more time to develop. A lot of times radio won't be there yet. Sometimes they will be there. Some artists, we know the song's going to be a huge hit, so we wait for radio to make it a hit, and then we play it. Other artists we want to jump on, we want to be a part of their development. It really depends on the kind of music, and it depends on the balance on the channel at the time. There are certainly people in my department out there in radioland all the time; they feel that out and talk to those people. Though I'm not one of them, I'm aware of what's going on in radio, and I'm really aware of how radio can break artists and help to keep an artist on MTV as well. If people are wanting to pull a band off of the air, and you want that slot for your band, then it's easy to come in with a radio story."

Kates points out that MTV's new programming strategy defies attempts to introduce new artists. "MTV's point of view now is that they don't really want to step out and break artists," he maintains. "Or if they do, they want to be absolutely sure that the label is treating it as something that they have no choice but to break. MTV stepped out on the early side on Hanson, and it debuted in the top five. That's a case where, like Spice Girls, the label pretty much has to go to MTV and say, 'This is a major, mainstream, top-forty priority to us, we need you on this.' I think that the era of a video breaking a song may be over. I think the audience is a little bit dulled to the whole thing. Maybe the Chemical Brothers defy that. We'll see. When it comes to MTV we look at the impact very carefully. This is a down time for the record business, and everybody's looking at how they spend their money much more carefully, whether it's making videos or buying advertising, or however you look at the marketing of a record. Everything spent ultimately needs to be related to a SoundScan [sales] number."

Finnerty maintains that MTV wants to break new acts, but that it has been a searching period in music as audiences as well as labels restlessly latch onto and then discard new bands. "Years ago we were in a time for music in which there were a lot of artists being developed, in radio and MTV, and they were artists that had some staying power. For the last couple of years, we've been in this realm where we see one hit here and there. And that's difficult for us, because we're trying to develop artists that will play at the VMAs [MTV Video Music Awards] and come do fun things with us, but we're finding that the audience isn't that loyal right now. Only in underpockets of music is there any loyalty going on. Metal loyalty will be there forever and ever, even though we don't have a metal show. There's certainly a really big feel in electronic music, there's a lot of loyalty there; it's a really good punk-rock scene; and there's definitely the same kind of feel with hip-hop. I feel like right now is a really incredible time in music, that we're just about to come upon an age when we develop artists again that have some staying power, that we can work on for two, three or four records. People ask, 'How can you say that? Green Day sold seven million records,' and, no offense, but they didn't come back and do that well. It kind of shows this weird non-loyalty, do you know what I mean? Right now our focus is helping people make careers. We want them to have long careers with us. That's hard to do. My theory with a lot of things in life, but especially MTV, is one time is an accident, second time is a coincidence, and the third time is a habit. We just have a lot of one- and two-time acts. But I really feel that there are artists coming up that we're going to be able to do things with for a long time. For the last couple of years, it's kind of sucked, don't you think?"

In fact, the Recording Industry Association of America (RIAA) and the National Association of Recording Merchandisers released a joint survey in March 1997 that purported to show that MTV no longer influences music consumers. That brought a sharp response from Andy Schuon, vice president of programming for MTV. He told the press that "Out of nowhere, MTV can push the button to ignite sales and sell records. That being said, there are more record companies now than when we started in 1981. More videos are being made, and there are more people to say no to. The increased frustration is from the increased amount of supply, not the fact that MTV has cut back." And he asserted that music still occupies 80 percent of MTV's programming. Critics respond that MTV simply programs more showings of the same stunted playlist.

But given the long, tortuous road of finding a rep, dealing with label video commissioners and the selective programming process, it's difficult to imagine the video we've encouraged you to make finding its way to MTV. The truth: If you've made a video for an up-and-coming band without a record deal, it's highly unlikely that the video will get shown on MTV. But guess what? The decks will soon get cleared by new sounds and new images from the margins, sounds and images that play way below the frequencies picked up by MTV. Like the larger music industry to which MTV belongs, the music-video programmers are searching for the next pop movement that will lift the business out of the doldrums. It's undoubtedly coalescing now, and you might be part of it. Just as in the late '70s, a new rock generation will surely rise to obliterate the old. And, given the near-universal access to TV, computer technology and the Web, it will be driven in part by visual information.

There are also other outlets for your work besides MTV. Video commissioners at labels service videos to local cable access stations across the country that have weekly video shows specializing in obscure or local bands, and Susan Solomon makes the point that videos help with in-house hype at a label, introducing the band to sales and marketing people in regions that might not get the chance to see them. If you're servicing your own first low-budget video, definitely send 3/4" cassettes to local cable affiliates. You can find playlists for these local shows in the music-video tradepaper, *CVC*. Also, the clubs in your town may show videos in the bar or on a screen between bands. Make sure you give a copy of the video to the band before they go on tour; they may be able to get it shown in clubs around the country as they travel. Send a copy of your opus to the local-music specialist at your city's newspaper or the local fanzine. Many fanzines, and some large metropolitan newspapers review local videos and a good clipping can't hurt when you're looking for your next project or for a rep. Billy Proveda, president of the Music Video Production Association (MVPA) thinks that digital video disks (DVD), will create new markets for the music video industry. "The advent of DVD will keep the industry viable because consumers will expect to have visuals every time they hear music," he told an industry press conference.

MUSIC VIDEO FOR FUN AND LEARNING . . . NOT PROFIT

Once you acknowledge the career struggles that surround making music videos, making them becomes more purely an excercise in the creative process. The urge to be part of that process is the reason you've met everyone in this book. Phil Morrison directs huge ad campaigns for Nike sneakers and Energizer batteries but still jumps at the chance to direct a video for Yo La Tengo with a budget that wouldn't be adequate for the craft services table on one of his commerical jobs. Kevin Kerslake, too, in the midst of a burgeoning directing career, agrees to do a $15,000 Mazzy Star video. Just like directors who are still struggling, they, too, are addicted to the rush of making music videos.

What's that rush feel like? When a performer rocks out in an atmosphere you created, you feel like you've hosted the greatest party ever — a surreal usurping of the normally quiet, orderly film set. On a music-video set, if the song is good, the crew tap their feet and mouth the lyrics. The music pounds in your chest, and, if you get beyond lip-synching freeze-ups, the performance can be a strangely moving experience. When rockers you respect are pleased with the results, you're elated because you've been an important part of their creative process, too.

We hope you've felt that sense of collaboration throughout the production process. Your ideas grow and change from the very beginning, when you conceive the treatment with a band, budget with a producer, shoot with a DP, and edit with an editor. Even if you perform all the production duties yourself, a successful music-video experience can be much more fluid and organic than other kinds of filmmaking. The final cut can be quite different from what you originally dreamed, and that in itself can be a rush.

If you saw your first video through to the end, you will want to direct another one. A filmmaker walks a long road to visual fluency, and there's nothing more addictive than seeing what you could have done better and wanting to get it right the next time. You'll want the opportunity to try it again; even Spike Jonze told me he sometimes comes up with shots that would have improved a video a year later.

After one video, you get the urge to make a better one once you feel more in control and know what to cover. You begin to fantasize about the ever-elusive ability to execute your ideas without budgetary constraints or compromises. At the same time, you recognize that constraints and compromises are a part of the learning experience. By opening a little window into the world of "real" film and television production while making your video, you realize that compromises and constraints define the filmmaking dynamic in the real, big-budget world as well.

Spike Jonze's "Southern California" video for Wax is one of the best short films of the last twenty-five years, a bold haiku of a movie. Of course, had Spike strayed from his original vision, and if the record company forced him to insert performance shots, the video would have been reduced to banal bullshit. Given the opportunity to simply execute one pure idea, Jonze created an unforgettable image, a crystalline moment. The odds are stacked against most directors making a good video. Too many other folks get involved, and there are too many agendas to fulfill. This makes music videos a microcosm of Hollywood filmmaking, though, and given music video's short production schedules, the issues reach critical mass quickly. For personal expression to break through this web of competing interests, the director has to have bold ideas, like Spike's Wax video. Let's not shy away from stating the obvious: Music videos are advertisements for bands. They are a completely commercial medium.

Can a commercial medium become an art? Look at what happened to mass-market, commercial rock-and-roll in the '70s. Espousing a DIY philosophy, employing subversive irony and scratching at a slick medium with deliberate low-fi, punk revolutionized rock and elevated it to an art form, making a lasting cultural impact on film, fashion, politics, fine art — and television.

In a world ruled by consumer capitalism, the notion that a mass medium can be re-appropriated, reinterpreted and reinvented is a shining ray of hope for anyone in search of his or her creative voice. Music videos will make the shift from being the ultimate commercial medium to guerrilla art only if you seize the opportunity and recognize music videos as a viable medium for expression. The tools are more readily available than you might think and the processes learnable. All you need is the desire and the imagination to tell yourself, willing musicians and everyone on your crew, where to stand.

GETTING STARTED: DAVID KLEILER

"At various points throughout my childhood, both my parents taught cinema studies courses. Naturally, I always wanted to be a film director. In high school, when I wasn't playing in rock bands, I was at the movies. After high school, I started working as a production assistant. I went to film school, and though I dropped out and moved back to Boston to be in a rock band, my day job was as a PA. When you PA, you get hungry for more production work, or at least a better job. I moved back to New York to go back to film school, but my experience there was so fragmented that my final film felt inconclusive. I worked at odd jobs until I decided that I was going to direct music videos.

Now, like any good post-punker, music videos represented for me a further vulgarization of music, so I approached music videos from an ironic distance. I didn't really like music videos at all. However, as a pop-culture vulture, I was extremely MTV literate and watched videos constantly in the mid- to late-'80s. What fascinated me about music videos was their unequivocal statement of what they were. There was no artifice, no attempt to say that a music video was anything more than an advertisement, a billboard for a band and a song.

I think I came to the decision to make music videos because at certain points in your life you don't think about your ultimate goal, the end of the career path. You just look around and see which of your peers are leading the kind of life you might want to lead. My punk-rock experience prepared me to view music videos as ridiculous, but I realized that people such as Jesse Peretz and Phil Morrison were having fun with music videos and making creative, challenging work. I also realized that film-school cronies who weren't shooting battled chronic depression. Just wanting to get started made it an easy decision to do the first Wider video. I genuinely liked the band and the people in it, and they had a song that was supposedly going to be on a record. I thought I would borrow some money, make, say, three videos, and then I would be on my way — I'd have a directing career.

My supportive friends at Matador Records gave me $5,000 to do a Bailter Space video. From that point on, I didn't pay to make videos, so I had a career or, at least, the illusion of a career. I still had no money, and I lived in completely low-budget circumstances. Then, after my fourth or fifth video, I got a rep. That becomes the carrot on a stick dangling in front of you. Attached to the carrot is a sign that reads, 'This is a job you could get,' or, 'This is a few thousand dollars that could be in your pocket.'

You've heard the production stories of many of the videos that followed. The experience of each one (from the blissful to the truly insane) has given life to my directing dreams and the confidence to fulfill those dreams. I hope this book inspires similar dreams."

<<<

appendix >

FILM PRODUCTION COST SUMMARY

[X] Firm Bid   [ ] Cost Plus   Bid Date: 5/30/97

	Job#:
Job#:	
Production Contact:	Client/Product:
Director:	Producer: ___ Tel:
Dir. of Photography:	Art Dir: ___ Tel:
Producer:	Writer: ___ Tel:
Editor:	Bus. Mgr: ___ Tel:
No. pre-pro days:	Commercial Number/Title/Length:
No. pre-light days:	1.
No. build/strike days:	2.
No. studio shoot days:	3.
No. location days:	4.
Location sites:	5.

SUMMARY OF ESTIMATED PRODUCTION COSTS		ESTIMATED	ACTUAL		
1. Pre-production and wrap costs	Total A & C				
2. Shooting crew labor	Total B				
3. Location and travel expenses	Total D				
4. Props / wardrobe and animals	Total E				
5. Studio & set construction costs	Total F/G/H				
6, Equipment costs	Total I				
7. Film stock develop & print	Total J				
8. Miscellaneous	Total K				
9. SUB-TOTAL	A thru K				
10. Director/Creative fees	Total L				
11. Insurance					
12. SUB-TOTAL	Direct Costs				
13. Production fee					
14. Talent costs and expenses	Total M & N				
15. Editorial and finishing	Totals O & P				
16.					
17. GRAND TOTAL	(Incl. Director fee)				
18. Contingency					

Comments:

This bid is submitted under the stipulation of the adherence to the AICP Production Guidelines.

197

		A:PRE-PRO/WRAP									B:SHOOT								
	CREW	ESTIMATED				ACTUAL						ESTIMATED				ACTUAL			
		Days	Rate	OT Hr	Total	Days	Rate	OT Amt	Total			Days	Rate	OT Hr	Total	Days	Rate	OT Amt	Total
1	Producer									51									
2	Assistant Director									52									
3	Dir. of Photography									53									
4	Camera Operator									54									
5	Asst Cameraman									55									
6	Outside Prop									56									
7										57									
8	Inside Prop									58									
9										59									
10										60									
11	Electrician									61									
12	Best Boy									62									
13										63									
14										64									
15										65									
16	Grip									66									
17										67									
18										68									
19										69									
20	Mixer									70									
21	Boom Man									71									
22	Recordist									72									
23	Playback									73									
24	Make-up									74									
25	Hair									75									
26	Stylist									76									
27	Wardrobe Attendant									77									
28	Script Supervisor									78									
29	Home Economist									79									
30	Asst Home-Economist									80									
31	VTR Man									81									
32	EFX man									82									
33	Scenic									83									
34	Teleprmt Operator									84									
35	Generator Man									85									
36	Still Man									86									
37	Loc. Contact/Scout									87									
38	P.A.									88									
39	2nd A.D.									89									
40	Nurse									90									
41	Craft Services									91									
42	Fireman									92									
43	Policeman									93									
44	Welfare/Teacher									94									
45	Teamster									95									
46										96									
47										97									
48										98									
49										99									
50										100									
		Sub Total A										Sub Total B								
		PT P&W										PT P&W								
		TOTAL A										TOTAL B								

Page 2

C PRE-PRO AND WRAP - MATERIALS/EXPENSES	ESTIMATED	ACTUAL	
101. Auto Rental			
102. Air Fares ( ) people @ ( ) per fare			
103. Per Diems ( ) people @ ( ) per day			
104. Still Camera Rental & Film			
105. Messengers			
106. Trucking			
107. Deliveries & Taxi			
108. Home Econ Supplies			
109. Telephone & Cable			
110. Casting Prep(@) Cast(@) CallBk(@)			
111. Casting Facility			
112. Working Meals			
113.			
Sub-Total C			

D LOCATION EXPENSES	ESTIMATED	ACTUAL	
114. Location Fees			
115. Permits			
116. Car Rentals			
117. Bus Rentals			
118. Camper/Dressing Vehicles			
119. Parking/Tolls/Gas			
120. Trucking			
121. Other Vehicles			
122. Other Vehicles			
123. Customs			
124. Air Freight/Excess Bag			
125. Air Fares ( ) people @ ( ) per fare			
126. Per Diems ( ) people @ ( ) per day			
127. Air Fares ( ) people @ ( ) per fare			
128. Per Diems ( ) people @ ( ) per day			
129. Breakfast ( ) people days @ ( ) per meal			
130. Lunch ( ) people days @ ( ) per meal			
131. Dinner ( ) people days @ ( ) per meal			
132. Guards			
133. Limousines (Celebrity Service)			
134. Cabs/Other Tras			
135. Kit Rental			
136. Art Work			
137. Gratuities			
138.			
139.			
Sub-Total D			

E PROPS/WARDROBE/ANIMALS	ESTIMATED	ACTUAL	
140. Prop Rental			
141. Prop Purchase			
142. Wardrobe Rental			
143. Wardrobe Purchase			
144. Picture Vehicle			
145. Animal & Handlers			
146. Wigs & Moustaches			
147. Color Correction			
148.			
149.			
150.			
Sub-Total E			

F STUDIO RENTAL AND EXPENSES - STAGE	ESTIMATED			ACTUAL		
	Days/Hrs	Rate	Total	Days/Hrs	Rate	Total
151. Rental for Build Days						
152. Rental for Build OT						
153. Rental for Pre-Light						
154. Rental for Pre-Light OT						
155. Rental for Shoot Days						
156. Rental for Shoot OT						
157. Rental for Strike Days						
158. Rental for Strike OT						
159. Generator & Operator						
160. Set Guards						
161. Power Charge & Bulbs						
162. Misc (cartage/phones/coffee)						
163. Crew/Talent Meals (lun/din)						
164.						
165.						
166.						
167.						
Sub-Total F						

G SET CONSTRUCTION CREW (BUILD/STRIKE/PRELIGHT)	ESTIMATED				ACTUAL			
	Days	Rate	OT Hr	Total	Days	Rate	OT Amt	Total
168. Set Designer								
169. Carpenters								
170. Grips								
171. Outside Props								
172. Inside Props								
173. Scenics								
174. Electricians								
175. Teamsters								
176. Men for Strike								
177. PA's								
178.								
179.								
180.								
Sub Total G								
PT P&W								
TOTAL G								

H SET CONSTRUCTION MATERIALS	ESTIMATED	ACTUAL	
181. Props(Set dressing purch)			
182. Props (Set dressing rental)			
183. Lumber			
184. Paint			
185. Hardware			
186. Special Effects			
187. Special Outsd. Construction			
188. Trucking			
189. Messenger/Deliveries			
190. Kit Rental			
191.			
192.			
Sub-Total H			

I EQUIPMENT RENTAL	ESTIMATED	ACTUAL	
193. Camera Rental			
194. Sound Rental			
195. Lighting Rental			
196. Grip Rental			
197. Generator Rental			
198. Crane/Cherry Picker			
199. VTR Rental			
200. Walkie Talkies /Bullhorn			
201. Dolly Rental			
202. Camera Car			
203. Helicopter			
204. Production Supplies			
205. Teleprompter			
206. Stabilizer			
207.			
208.			
209.			
210.			
Sub-Total I			

J FILM STOCK / DEVELOP AND PRINT	ESTIMATED			ACTUAL		
	Footage	Rate	Total	Footage	Rate	Total
211. Purchase of Raw Stock						
212. Develop Negative						
213. Print Dailies						
214. Transfer to Mag						
215. Sync/Screen Dailies						
216.						
Sub-Total J						

K MISCELLANEOUS COSTS	ESTIMATED	ACTUAL	
217. Petty Cash			
218. Air Shipping/Special Carriers			
219. Phones & Cables			
220. Accountable Cash Under $15			
221. External Billing (Computer etc)			
222. Special Insurance			
223.			
224.			
225.			
226.			
Sub-Total K			

L DIRECTOR/CREATIVE FEES	ESTIMATED	ACTUAL	
227. Prep			
228. Travel			
229. Shoot Days			
230. Post-Production			
231.			
232.			
233.			
Sub-Total L			

M TALENT	No.	Rate	Days	Travel Days	1½ X hrs	2 X hrs	ESTIMATED	No.	Days	ACTUAL
234. O/C Principles										
235. O/C Principles										
236. O/C Principles										
237. O/C Principles										
238. O/C Principles										
239. O/C Principles										
240. O/C Principles										
241. O/C Principles										
242. O/C Principles										
243. O/C Principles										
244.										
245.										
246.										
247.										
248. General Extras										
249. General Extras										
250. General Extras										
251. General Extras										
252. General Extras										
253. General Extras										
254.										
255.										
256. Hand Model										
257.										
258. Voice Over/Narration										
259. Fitting Fees SAG										
260. Fitting Fees SEG										
261.										
262. Audition Fees SAG										
263. Audition Fees SEG										
264.										
265.										
266. Payroll/P&W Taxes										
267. Wardrobe Allowance										
268.										
269. Other										
270. Mark-Up										
				Sub-Total M						

N TALENT EXPENSES	ESTIMATED	ACTUAL	
271. Per Diems ( ) man days X ( ) per day			
272. Air Fares ( ) people X cost ( ) per fare			
273. Cabs And Transportations			
274. Mark-Up			
275.			
276.			
Sub-Total N			

O EDITORIAL COMPLETION	ESTIMATED			ACTUAL		
	Quan	Rate	Total	Quan	Rate	Total
277. Editor						
278. Assistant Editor						
279. Coding						
280. Projection						
281. Artwork for supers						
282. Shooting of artwork						
283. Stock Footage						
284. Still photographs						
285. Opticals (incl. pre-opticals)						
286. Animation						
287. Stock music						
288. Original music						
289. Sound effects						
290. Dubbing studio						
291. Studio for narration						
292. Studio for mixing						
293. Negative tracks						
294. Answer & corrected prints						
295. Contract items						
296. Film-to-tape transfer						
297. Film to tape transfer - editorial fee						
298. Film Release Prints						
299.						
300.						
Sub-Total O						

P VIDEOTAPE PRODUCTION AND COMPLETION	ESTIMATED			ACTUAL		
	Quan	Rate	Total	Quan	Rate	Total
301. Basic crew						
302. Additional crew						
303. Labor overtime						
304.						
305.						
306. VTR/Camera rental						
307. Additional VTRs/Cameras						
308. Equipment overtime						
309. Special equipment:						
310. Special processes:						
311. Trucking						
312. Moble unit						
313. Stock rental						
314. Screening						
315. On-line editing						
316. Off-line editing						
317. Videotape /VB roll preparation and stock						
318. Audio mix with VT projection						
319. Video air masters						
320. Video printing dupe						
321. 3/4" video cassettes						
322. Tape-to-film transfers						
323. Markup						
Sub-Total P						

photo credits